THE ESSENTIAL
GUIDE TO SKIING

201 THINGS
EVERY SKIER MUST KNOW

Ron LeMaster

PEAK SPORTSpress®

BOULDER, COLORADO

An imprint of VeloPress®
1830 North 55th Street
Boulder, Colorado 80301–2700 USA
303/440-0601 Fax 303/444-6788 E-mail velopress@insideinc.com

To purchase additional copies of this book or other VeloPress books, call 800/234-8356 or visit us on the Web at velopress.com.

Cover design by Shannon Saddler. Cover photo © Getty Images. Interior art direction by Megan Selkey. Interior photos © Ron LeMaster unless otherwise noted.

To Dee,
my wife and my best friend

TABLE OF CONTENTS

201 THINGS

Gearing Up

EVERY SKIER MUST KNOW

Accessories and Soft Goods

201 THINGS

Going Skiing

201 THINGS

Racing

Photos and Video

ACKNOWLEDGMENTS

I want to thank Bill Grout for conceiving of this book, suggesting I write it, and shepherding it (nearly) all the way through its development and publication. Amy Rinehart gets my sincere thanks for picking up where Bill had to leave off and seeing the job through to the end.

Rick Kahl, during hundreds of miles of bike rides, provided invaluable information and insight on the ski industry. Rick also gave me critique and encouragement when I needed it most. Once again, I want to thank Paul Fargis for being my go-to guy for advice on the business of publishing.

Seth Masia did a great job of reviewing and improving the equipment sections, for which Jeanne-Marie Gand at Rossignol also provided important information and support. Thanks to Larry Houchen at Boulder Ski Deals and Jim Lindsay at BooTech in Aspen for sharing their knowledge on ski boots and the art of fitting them, and to Matt Carroll at Kenny's Double Diamond in Vail for his help with the section on selecting skis. I hope my readers come away with an understanding of the importance of specialists like these and the specialty shops in which they work.

Finally I want to thank Carol Levine at the Vail/Beaver Creek Ski and Snowboard School (and who appears in many of the pictures), Jesse Hunt of the U.S. Ski Team, and Curt Chase for being the best colleagues and mentors a guy could hope for.

FOREWORD

When I think back to skiing as a kid I remember waking up on those early mornings and waiting for my parents to take my sister and me to the ski area. On these mornings my mom and dad would feed us and make sure we had sunscreen on and all of the right clothes to wear for that day. Then we would drive up to the mountain and go to the locker room to get our skis and poles. Shannon and I would hit the slopes early and put in a full day. We were lucky enough to have our mom and dad taking care of all of the details us so that we didn't have to think about anything but skiing. That's how it should be, but now I have to make sure I do all the little things for myself in order to have the most fun on the hill.

To many people, skiing is a sport. To me it's a lifestyle. It's a way to experience life's challenges, a way to feel free, a way to express myself, a way to be out in nature, and a way to have fun. I love to ski. Skiing has filled my life with rewarding experiences. I have learned to overcome challenges, reach goals, and live life to the fullest.

When I snow ski I get to experience one of the best feelings in life. I love the days up on the hill skiing powder; heli-skiing; back country skiing in the trees and open bowls; skiing on groomers; hitting jumps; training on giant slalom, super G, and downhill courses; and racing. Pretty much any day on skis is fun for me, and every day on the hill is a challenge.

Think of all the terrain and different situations you can encounter. When you're looking down a steep chute or standing at the top of an icy groomer, you'll want to feel confident and have no distractions. Even if you're just walking out of the tram for a nice mellow run, you want to have everything dialed so you can ski and have nothing else on your mind except for making it down in one piece. Just kidding, you'll be fine. Just as you should consider the terrain and snow conditions, you should be ready for variable weather. It's good to know things like what sort of ski setup you want, how to stay warm and not sweat, and plenty of other little things that may not have crossed your mind. You have to plan ahead for every day on the ski hill to make life easier and ultimately enjoy your day skiing.

The Essential Guide to Skiing will give you good ideas to eliminate the hassles that can be avoided before you show up at the slopes. You will learn efficient ways to do almost anything throughout your day. Then you can focus more on just skiing and not the little annoyances that seem to creep up on those who are not prepared. Skiing is challenging enough. Why make it more trouble than it is?

Take this knowledge and use it to your advantage. Get out and ski!

Daron Rahlves
World Champion in super G, 2001

PREFACE

I started skiing in 1957 at the age of 8. It was a trip to Winter Park, Colorado, with my sister's Brownie troop. We rode the Denver and Rio Grande Ski Train up from Denver, an adventure in itself for an 8-year-old. My sister and I shared a pair of old, wooden skis that belonged to another family, and we made maybe three runs each on the bunny slope the entire day.

But I was hooked. From then on it became a Sunday ritual in our family to get up before dawn and drive the family station wagon from our home in Denver to the mountains for a day of skiing. My father remembers that while he often had to pry my sister out of bed and cajole her into going, he never had to ask me twice.

Like anyone who loves the sport and has an opportunity to pursue it, I learned to ski passably well. Over the decades I learned Hannes Schneider's Arlberg Technique, the official Austrian and American technique of the 1960s, and other systems of technical maneuvers too numerous to mention.

I also picked up lots of skiing lore along the way, much of it from other skiers: things like how to keep goggles from fogging on a snowy day, how to avoid lift lines, how to dry boots overnight, and how to find pockets of fresh powder several days after a storm.

This is the sort of information you won't find in ski instructors' manuals, and even though the ski magazines sometimes provide it in bits and pieces, it's not easy to find when you need it. But it's just this kind of insider's knowledge that every skier needs. In some ways skiing is a simple sport—it's just you, a mountain covered with snow, and gravity. But in other ways, it's extremely complicated, particularly when you factor in the planning, packing, traveling, schlepping, and all the intricacies of gear and clothing.

That's why I wrote this book: to give you a leg up on all those skiers out there who are learning the sport by trial and error, as I did. It took me forty-five years to learn everything that's in this book. You can learn it in a day.

Good luck and good skiing.

Ron LeMaster
Boulder, Colorado

Skis, boots, bindings, and poles. These are friends with whom you spend some of the best days of your life.

GEARING UP

With the advent of Howard Head's aluminum skis in the 1950s and Bob Lange's plastic boots in the 1960s, ski and boot design leaped from craftsmen's workshops in the Alps into unlikely engineering labs in Maryland and Iowa. Since then, all sorts of exotic engineering materials and manufacturing processes have been tried, many successfully, to make our equipment better. Genius and hard work have been applied not only to skis and boots, but also to bindings, poles, clothing, goggles, and accessories of all types.

Every year we can ski better and more comfortably in a wider range of conditions thanks to new and better equipment. With such constant innovation, how are you to know when and what to buy? Is it time for a new pair of skis? And, if so, what should you get? Do the new boots just look different or are they functionally superior to what you're wearing now?

Here is some information to help you sort it out.

Where to Shop
SKI SHOPS

Picking a good ski shop is an important first step. Some have a lot of staff turnover, while others retain their employees for years and train them well. For the best service, seek out a specialty shop that has been around for a long time. Avoid chain stores that emphasize price over performance in their advertising. The money you might save at such a place (and there's a good chance you won't save any) will be a poor trade-off for the level of knowledge and service you're likely to get, especially if you end up with inappropriate skis or poorly fitted boots. I don't know about you, but I'd rather discuss my ski equipment needs with someone who specializes in ski equipment, not someone who was selling jockstraps and baseball gloves in another section of the store last week. As one friend puts it, "I don't buy my skis at the same place I buy my fishing license."

If you're thinking of buying new equipment before leaving on a ski vacation, consider waiting and buying it at your destination. When you get to the mountains, you can try different models of skis in different lengths to find just the right pair. If you're in the market for boots, this could be a good time to buy, as you'll be able to return to the shop—several times if need be—to get them set up just right.

A ski town will have a lot of ski shops, and some will be better than others. To find a good one, ask for recommendations from ski instructors, patrollers, and other locals. Go to the shops that get the most votes. Ask for recommendations on specific salespeople, too. Ski town populations are transient, and not everyone has the same level of expertise. This goes double for boots.

Regardless of where you shop, go when the store isn't busy and you've got some time to spend. Try shopping on a weekday, when the salesperson can spend time with you. This is true when shopping for boots, in particular. Boot selection and fitting take time.

Human nature compels us, some more than others, to say what we think will impress the salesperson. Impress him or her with your frankness and candor; don't oversell or undersell yourself.

SALES

Ski shops start to put equipment on sale as early as February and March, and this is the best time to pick up good deals. If you see something you like in December or January, don't be afraid to ask when the store will start its spring sale. Find out who else carries the product you're interested in.

By the time the fall sales come around, you'll have to look harder to find the good stuff, as these sell-offs emphasize leftover gear from the previous season that nobody wanted.

HARD GOODS VERSUS SOFT GOODS

Skis, boots, bindings, and poles are, in the lexicon of the ski industry, "hard goods." This is the stuff that ski junkies get worked up about every fall as they prepare for the upcoming season. The term "soft goods," in contrast, refers to ski clothing—parkas, shells, pants, vests, fleece jackets, underwear, socks, gloves, and hats.

SKI SWAPS

Virtually every town with a sizable ski club or ski team has a decent ski swap in the early fall. Every year overequipped skiers bring in their old gear, hoping to clear out a bit of space in the garage for that new snowblower. The ski club keeps a cut of the proceeds. Some ski swaps also accept merchandise from retailers who have overstock from previous seasons.

Swaps are good places to find not only hard goods, but clothing, too. They are also good places to unload some of your old stuff. Watch your local newspaper in September and October and ask around at the local ski shops to find out when the swaps are scheduled.

The problem with ski swaps is that it's easy to buy the wrong stuff. Again, the best approach is to go looking for specific things. If you don't know exactly what you're looking for, seek out a counselor. At a swap organized by a competition-oriented ski club, ask to talk to one of the coaches.

USED SPORTING GOODS STORES

Stores specializing in used sports equipment are very good places to shop if you know what you are looking for and how to evaluate it. They are also good places to sell your old equipment. Good gear can also be found on eBay.com, but of course you won't be able to handle or try on the merchandise before you buy it.

Find a good shop that specializes in skiing, with a stable, knowledgeable staff.

Where to Shop

Preparing To Shop

A good ski shop salesperson will ask you a lot of questions in order to match you with the right gear. So before you walk into a shop, be prepared with answers to the following:

- Why do you ski? Do you ski for excitement or for pleasure? Do you ski because you love being outdoors with your friends and family, feeling the wind in your face and the snow under your skis, or because you love the feeling of slicing a tight arc at warp speed?
- How much do you ski? How many years have you been at it, and how many days a year do you ski? If you plan on skiing more often than you have in the past, you'll be improving more quickly, so take that in to account, too.
- How accomplished a skier are you, and how keen are you on improving? Think about the specific runs and conditions on which you feel comfortable and the ones you don't and mention them to the salesperson. Be honest with yourself. If you get skis or boots that are designed for a much better skier, you won't have as much fun, which is what skiing is all about.
- How aggressive a skier are you? Are you looking primarily for high performance or comfort and convenience? Some skis and boots want to be your chauffeur. Some want to be your co-pilot. Which are you looking for?
- In what part of the country do you do most of your skiing? On soft snow or hard snow? If you ski a lot in the East or Midwest, where the snow is likely to be hard more often than not, you'll be looking for a ski with a narrower waist

and more edge grip, and more precise, stiffer boots. If you ski in the West most of the time, a somewhat wider ski and softer boot may make you a happier skier.

- How do you like to ski? Do you spend most of your time on groomed slopes, unpacked snow, or in bumps? Do you prefer blue-square or black-diamond runs? Do you like to make short, quick turns, long cruising turns, or a combination of both? Moguls favor a narrower ski, from tip to tail, and boots that allow a lot of ankle flex. Ungroomed snow favors wider boards. Most people ski steep, challenging terrain better on short, deeply shaped skis derived from slalom racing designs. For big-mountain cruising, look to bigger types of skis from the giant slalom family tree. Short, snappy turns are facilitated by stiffer boots.

EQUIPMENT FOR WOMEN

In case you haven't noticed, women are physiologically different from men. Of particular importance in skiing are the differences in mass distribution, relative limb length, hip width (specifically, the distance between the ball-and-socket joints where the legs join the pelvis), angle of the upper leg as it comes out of the hip, and shape of the calf muscle. If you are a woman, the more typically feminine you are in these respects, the more seriously you should consider women-specific boots and skis.

EQUIPMENT FOR CHILDREN

Most good ski shops have special equipment programs for children that enable kids to ski on gear that matches their bodies and skills as they grow without

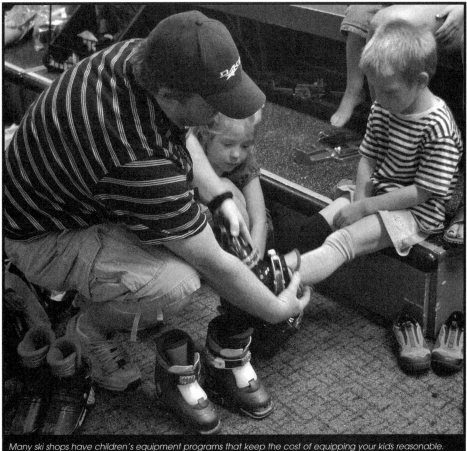
Many ski shops have children's equipment programs that keep the cost of equipping your kids reasonable.

putting their parents in the poorhouse. A typical setup goes like this: You pay $100 for skis, boots, and bindings. The next season, if your child needs bigger skis, you swap the skis from the previous year for a longer pair at a cost of $20. Larger boots also cost $20. If you need to change anything in the middle of the season, there is no additional charge. The initial buy-in of $100 keeps you in the program until your kids are too big for the equipment the shop uses in the program, usually at around middle school age.

GETTING ADVICE
Instructors

A ski instructor from whom you've taken a lesson is an excellent source of advice on equipment. He or she will know your skiing style, ability, and temperament. Instructors will usually be happy to help you shop for skis or boots after your lesson. This is an opportunity you should take advantage of.

Friends

Don't rely on advice from your friends and acquaintances. Most people, even your

Where to Shop

good friend who spent two years ski-bumming in Lake Tahoe after college, will only know the gear he himself owns and will have few points of comparison with other brands and models.

Magazine Tests

Some skiers think that the major ski magazines are pawns of their advertisers, and that the equipment tests they do every year are either rigged, inaccurate, biased, or simply a pack of lies penned by the manufacturers' marketing departments.

I've worked as an independent ski tester for *SKIING* magazine, and my experience is that the tests are none of the above. But they are not easy to interpret. Here are some tips that will help you. They apply both to ski and boot tests:

Each fall the major ski magazines publish extensive equipment tests. Interpreted properly, they're good sources of information.

Photo courtesy *Ski* magazine.

- Look for the comments of testers who are about your build, age, and gender.
- Consider the testers' comments in light of what you like in a ski or boot. There are a lot of great examples of both out there, but they are different in character. Just because a restaurant has some fabulous oysters on its menu doesn't mean you should order them if you don't care for oysters.
- Keep in mind there are some skis and boots that women universally love and men don't. And vice versa.
- If there is a ski or boot that all the testers love, you'll probably love it, too. If there is one that a couple of the testers love, you are less likely to love it yourself.
- Brand loyalty is often based on real, tangible characteristics that express the design philosophies of the manufacturers. A person who really likes K2s will probably continue to like them. Another may be an Atomic devotee, for his or her own good reasons.
- When considering boots, the shape of your foot should override all other considerations. In a choice between a boot that fits your foot perfectly or one that matches your ability level, go for the fit.

Boots

Any professional skier will tell you that your boots are your most important piece of equipment. I know if I had to choose between an airline losing my skis or my boots, the choice would be simple. Good-bye, skis.

Dollar for dollar and hour for hour, your skiing will benefit more from getting into the right pair of boots and getting that pair set up right than anything else you can spend your time and money on, including skis or lessons. Boots are your most personal piece of gear. They must fit not only the shape of your feet, but their geometry must be in sync with your body's geometry—the relative lengths of major body segments, the angles between them and the distribution of body mass along them.

Shop for boots when you've got some time to spend. Be ready to spend an hour or more trying on boots before you pick a pair. Plan on trying boots from at least three different ability ranges and from two or three different manufacturers. It doesn't end there. Be prepared to

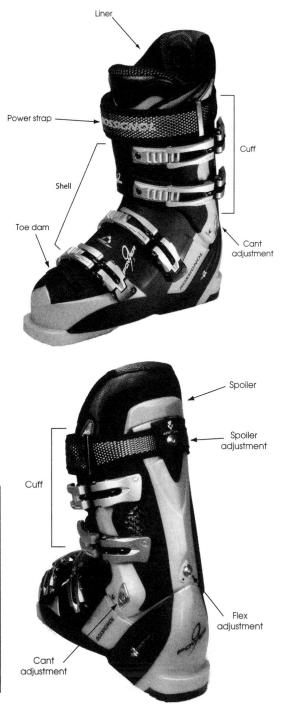

Boots

Boots intended for rental have to fit comfortably on a lot of different feet. That means they have thick, soft liners. They'll be okay for your first five or ten days, but once you're spending most of your time on intermediate runs (the ones marked by blue circles on the trail map) you should get a pair of your own. When you do, you will see a quantum improvement in your skiing.

Design Terms

CANT: n. The angle between the cuff of the boot and a vertical line when viewed from the front. A cant adjustment allows the position of the cuff to be set so that the skier applies pressure evenly across the width of the boot. Properly canted boots are important for good edge control, proper edge grip in turns, and fast, secure straight-running. Improperly canted boots can cause a wide range of skiing problems.

OVERLAP BOOT: n. A boot that has a two-part overlapping shell—a lower shell, which wraps around the forefoot with overlapping flaps and an upper shell, called the cuff, which is attached to the lower, often by a hinge at the ankle, and wraps around the ankle and lower leg.

CUFF: n. The part of the shell that surrounds the ankle and lower leg.

CUSTOM FOOTBED or CUSTOM INSOLE: n. Boot insoles molded to match the sole of an individual skier's foot. Many specialty ski shops make custom insoles. Similar, but not identical, to an orthotic. (See below.)

FOOTBED: n. See INSOLE.

FORWARD-FLEX ADJUSTMENT: n. A mechanism on a ski boot that allows the skier to change the resistance the boot presents to the skier bending his or her ankle.

FORWARD-LEAN ADJUSTMENT: n. A mechanism that changes the angle between the boot's cuff and a vertical line when viewed from the side. Proper forward lean allows the skier to flex and extend the entire body through a long range while maintaining good balance fore and aft.

INSOLE: n. The piece of material in the boot, inside the liner, on which the skier's foot rests. For optimum comfort and performance, the insole should conform to the shape of the sole of the skier's foot and support it so it remains stable under the forces of skiing.

LINER: n. The soft, cushioned inner boot. The thinner and firmer the liner, the better the boot will perform, but the harder it will be to fit the boot to the skier's foot. The thicker and softer the liner, the more comfortable the boot is out of the box, and the easier it is to fit, at the expense of performance.

ORTHOTIC: n. A custom insole made by a board-certified and licensed specialist. (These include pedorthists, podiatrists, and orthopedists). Skiers sometimes speak of having orthotics in their boots when what they actually have are custom footbeds.

POWER STRAP: n. The nylon strap with Velcro closure that is attached to the top of the boot cuff. Provides additional control over the stiffness and flex of the boot.

REAR-ENTRY BOOT: n. A type of boot, popular in the 1980s and early 1990s, with a two-piece shell consisting of a continuous piece of plastic across the front and sides of the foot and shin and another that forms the back spine of the boot. The back hinges at the bottom, allowing it to act like a door. Characterized by ease of entry and exit, warmth and comfort, this style of boot fell out of favor because many were too stiff in flex and imprecise in their performance. There were, however, several models that skied quite well.

SHELL: n. The rigid plastic outer boot.

SPOILER: n. The hard plastic tab that forms the top of the cuff behind the skier's leg. Assists in applying pressure to the tail of the ski.

WALK MODE: n. A feature found in some boots that lets a skier change the cuff to an upright position to facilitate walking.

Performance Terms

FLEX: n. The resistance that a boot has to being bent fore and aft. Generally, the stiffer-flexing the boot, the faster it responds to a skier's movements and the less tolerant it is of technical errors, particularly at speed and in moguls.

FORGIVENESS: n. The extent to which the boot allows the skier to make mistakes in technique without transmitting inappropriate maneuvers to the skis. Generally this is a function of soft flex.

LATERAL SUPPORT: n. The degree to which the boot resists bending side to side. Generally the greater the lateral support,

the more stable the boot feels at higher speeds and in aggressive maneuvers, and the better the ski will grip.

QUICKNESS: n. The speed with which the boot causes the ski to react; related to flex. Syn.: Responsiveness. Ant.: Forgiveness.

STABILITY: n. The degree to which the boot allows the skier to maintain control of the arc of the turn or keep the ski tracking in a straight line, whether in difficult or changing snow conditions or at higher speeds; related to lateral support.

STANCE: n. The skier's overall position when standing in the boot.

It's the most critical piece of your ski equipment. And somewhere out there is the perfect boot for you.

Fit Terms

CALF SIZE: n. Two things determine how a boot will fit the lower leg: the size of the calf muscle and the point where the calf muscle merges into the Achilles tendon. If your calf muscle extends lower on your leg, look for a boot that is designed to fit a large calf or can be adjusted to fit one.

FOREFOOT: n. The front of the foot, from the arch forward, especially the widest part of the foot or "ball."

HEEL POCKET: n. The sculpted-out area at the base of the back of the boot. The better defined the heel pocket, the more secure the fit. A snug fit at the instep and heel pocket will help keep the foot from sliding fore and aft, up and down, and side to side. The lower buckle on the cuff of a four-buckle boot has the greatest effect on seating your foot in the heel pocket.

INSTEP: n. The top of the midfoot; the part of the foot above the arch. The fit over and around the instep is the most critical to good control of the ski.

LAST: n. The interior shape of either the shell or the liner. Literally, the mold around which a shoe or boot is built.

MONDO POINT: n. The international length-measurement system used for ski boots. It is also used for some other sports equipment, such as inline skates. It bears no clear relationship to any other common system of foot measurement. I wear a size 9 shoe and a Mondo Point 26 ski boot.

PRONATE: v. A rolling of the foot toward the inside as the skier applies weight to it. The arch usually flattens as this happens. This is a common condition that can be addressed with a custom insole or orthotic. Ant.: Suppinate.

RAMP ANGLE: n. The angle of the footbed inside the boot due to the heel being higher than the toe. There are differing opinions among experts on the effects of ramp angle.

SUPPINATE: v. A rolling of the foot toward the outside as the skier applies weight to it. Not as common as pronation. Ant.: Pronate.

TOE BOX: n. The very front of the boot liner or shell.

VOLUME: n. A general description of the interior size of a boot, independent of length. Boots are generally characterized as low, middle, or high-volume. Incorporated in this loose metric are width, instep height, and cuff diameter.

spend another hour or more getting the boots to fit just right and to make a couple of return visits to get them tweaked. I go through this myself every time I get a new pair of boots. It's a ritual I've come to enjoy.

FINDING THE BOOT OF YOUR DREAMS

The best boot fitter I know in my hometown, Larry Houchen at Boulder Ski Deals, says the most common criteria people use in choosing boots are friends' recommendations, price, and cosmetics. The proper criteria, he says, are fit and flex.

Larry also estimates that 90 percent of skiers are in boots that are too big and too stiff, an opinion I have heard echoed by virtually every good boot fitter I've talked to. People buy them too big because they don't understand how boots are supposed to fit, and too stiff because they overestimate their abilities and think that a better skier needs a stiffer boot.

A ski boot is not a shoe and shouldn't fit like one. It's the control stick with which you manipulate your ski and should feel like it was molded around your foot and lower leg. I recommend trying on boots with a very thin ski sock or even a street sock rather than a thicker one that you might use while skiing. You will be better able to feel conflicts between the shape of your foot and the shape of the boot and be less likely to get a boot that is too big.

The boot fitter should start by measuring your feet. The best way to do this is with a Brannock device, one of those metal measuring plates used in shoe stores. If your boot fitter uses one of these, it's a good sign. The device measures length in two ways. It measures the distance from

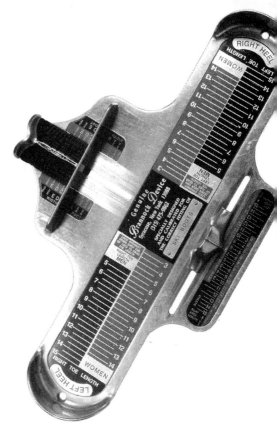

The Brannock device will tell you and your boot fitter a lot about your feet.

heel to toe, but more importantly, it measures your foot from the heel to the knuckle just behind the big toe. This point corresponds with the widest part of your foot and the start of your arch, and it must jive with the shape of the boot as precisely as possible. The overall length is much less important, as long as your toes don't bang against the end of the boot. The Brannock also measures the width of your foot at its widest point.

After measuring your feet, a good boot fitter will take a look at their general shape and volume. Now he or she will know which brands and models of boot are likely to fit you. High instep, low

Boots

instep, wide forefoot, narrow heel . . . every boot is designed to fit a certain type of foot. Just because your best friend—a great skier—loves his or her Langes doesn't mean it's the brand for you. Also, you may need to visit several shops to find the right make and model.

A boot's flex is crucial to its performance. Generally speaking, if you ski a lot in moguls or soft snow, your boots should be softer flexing. Big turns at speed favor a softer flex, too. If you ski mostly hard snow and make lots of short turns, a stiffer boot may be appropriate.

It's not just a matter of stiffness, either. The way in which the boots flex is important. Some boots give a bit when you press your shins forward, then stiffen up fast. Other boots allow a longer flex range and stiffen up progressively. The latter type work better for most people than the former. Over the years, certain boots, such as the Raichle Flexon (which is now sadly out of production), have become legendary for their smooth, progressive flex.

Finding the right flex is tricky; count on the boot fitter to steer you in the right direction. If the fitter recommends boots that feel too soft to you, remember that boots are always stiffer in the cold air of the mountains than in the warmth of the store. Some boots are more affected by cold than others. Depend on your boot fitter to know the differences.

Virtually every boot on the market is stiffer out on the snow than it is in the shop. Some materials are more temperature sensitive than others, and some shell designs do a better job of dealing with temperature-dependent stiffness than others. High-performing boots in general, and race boots in particular, are more difficult to get into and out of than lower performing boots, which are softer and designed for ease of entry and exit.

If you ski in a cold part of the country, such as the Upper Midwest or New England, take this into account when buying a boot. Just getting out of some boots after skiing all day at 10 degrees Fahrenheit is an athletic event in itself. I once cut my foot getting out of a pair of boots when the plastic was cold.

WOMEN'S BOOTS

Women vary more in certain physiological parameters than men do, and nowhere does this play a more important role in skiing than in the selection and setup of boots. Years ago, manufacturers thought the most important differences between

BUCKLING UP

The right way to put on a ski boot is not as obvious as you might think. You can buckle from the top down or from the bottom up, but in either case, once you've closed the lower buckle on the cuff, take a moment to push your knee forward as far as you can. This will drive your heel into the back of the boot, seating it properly in the heel pocket. Once you've done this, you may want to snug up the other buckles again. Finally, hook up the power strap, but don't cinch it down super-tight.

The most common cause of painful feet is overtightened boots. Start the day with your buckles on the loose side, particularly the top one. After you've made a run or two and your feet have settled into the liners, you can start tightening them up. When you take breaks during the day, loosen your buckles to let your feet expand a bit. If you don't, your boots will feel looser as the day goes on.

Boots

Look carefully at your boots from the side and you'll see there is a point, about an inch behind the toe, where the boot sole angles up slightly. The angle of this bevel and its distance from the front end of the sole conforms to an international standard carefully engineered to make bindings work more reliably. When your boots' soles get worn and rounded off under the toes, those angles and distances change and they are no longer safe for skiing. Walking a lot on hard surfaces (like parking lot asphalt) can ruin them.

The soles of some boots have replaceable toeplates. (Lange and Atomic are examples.) This solves the problem, but only if you keep an eye on them and replace them when necessary.

Many people who live in their ski boots use gizmos called Cat Tracks to protect the soles. These are removable plastic treads that you slip onto the bottom of your boots for walking around, then fold up and put in your pocket when you put on your skis. Cat Tracks serve two important purposes: First, they make walking in your boots safer and easier, gripping on snow and ice much better than the boots' soles and cushioning your joints from the blows of clunking around in those hard plastic boots; second, and just as important, they protect your boot soles from wear.

Cat Tracks come in only a few sizes, and they are not very stretchy, particularly in the cold. The manufacturer suggests that if your boots are a bit bigger than the Cat Tracks, you should stretch them hard a few times in the warmth of your home before using them on the hill. If your boots are smaller than the Cat Tracks, you can make them fit by twisting them when you put them on, as shown in the photograph.

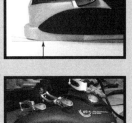

The boot's sole is beveled under the toe. The angle of the bevel and the distance at which it starts from the end of the sole are critical to the proper function of your bindings.

Some boots soles have replaceable toeplates—a notable safety feature.

Cat Tracks protect your boot soles and improve your traction on slippery surfaces. You can make them tighter by twisting them in the middle.

Use your pole for support when you put on or take off Cat Tracks on the snow.

Boots

men and women were in their tastes. Fortunately, they now also recognize and address the physiological ones.

I suggest that all women look first at women-specific models. Top manufacturers make them at most performance levels. Try unisex (i.e., male) boots, too, but understand that a boot designed for an average man's foot, shrunk down to the size of an average woman's foot, is likely to get stiff in the process. So it's important, if you have small feet, to make sure you don't walk out of the store with a pair of boots that you can't flex.

Katie Fry, director of the Aspen Highlands Ski School, a member of the Professional Ski Instructors of America Demo Team, and one helluva skier, is a woman with small feet. She recommends that women with similar foot sizes consider junior race boots. Some of these are high-performance boots with all the bells and whistles of their adult counterparts, but they're sized for smaller feet, are a bit softer (which is usually a good thing for an adult anyway), and are less expensive. If the cuff of the boot is a little too soft, a good boot fitter can easily stiffen it with rivets.

Seth Masia, an expert in the industry, notes that most manufacturers build adult boots down to size 3 for the Japanese market. A good specialty shop may be willing to special-order some for you.

Cuff height and shape are more critical parameters for women than men. Make sure that the cuffs are not overly tight around your calves and that the top of the cuff does not dig in to your calf muscle. Be especially careful with boots that have very high backs, such as some Lange unisex models.

The other design parameter that is more critical for women is the forward lean of the cuff. Pay particular attention to the advice given in the Forward Lean section on page 24.

CHILDREN'S BOOTS

Kids learn to ski better and more quickly in boots that let them bend their ankles a lot. So look for boots that your child can flex, that he or she can get into and out of with minimal assistance, and that have simple buckles. Be sure the buckles don't require more strength to open and close than your child has.

A kid's boot should have a minimum of two buckles. In general, more buckles are better than fewer. Avoid rear-entry boots; they are easy to operate but hard to ski in, are usually too stiff, and encourage the development of poor skiing skills.

Buy boots that fit your child. Don't buy them big, figuring your child will grow into them. By that time, he will have probably learned to hate skiing from being made to do it in ill-fitting equipment and refuse to go anymore. Used boots for kids are a good idea, but make sure the soles are not worn down, as they will not operate reliably in release bindings.

THE FIVE FIT POINTS

There are five critical ways in which a boot must fit your foot and leg, according to master boot fitter Jim Lindsay of BOOTech in Aspen.

LENGTH: As Lindsay puts it, "When standing neutral in the boot, neither pressed forward or back, your toes should be fully extended and aware that the end (of the toe box) is near. If you try to stand up straight your toes should hit the end, but not enough to bend them."

In addition to measuring your feet with a Brannock Device, the boot fitter will do what is called a *shell fit*. He'll take the liner out of the boot, then ask you to stand in the boot with your toes against the end. Then he'll shove his hand down the back of the boot to see how much space is behind your heel. If you ski less than fifteen or so days a season, there should be about one inch, or two fingers, of space. If you ski more than that, the space should be about half that, or one finger's width. Why the difference? How much you ski will determine how much the liner will compress, or *pack out* over time. When this happens, the boot will, in effect, get bigger.

Next, the boot fitter will put the liner back in the shell and you'll buckle them up. Don't worry if they feel a little short. As the liner packs out over time, your foot will move back a bit in the boot, giving your toes more room. If you feel the liner against your toes, don't worry. If, on the other hand, you feel the hard plastic of the shell, tell the boot fitter.

Ski boot lengths are measured in *Mondo Point* units, which bear no resemblance to standard American or European sizes. I wear a size 9 shoe and a Mondo Point 26 ski boot.

WIDTH: A ski boot should feel tight when it's new—to the point that your foot feels a little cool from reduced blood circulation after you've buckled them down snugly for ten or fifteen minutes. After you've skied in them for an hour, they'll loosen a bit and

Expect to try on several pairs of boots in your quest for the best fit.

Boots

stop restricting your circulation. After you've spent ten or twenty days in them, they will have packed out and loosened considerably. As Lindsay puts it, it's easier to make a boot wider than it is to make it narrower.

If you have to close any buckle tighter than the second notch to make it feel good and snug, the boot is too big. On the other hand, if you feel the hard plastic of the shell against the knuckle behind your big or little toe, or the sides of your heel, the boot is too narrow. The shell can be modified to address these fit issues, but it's best to start with one that doesn't have them.

INSTEP HEIGHT: If the boot is designed for a lower instep than yours, you'll have cold, painful feet. If your instep is lower than the boot's, you'll have a sloppy fit and poor control of your skis. It's easier to modify a boot to deal with the second problem than the first. Some Salomon boot models have a buckle with a special fore-aft adjustment that is effective in adjusting the boot's instep height.

TIBIAL ANGLE: This is the angle at which your lower leg rises from your foot. Almost everyone's angles outward a bit, but there are wide variations, even between an individual's left and right legs. Some boots have decent adjustment for this, within a limited range. A good boot fitter can make these adjustments on any boot.

FORE-AFT BALANCE: A number of factors in the design of a boot contribute to its overall effect on your balance, fore and aft, as you move up and down from a tall stance to a low crouch and back. With the boots buckled tight, you should be able to comfortably move through this range. The bottom line is this: if you can't, either the boot needs to be adjusted or you're in the wrong boot. A good boot fitter will know what to do.

CUSTOM UPGRADES
Liners

Your boot's liner must do two things well: It must conform to the shape of your foot to provide a comfortable fit, and it must transmit forces and vibrations between the shell and your foot and leg. If you focus only on the first requirement, you'll end up with a thick liner filled with soft, mushy foam. Controlling the ski with a liner like this is like trying to sign your name wearing a boxing glove. The second

The firmness and thickness of a boot's liner has a big effect on the boot's performance and comfort.

requirement begs for a liner so thin and firm that there is almost no liner at all. Unless the shape of the shell exactly matches that of your body, and no shell does, skiing in a boot like this will be a painful experience.

Traditional boot liners balance these requirements with varying degrees of success. Rental boots typically have thick, soft liners that will be acceptably comfortable for a wide range of renters and suitable for beginners, but once you've reached the ranks of aspiring intermediate skiers, you need something better. This is when you need to take your boot shopping seriously and find the right fit.

Thermo-fit Liners

Much-improved fit and performance are now available in many boots with the arrival of heat-molding, or what I call *thermo-fit* liners. Pioneered by Raichle in the mid to late 1990s as an after-market item, many boots now come with them. Versions are still available as after-market items to replace the conventional liners that came with your boots.

These liners are filled with a material that becomes soft when heated, then sets to shape as it cools. After heating the liners in a special oven, your boot fitter puts them in your boot shells. You buckle up the boots, stand in them for awhile, and you're good to go with a liner that matches the contours not only of your foot, but the inside of your shell. The process can be repeated if necessary.

The fit is an improvement over traditional liners because it matches your foot and leg precisely. The material in some of the higher-performance models is firmer than the padding in a traditional liner,

An after-market thermo-fit liner that has been molded to its owner's foot and boot. Note how the liner has molded to the inside of the shell.

too, and so performs better. Since the process does not add material to the liner, however, a thermo-fit liner will not make a boot tighter if you have narrow feet or your instep is low.

If the stock liners that came with your boots are packed out to the point where you just can't make them snug, but the shells are still good, a new thermo-fit liner is something to consider.

One company, Tecnica, makes an ingenious thermo-fit liner that is heated electrically. Instead of putting them in an oven, you plug them in to a special controller. As with other thermo-fit liners, this process can be repeated. They also come with a lower-wattage electrical source that heats the liners just enough to dry them out overnight and make them toasty in the morning but not enough to disturb the fit.

Boots

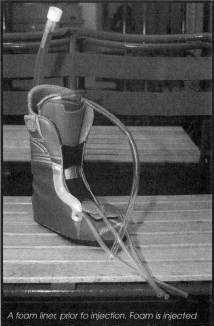

A foam liner, prior to injection. Foam is injected into the large tubes on the back of the liner and top of the tongue. As the foam expands through the liner, the excess comes out the other tubes.

Injected Foam Liners

At the high end of the performance spectrum are foam liners, of which I am a devotee. They are injected with a material that expands and forms to the shape of your foot—and then sets in that shape. This has three important benefits: First, material is added to the liner, filling in space so the volume of the boot matches that of your foot. This can make a world of difference, particularly to a skier with a very narrow or low-volume foot. Second, the fit is exact, so you have even pressure all around your foot, and no hot spots. Have you ever stuck a big spoon into a bowl of Jell-O and pried out a scoop? That's how my boots feel when I take them off at the end of the day. Third, because the fit is exact, you

can use a firmer material that enhances boot performance.

Done right, nothing fits or performs better than foam. If you have a great pair of boots whose liners have bit the dust, replacing them with foam liners will give you a pair of boots that ski even better than the originals and save you money over a new pair. The difference in fit and performance between a boot with a stock liner and the same boot with a foam liner is remarkable, with little or no sacrifice in comfort. And while you are lucky to get 100 days of skiing out of a stock liner, a good foam liner will last up to 300 days or more.

Done wrong, nothing is more frustrating and hurts worse than a foam liner. The secret is finding the right person to "shoot" your boots. You *must* do background research before picking a boot fitter to foam your liners, or you could live to regret it. I have, on several occasions, driven 120 miles each way to get my boots foamed by the guy I trusted most to get it right. First and foremost, find one who has years of experience injecting foam liners and who will guarantee the results. Research is essential. This is like shopping for a knee surgeon; you want the guy who does 100 a year, not 10.

The process of foaming a pair of liners could be the most painful ten or twenty minutes you will ever spend in ski boots. You put the empty, unfoamed liners in your boot shells, then step in and buckle up. The boot fitter mixes two chemicals in a plastic bottle, then hooks the bottle up to the tubes going into the liner. The chemicals react to produce a foam that expands and flows through the tubes into the liner.

As it expands inside the liner, the foam

Boots

gives off a lot of heat and crushes your foot like a boa constrictor. After the foam sets, it backs off a bit, leaving a perfect impression of your feet and ankles.

Many boot makers produce foam liners for their high-performance models. You can often use one brand's liner in another brand's shell. You can also buy generic foam liners that work in just about any shell, and these are often the best. A particular favorite of many experts and World Cup racers is the one made by Conform'able. A top boot fitter will know which liners will work with which shells.

I recommend using a liner that takes foam in the tongue as well as in the rest of the liner. A good foamed tongue will hold your foot in place without you having to close the shell tightly, giving you great performance with no discomfort.

Cutting-edge Goop

Another approach to a custom fit is the new injected liner from Sven Coomer, a legend in the ski industry who designed some of the most important and innovative products of the last thirty years. Among Sven's masterworks is the Nordica Grand Prix, the 1970s ski boot to which many of the best racing designs of today trace their lineages. Sven's liner can be used in many different brands and models of boots, and is much simpler to inject than a foam liner. Instead of chemical foam, they are injected with a goop that softens in a microwave oven, so you can fit and refit them yourself, adding more goop when needed.

This product is still in its infancy, but it is a sign that things are improving in the comfort, performance, and convenience categories.

"SOFT" BOOTS

A new species of soft ski boots has appeared on the market in recent years. These designs are based on the philosophy that a ski boot needs to be stiff laterally (side to side), to provide precise and firm edge control and grip, but doesn't need to be very stiff front and back. Compared to traditional overlap boots, soft boots are much softer in the front and a bit softer in the back. Some of these designs ski remarkably well. They are warmer, lighter, and more comfortable than conventional ski boots and easier to get in and out of. Most of them have more aggressive treads on their soles, too, for more security while walking on snow and ice.

If you do most of your skiing on groomed slopes, in soft or junk snow, or do a lot of heli-skiing, you should give this type of boot serious consideration. As of this writing, some specialty shops that carry them are selling one pair of soft boots for about every four pair of conventional ski boots. Expect to see soft boots become more and more popular as the skiing public becomes aware of them and manufacturers increase performance while maintaining comfort.

Plug Boots

The most recent bit of boot technology to descend from the World Cup to high-end recreational skiing is the so-called *plug boot*. This genre of ski boot was first developed during the era of Italian Olympic gold medalist and World Cup champion Alberto Tomba. Lange made boots for Tomba with thick shells and thin liners—and ground the insides of the shells to fit Alberto's feet. This approach has been adopted by a number of boot makers who support World Cup racers. It works very well, as long as you have the time to test and grind—and have someone knowledgeable to do the grinding.

Footbeds

You put a lot of force on the soles of your feet when you ski, so your boot should give you good support from below along the entire length of your foot. For this reason, a lot of serious skiers replace the stock insoles that come with their boots with either better after-market athletic footbeds, called *trim-to-fits*, or custom footbeds made specifically for their feet. Just about every good ski shop deals in both.

Russel Bollig, who as owner and operator of Podium Footwear has made innumerable orthotics for top athletes (including Lance Armstrong and members of the U.S. Ski Team), puts it this way: Your footbeds should be like "boot gaskets," filling in the spaces between your feet and your boot soles and providing firm, uniform support. In fact, he thinks of shoe- and boot-fitting in general that way.

The key issue for footbeds is how much your feet pronate (flatten or roll inward), when you put skiing-type pressures on them. A little bit is ok, but too much compromises your control of the ski. If your foot supports itself adequately, you can ski with no footbed at all. Most skiers need some support from the footbed to achieve adequate stability, and that often means replacing the ones that come in your boots with something more substantial.

Trim-to-fit Footbeds

These are after-market insoles that fall somewhere between stock insoles and

The tops (left) and bottoms (right) of different types of footbeds. The minimal support provided by stock footbeds (middle) is sufficient for some, but many skiers will benefit from upgrading to either trim-to-fit (bottom) or custom-molded (top) footbeds.

custom footbeds with regard to support and performance. Models from DownUnders and Superfeet, who also make moldable cork custom footbeds, are good examples. At around $25, these are much more supportive than stock insoles and mold slightly to your feet with a couple of days' use.

Different brands have different shapes and are therefore suited to different feet. Try a few to find the ones that match you.

Bollig and many other experts recommend that before you toss significant money at custom footbeds, you first try trim-to-fits. Don't be afraid to augment them yourself with small foam shims to improve their fit. Your feet will tell you if you're doing the right thing. The custom jobs should be Plan B if you can't get a good "gasketlike" fit.

Custom Footbeds

Most people who really need custom work do so because they have hypermobile sub-talar joints, which results in excessive prona-tion, often as the result of injuries, according to Bollig. Feet with high arches tend to be more rigid and are less likely to require spe-cial support. It's the flatter ones that most need the extra support in a ski boot.

Custom footbeds are made of plastic or cork that is molded to the shape of the bottoms of your feet. Most are molded under heat directly against your feet, with prices ranging from $75 to $200 a pair. This is an item whose quality will depend not so much on how much you spend but rather on the experience and skill of the individual who makes them for you. You can get a good pair just about anywhere in the price range, if the right person makes them. So ask around for recom-

mendations before you select a boot fitter to make your custom footbeds.

This may sound like a lot of money, but consider that a good pair will last you for many years. I used one pair of footbeds for eighteen years, until my boot fitter refused to put them into yet another pair of boots. (It might have been the smell that finally got to him.)

Orthotics

For people with problem feet, there are *orthotics*. These are generally molded from plaster casts taken of your feet by a licensed podiatrist, podorthist, or ortho-pedic doctor. Lots of skiers talk about the great orthotics they have, when what they really have are custom footbeds.

TUNING THE SHELL SETUP

Once you've found the right boots and fitted them with the right footbeds, you're not done. You need to consider some setup parameters.

Canting

The cuff of a ski boot does not rise per-pendicularly from the sole of the boot. Instead, it is angled outward slightly to conform to the shape of your leg. Just how much it is angled is important, because it has a lot to do with how well the ski will grip and turn. The technical term for this angle is *lateral cant*, or simply cant, and there are several ways to adjust it so it will be just right for you.

Here is a simple, commonly used method of checking if your boots are canted more or less correctly: Put them on and buckle them up snugly. Tie a small weight, like a wedding ring, to a three-foot-long string. (If you have a plumb bob,

To conform to human anatomy, the cuffs of ski boots are angled, or **canted**, outward.

and tell you if you need more or less cant, but there are a lot of charlatans out there, too. The best approach is to start with the weight-on-a-string method, then experiment with temporary cant adjustments until you find what works best for you. If you're diligent, you'll know the right setup when you hit it.

If your boots have a cant-adjustment mechanism, start by experimenting with different settings until you find the one that works best for you. Seth Masia, an industry expert and former equipment editor for *Ski* magazine, recommends the following method for getting a pair of such boots in the ballpark. Loosen the cant-adjustment screws, then put the boots on, buckle them up, and flex them back and forth a few times. Finally, tighten the adjustment mechanisms *before* you unbuckle the boots and take them off. Bear in mind that many of these adjustment mechanisms are not very effective, so you should still check them with the weight-on-a-string method.

If your boots have no cant adjustment system the system is ineffective, or the range of adjustment is too small experiment by putting a sheet of some firm material between the boot's liner and shell over the inside of your ankle. Trail maps, cork, and neoprene work well. Go take a run or two on some firm, packed snow. (You'll have a hard time feeling any difference on soft snow.) If you don't feel any difference, put more material in there until you do. Keep putting in more material until you know you've got too much. Next, take all the material out and go through the same process with material on the other side of the cuff. If your boots were already tight around your calves

use that.) Standing on a hard, level floor, hold the string against the middle of your kneecap, dangling the weight just above your foot. As a rule of thumb, the weight should fall between the middle of your big toe and the middle of the toe next to it. If you are outside that range, your boots probably need adjustment.

There is no shortage of whiz-bang gizmos for measuring your stance in your boots and spitting out the "correct" amount of cant, but I am skeptical that they are any better than the method described above. A top-flight ski instructor or boot fitter will be able to look at you

Boots

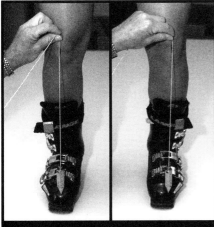

The boot on the left is canted well. The boot on the right is overcanted.

This is what a skier looks like in boots that are undercanted (top photo) and overcanted (bottom photo).

and ankles, you may need to move the buckle attachment points on the cuffs first.

You'll know when you've found the right setup.

If your optimum setup requires putting material in the boot, you have three choices for a long-term adjustment. First, you can glue small sheets of cork or neoprene to the liner. This you can do yourself. Second, you can have special beveled shims put under your bindings by a knowledgeable ski shop. This works well but has a couple of drawbacks: You'll now have specific left and right skis, and you won't be able to ski your best on any other skis. Third, you can have the soles of your boots shaved to achieve the same cant angle. This is a very specialized task that should only be done by a highly qualified boot fitter who does such work regularly, and whose track record you know.

There are those who argue that these methods of adjustment have very different effects on your skiing. I'm skeptical of this. Except in cases that involve gross adjustments of four degrees or more, I think they are equivalent. Some also claim that making adjustments to the footbed can solve such problems. I believe footbed adjustments are important, but that they address different issues.

Boots

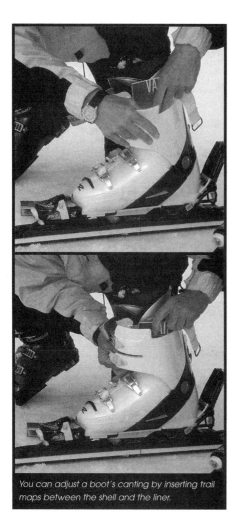
You can adjust a boot's canting by inserting trail maps between the shell and the liner.

commonly, *forward lean*. Boots have forward lean so you can flex into a low stance without losing your balance backward. If your boots have too little forward lean, you won't be able to move up and down through an adequate range. This will have a particularly adverse effect on your ability to ski in moguls.

You can easily determine if a pair of boots has the proper amount of forward lean. Put on the boots and buckle them up snugly. Standing on a hard, flat floor, crouch as low as you can without falling over backward. If you can't get your hips down to the level of your knees, you need more forward lean. If you can easily get your rear end well below your knees, you may have more than you need. A lot of World Cup racers can get their hips well below their knees in this exercise (many can touch their butt to their heels), but this is one of many examples of World Cup equipment characteristics that are inappropriate for all but a few skiers.

Many women need more forward lean than their boots provide. This is due to the distribution of mass in a typical woman's body and the fact that so many boots are really designed for a male physiology.

Some boots have forward lean adjustment devices built into them. Many don't. Tecnica makes some good examples. You can increase any boots' forward lean by putting material in the back of the boot between the shell and liner, or by adding a *spoiler*—a plastic extension on top of the back of the shell. Some Lange models have interchangeable heel plates of different thicknesses for the boot's sole that change the boot's forward lean.

Some bindings place the heel of the boot higher than the toe; these will

After the first thirty or so days of skiing in a pair of boots, check the canting again. As the liner packs out and gets thinner between your leg and the cuff, the cant will be effectively reduced, and you may need to make adjustments.

Forward Lean

Not only is the cuff of your boot angled outward, it is also angled forward. This is referred to as forward cant or, more

The degree to which a boot's cuff is pitched forward is its forward lean. This helps you stay in balance in a deeply flexed position.

If you can't crouch this low without losing your balance backward, your boots need more forward lean. If you want to ski well in moguls, you should be able to get even lower.

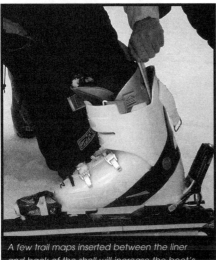

A few trail maps inserted between the liner and back of the shell will increase the boot's forward lean.

effectively increase the boots' forward lean a bit, too. Some of Rossignol's bindings, for example, can be mounted in such a way that they add two degrees of forward lean to a size 26 (Mondo Point) boot, around a 15 percent increase for most high performance boots. (These particular bindings can also be mounted flat.) Other bindings, such as those from Atomic, hold the boot sole parallel to the ski's base and have no effect on the boots' forward lean.

Tracking

Try this experiment: Stand with your feet about six inches apart, as if you were standing on skis. It is critical that your feet be parallel and not splayed. Look down at your knees, then bend your ankles so your knees move over your toes. Do your knees move straight forward or do they move to the inside or outside? A large discrepancy between this and the way your boots flex could be a problem, especially

Boots

for high-performance boots on advanced skiers. I personally like a boot that tracks a bit straighter than my legs, because it makes the tips of my skis bite more when I bend my ankles.

Changing the tracking of your legs is relatively easy. Simply put a wedge under your insoles or footbeds that tilts them to one side or the other. Tilting them toward the outside will make your knees track outward more. Tilting them the other way will make your knees track more toward the inside.

Your boot fitter can easily make minor adjustments to the boot's tracking. Major adjustments require major surgery (to the boot).

ADJUSTING THE FLEX

Some models of boots have good shell-stiffness adjustment mechanisms. Some have mechanisms that don't do much. Ask the boot fitter to show you the ranges of adjustment of the boots you try on. See if you can feel a big difference. Tecnica and Rossignol have some of the more effective adjustments. If your boots don't have such an adjustment, they can be softened or stiffened by a knowledgeable boot fitter. He can soften them by making strategically placed cuts in the shell or remove certain rivets or screws. If your boots are too soft, they can be stiffened with a couple of well-placed rivets or bolts. This work should be delegated to someone who does it for a living.

You can adjust the forward flex of your boots in a couple of ways, right on the hill. Make coarse adjustments with the top buckle. Leave it loose and you've got a lot of leeway, suitable for bumps,

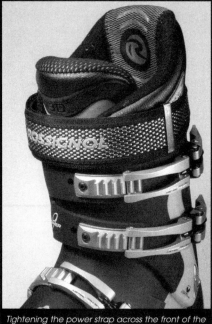

Tightening the power strap across the front of the plastic cuff stiffens the boot considerably.

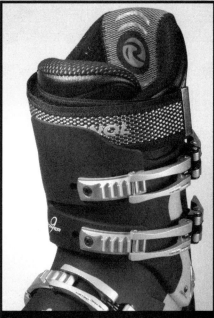

Tightening the power strap against the tongue under the plastic cuff provides a more progressive flex.

powder, and fast cruising. Clamp it down and the slack disappears, giving you more immediate response for short, snappy turns on firm snow.

Make fine adjustments with your power strap—the Velcro-closure nylon strap attached to the top of the boot cuff. It's like another buckle, farther up your leg. You can exercise a lot of control over the boot's flex by how tightly you cinch it down and by where you place it. For maximum stiffness and bite, wrap the strap around the outside of the front part of the plastic cuff. But you can achieve more subtle flex control by putting it under that piece of plastic so that it bears directly on the tongue. Carol Levine, a respected authority on ski technique and instruction, recommends using your power strap in this position most of the time. That's where I put mine.

While most top skiers regard their power straps as something of an essential sixth buckle, not everyone does. Olympic medalist and World Champion Bode Miller hardly closes his.

A final note about power straps: Most ski pants have an elastic powder cuff that fits snugly over the top of your boots. If you pull the cuff over your power strap, it will be a pain to adjust the power strap on the hill. Pull the pants' powder cuff over the boot tongue before cinching down the power strap, then close the strap over the outside of the powder cuff. This way, you can adjust the strap easily on the hill.

TUNING THE FIT

Professional skiers are notorious for tinkering with their boots. If you're going to spend six hours a day, five or more days a week,

The shaded areas are where you exercise the most control over the ski, and need the most precise fit.

twenty or more weeks a year in footwear that is unforgiving, you'd better get it right. But beyond comfort, we're talking about the control system for your skis. Like tuning a race car's suspension, tuning your boots will pay big dividends in your skiing.

The Essential Fit Kit

More than half of the fit adjustments you will make to your boots will involve adding material in order to fill in loose places or shift the position of your leg slightly in relation to the cuff. You can do a lot of this with simple materials and tools found in a hardware store and around the house. The monetary investment is small, and you can do the work on your kitchen table.

Shim Material

The first essential is some firm, pliable material about one-eighth-inch thick, such as rubber or cork, that you can cut with scissors or a knife. You'll cut this material into shims of various sizes to take up volume at critical places in your boots. Most often you'll glue it to the outside of the liner.

The most commonly used material is neoprene rubber. If you can find it with an adhesive backing, you're ahead of the game.

A favorite material of mine is cork. I buy it by the foot off of a three-foot-wide roll

A sheet of cork or neoprene and a can of contact cement are your primary tools for improving boot fit.

at my local hardware store. I like it because you can cut it with a plastic knife in the base lodge cafeteria. And if you can't find a plastic knife, you can cut it with the corner of a credit card or tear it into shape with your hands. It doesn't slip around in your boot and is remarkably durable. I carry four-inch squares of it in my boot bag and sometimes a few in a jacket pocket for on-the-hill adjustments.

Glue

The second essential material is some type of contact cement for gluing the shims to the outside of your liners.

You want glue with just the right balance of holding power and removability. The most commonly used contact cement is Barge, available at hardware stores. Household rubber cement will work but is a little on the weak side.

Solutions to Common Problems

Your Boots are Too Big

If your liners have packed out and you find yourself clamping your buckles down on the fourth notch to get a modicum of control, you need to reduce the overall volume inside your boot.

The most important places for your boots to be snug are around the top and sides of your instep and around and above your heel. If you have much slop in these spots, you're in trouble. With that in mind, try one of these remedies:

- Wear thicker socks.
- Take up some volume from the bottom of the boot. Pull out the liners and trace the outlines of their soles on a sheet of shim material, then cut it to shape. If you don't have any cork or neoprene, use the cardboard backing from a

Boots

A piece of cardboard cut to the shape of the footbed and placed under the liner will help tighten a loose boot.

L-shaped pads like the one shown here (and another on the other side) will help snug up a loose heel area.

couple of pads of 8 x 11 paper. Put one inside each boot, then replace the liners. (If you're using cardboard, start with two in each boot.) If the boots are still loose, put in another layer or two. Note that cardboard is not a permanent solution. It will get wet and eventually disintegrate inside your boot. Once you know how thick your shims need to be, a boot fitter can provide you with ones made specifically for this purpose.

- Pad the liner around the sides of the instep and the bend in the tongue. If you don't have any shim material with you, you can make the adjustment on the hill with paper napkins or paper towels. Cut or tear the material into squares about three inches on a side, then put your boots on and place the pads on top of your foot, centered under the bend in the tongue. If you feel no effect, add more. If this works for you, replace the napkins with some cork or neoprene, applied to the outside of the boot liner and tongue. When you've got the right size and thickness figured out, glue the shims to the liner and tongue. If the shim on the outside of the tongue doesn't hold up, you can try replacing it with some adhesive-backed felt on the inside of the tongue. (Dr. Scholl's Moleskin, available in supermarkets and drugstores, works well.)

- Be careful with this remedy, as most

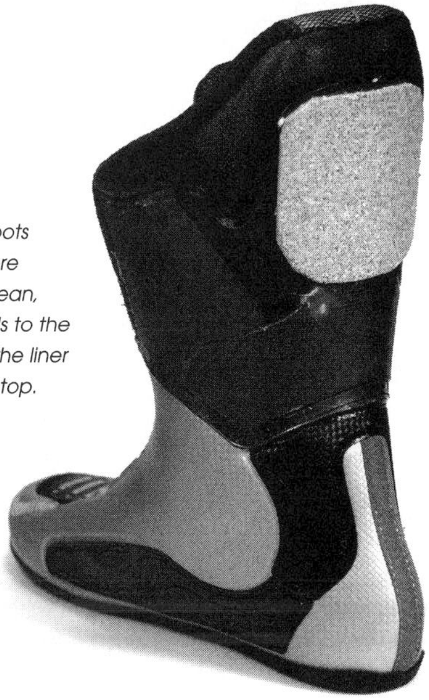

If your boots need more forward lean, glue pads to the back of the liner near the top.

Boots

The top buckles on most boots have multiple attachment points to accommodate legs of different thickness.

of the blood supply to your toes runs through your instep. Putting too much pressure on just the wrong spot is a recipe for cold feet. If this happens, cut a hole in the shim over the highest part of your instep.

And be careful not to add too much material over the navicular bone. This is the bony protrusion you can feel just below and ahead of your inside ankle bone. You will pay in agony for any excessive pressure on this bone.

• If your boots are loose around your ankles, try moving the buckles on the boot cuff. The parts of these buckles that are attached to the front of the cuff usually have a range of attachment points. The cuff of the boot can be tightened significantly by moving the buckle over. If you still can't tighten them enough, glue shims to your liners around the ankles above the level of your ankle bones.

The tongue on this liner attaches with Velcro. Moving it forward and back adjusts the instep height.

Increase your boot's cant and edge grip by applying a pad on the inside of the shin area. Placing the pad on the other side will reduce the cant.

Boots

- Get a custom-injected foam liner. This is a pricier option but is guaranteed to make the boot fit snugly.

YOUR HEELS MOVE AROUND

If your heels move side to side in your boots when you ski, you can snug them up by sticking L-shaped pads on the sides of the liner on either side of the heel. Any good ski shop will have pads specifically for this purpose.

If your heels move up and down more than a quarter of an inch when you ski, you need to do something about it. Follow the prescriptions in the section "Your Boots are Too Big" (page 28).

YOUR BOOTS GET WET INSIDE

This could mean one of two things. Either your boots leak or your feet perspire excessively. To determine which problem you have, spray one of your feet (not both) with antiperspirant (not deodorant) before you put your ski socks on in the morning. You should know by lunch if you've got a perspiration problem. If you do, try skiing in lighter socks and using the antiperspirant on both feet whenever you go skiing.

If your problem is leaky boots, you've got company. Many boots leak up near the toe where the shell closes on itself. There is usually a piece of rubber or plastic, called a toe dam, inserted into the shell whose purpose is to keep snow and water out. Sometimes toe dams fall out or tear, and some just don't do a very good job in the first place. You can try replacing the toe dams, but if this doesn't help, do what World Cup racers do: Put duct tape over the toe dam. A slightly more elegant solution is to run clear silicone caulk around the toe dam.

The black rubber piece just above the toe is the toe dam. This is the most likely place for a boot to leak.

Leakage is a particular problem with some of the first Rossignol models that have what is called an inverted overlap. This design allows snow thrown up by your inside ski to find its way between the overlapping pieces of the outside boot's shell. The best solution here is to have a ski shop pull open the flaps of the lower shell and lay them back down in the conventional, not inverted, position. If you can detect any difference in performance, I'll buy you a beer. If it doesn't make your boots drier, I'll buy you dinner.

YOU CAN'T MAKE YOUR SKIS GRIP

Your boots fit well, your skis are sharp, and your instructor says your technique has no serious technical deficiencies. Still, you just can't grip on hard snow. You may well need to increase the lateral cant of your boots. (See Canting on page 21.) You can do this by cutting some fitting material into four-inch squares and putting them between your liners and shells on the insides of your shins. Be careful not to insert them so far that they hit your anklebones. If your skis

Boots

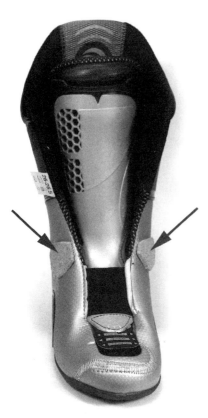

If your heel moves up and down, your foot rolls side to side, or you find yourself buckling your second and third buckles tighter and tighter, apply shims as shown here.

don't grip any better, add another layer. A custom insole may also help but will seldom be the complete solution.

Your Arches Ache

If your arch is lower or wider than the one your boot is designed for, your foot will ache. A heel lift will usually solve this problem; the ones available in drugstores and supermarkets, such as those from Dr. Scholls, work fine. Try putting them inside your liner, under the insole. If this raises your anklebone so it is uncomfortable, put the heel lift under the liner instead of under the insole, secured with duct tape so it doesn't move around in your boot.

Your Big Toenails Get Bruised

This is one of the most painful of boot problems. Many racers, in search of the ultimate fit, get boots so snug that they must constantly trim their toenails and suffer through the occasional blackened one. Fortunately, one of the following remedies usually works.

First, pull out the liners and look at the toes. Manufacturers achieve half-size steps in some boots by gluing rubber pads to the fronts of the liners. If yours have these, simply pull them off. Your boots will instantly be a half-size longer.

The next thing to try is a heel lift. This will pull your foot back a bit in the boot, giving your toes a little more room. If this doesn't work, it's time to take your boots to a good boot fitter, who will start by grinding away material inside the toe of the shells. If this doesn't give you enough room, the boot fitter will grind inside the heels. The last resort is heating up the

A boot press is often used to "punch out" areas in the shell that are causing painful pressure points.

Boots

plastic shells and pressing bulges into them in the vicinity of your big toe.

Your ski boots have cups molded into them to conform to the large lumps of your anklebones (anatomically speaking, your malleoli). The possible causes of pain here are the cups don't line up with your malleoli or they are not deep enough.

The first remedy to try is a heel lift placed inside the liner under the insole. If the cups are higher than your anklebones, this will lift your malleoli to a better level. If this doesn't work, your best bet is to take the boots to a boot fitter. He will be able to either lower your foot in the boot, if the cups are too low for your ankles, or make the cups deeper, if that is the problem. Both of these operations are routine.

THE KNUCKLE BEHIND YOUR
LITTLE TOE OR BIG TOE HURTS
This happens when you have a boot built on a last that is narrower than your foot or the arch length of the boot is too short. Take them to a boot fitter. Solving this problem usually requires work that can only be done in a good ski shop with some heavy-duty tools that you don't want to buy. The boot fitter may be able to solve the problem by trimming the liner or grinding the shell. He will heat up the shell in the problem area with a high-powered hot air gun, then put the boot on a press that will raise a bulge in the plastic. This is called "punching out" the shell. The bulge will look enormous at first, but the plastic will soon pull back a bit, closer to its original shape.

MAINTENANCE

Keep a close eye on the condition of the soles, paying special attention to the toe and heel. Look closely to see if the top, bottom, front, and back surfaces are rough, gouged, or rounded. Excessive wear will cause inconsistent binding release.

Replace worn or damaged parts right away. Skiing with a broken buckle can result in bigger problems, such as a tear in the plastic shell, which is virtually irreparable.

At the end of the season, buckle your boots up. Buckling the boot will help it keep its shape and be ready to go at the start of the next season. Make sure the tongue is positioned properly when you do this. Because mildew or mold will ruin the liner, check that the boots are dry inside before you put them away and store them in a dry place.

Warming Up Your Boots

Everyone's done it at one time or another: woken up in horror to find they left their boots in the car overnight. Your feet are facing a grim day of skiing when this happens. They will be cold most of the day, not to mention how hard it will be to get into those frozen boots in the first place. There is hope, however. Put your oven on about 200 degrees and stick your boots inside for five or ten minutes. This will warm them up quite well.

Drying Out Your Boots

Because everyone's feet perspire when they ski, even on cold days, boots get damp inside. And some boots just plain leak, especially in the spring.

Your boots should not be left damp inside for two important reasons: First, they will be miserable and cold when you

Boots

A boot drying system can also be used to dry gloves, hats, and shoes. Smaller, portable units are also available.

Many pros I know take the liners out of their boots at night. They will dry out quicker this way. It's not easy getting the liners back in some boots, however, and any fit-adjusting pads you have stuck to the liner can get knocked loose.

Get a heating pad at the drugstore for about $10. Place your boots on it overnight and they will be dry and warm in the morning.

The ultimate solution is to buy one of the many boot-drying systems available on the market. If you have a condo, cabin, or house in the mountains, consider a unit like the one pictured. Not only will it dry your boots, it will dry your hat and gloves, too. Smaller units, suitable for travel, are also available. Most portable ones don't work by blowing air into your boots but are simply low-wattage heaters that you stick down into the nether reaches of your boots. They are relatively inexpensive ($15–$30), and I am told by people who use them that they are quite effective.

ski in them. Second, the liner can easily develop mildew. If you find that your boots do not dry out overnight between days of skiing, here are a few tricks to try.

Put them on top of the refrigerator overnight. The boots will dry much faster in the warmer, drier air near the ceiling than they will in the cool air near the floor. This will solve the problem in most cases.

If you have access to a water heater, put your boots on top of it at night. They will be dry and toasty in the morning. Plus, the shells will be warm, so they'll be easier to get into.

Blow cool air into the boots with a hair drier. About fifteen minutes for each boot should do. Simply stick the nozzle of the hair dryer into the boot and turn it on. Do not blow warm or hot air into your boots. It can ruin both your boots and the hair dryer.

Boots

Skis

Something big happened to ski design in the second half of the 1990s. If you were around for the revolution, you know what I mean. All of a sudden skis were "shaped" with deep sidecuts and were much easier to ski well on. They turned easily and carved arcs that we had only dreamed of before. Whether this revolution was due to a rapid change in available materials and manufacturing techniques or a kick in the collective butt of the ski-engineering community delivered by the people designing carving snowboards is unclear, but the results are clear: Everyone skis better and has more fun.

The variety of skis targeted at particular sorts of skiing has ballooned since the new skis appeared. Every niche of terrain type and snow consistency is targeted with its own model. Some examples are shown on pages 38 and 39. But even though skis are focused on specific terrain and snow, they all seem to be much better at everything than the gear we used to use. How lucky can you get?

FINDING THE PERFECT SKI

Walk into a ski shop these days and you'll be confronted by an array of brands and models competing for your attention like boxes of children's breakfast food in the supermarket. Even picking a ski up and flexing it won't tell you an awful lot. This section is your equivalent of the nutritional information printed on the side of the cereal box, helping you decide which product is right for you.

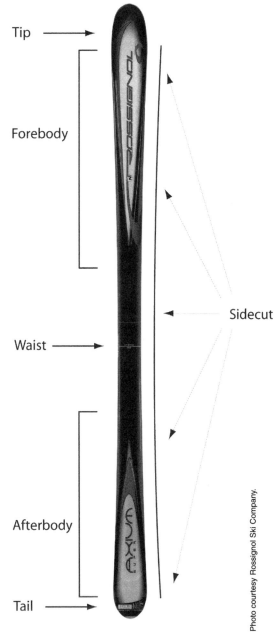

Tip

Forebody

Waist

Afterbody

Tail

Sidecut

Photo courtesy Rossignol Ski Company.

Traditional or Shaped?

Don't even think about buying a pair of skis that aren't "shaped." Regardless of how good a deal you might think you are getting on a brand-new, never-been-mounted pair of the best skis from the preshaped era, they are a waste of your time and money. If you can't afford a new pair of shaped skis, you are much better off buying a decent used pair than a pristine pair of old-school sticks.

Brand Personality

While all the manufacturers make good skis, they each have their own character. Dynastar, for example, always has and probably always will make skis that are light and lively. Some of K2 skis fit in this category, too. Volant, on the other hand, has always produced extremely quiet and smooth skis. Head and Fischer tend toward that end of the spectrum. Atomic and Rossignol have a reputation for producing skis that fall in the middle. If you don't have a strong opinion on this, plan on testing models from several manufacturers.

Waist Width

The width of a ski underfoot determines to a great extent how well it holds on hard snow, and how calm, collected, and forgiving it is, especially in ungroomed and unpacked snow. Have you ever wondered why ice skates hold so well? It's because the edge is right under your ankle. The narrower a ski is, the more it's like an ice skate. For this reason, a ski that has a narrower waist holds better on hard snow and goes from edge to edge more quickly. A wider-waisted ski, on the other hand, is easier to manage in loose snow, powder, and crud because it doesn't sink

as deeply into the snow, and because that pesky outside edge is less likely to catch when you're not careful. For this reason, beginner's skis are wider underfoot, too.

Matt Carroll, the hard goods manager of Kenny's Double Diamond Ski Shop in Vail, one of the best, classifies skis by waist width, as follows.

Snow Type	Ski Type	Waist Width
Powder and crud exclusively	Fat ski	88 mm and up
Terrain park, half-pipe	Free ride	80–85 mm
Mostly loose snow, some packed powder	Midfat	78–85 mm
Packed powder, some loose snow	All-mtn.	70–80 mm
Hardpacked snow and packed powder	Carving ski	64–66 mm
Ice, hardpack, and racing	Race carve	62–67 mm
All conditions	Beginner's skis	

Sidecut Radius

This is, of course, the design point at the forefront of the ski revolution. Prior to 1996, hardly anyone could quantify the sidecut of their skis. Now it's stamped on the ski's top in big numbers for the world to see. Although high-tech terms such as "parabolic" and "cycloidal" have been used to describe sidecuts, most often inaccurately, by ski marketing departments, in almost all cases, sidecuts are circular in shape.

The radius of the curve made by the ski's sidecut is the more important number than the absolute widths at the tip, tails

Skis

RENT OR BUY?

BEGINNERS

The best skis for your first forays to the slope will not suit you after three to five days of skiing, so it is best to rent. Once you can get around the easy intermediate slopes (marked by blue squares on trail maps) without too much trepidation, you're ready for a pair of skis you can stick with for awhile.

ADVANCED AND EXPERT SKIERS

All levels of equipment are available for rent these days, making renting a good option for everyone in some circumstances. If you are traveling far for a ski vacation and don't want to mess around with toting your skis, you can call ahead to your destination and rent your dream skis for the week. Or you can try a variety of skis.

The other situation in which renting makes sense is a ski trip to somewhere that has snow conditions not suited to your skis. If you do most of your skiing in New England, for example, and are going to Jackson Hole for a week of midwinter fluff, reserve a pair of midfat or fat skis for your trip.

making really big ones. They also require more attention and finesse when running straight. Wide-waisted skis cannot be given short-radius sidecuts, lest they become excessively wide and clumsy at the tip and tail.

To make a turn on skis, you tip them up on edge and push against them. The tip and tail, because they are wider than the middle, grab the snow, making the ski bend like a bow. The more deeply the ski bends, the more tightly and decisively the ski turns as it moves forward. (The ski's stiffness in torsion will also have an effect here and will be figured into the ski's design according to the ability level of the skier for which it is designed.)

Two-time overall World Cup champion Janica Kostelic bends her outside ski into reverse camber.

and waist. John Howe, a ski engineer who has had a long career designing groundbreaking skis, states that a radius of 15 meters or less is needed for making true arc-to-arc short-radius carved turns at recreational speeds. This number can be greater for large-radius turns on groomed intermediate runs, but skis with larger sidecuts will require skidded turns on steeper, narrow trails. Howe has made excellent skis with radii as small as 9.5 meters.

The trade-off is that skis optimized for carving short-radius turns are not so adept at

Size of Turn	Appropriate Sidecut Radius
Short turns	14 m and below
Medium radius and cruising	15–20 m
Big turns and high-speed open mountain cruising	20 m and up
Mogul skiing, exclusively	20 m and up

Skis

Type: Slalom race   *Waist: 65 mm*   *Sidecut: 13 m*

Description: Narrow waist helps the ski hold well on hard snow, and the tight sidecut radius makes for short turns. Recreational skis designed for short turns usually derive from this type of ski.

Type: Giant Slalom race   *Waist: 68 mm*   *Sidecut: 21 m*

Description: Dimensions, flex, and torsion are optimized for medium to long-radius turns on hard snow and ice at speed. Many recreational cruising models descend from giant slalom race skis.

Type: Packed snow cruising   *Waist: 65 mm*   *Sidecut: 16 m*

Description: Detuned giant slalom race design. Narrow waist holds well on packed snow and moderately deep sidecut carves medium to long-radius turns.

Type: All-mountain   *Waist: 70 mm*   *Sidecut: 18 m*

Description: An all-around advanced ski. Design parameters are balanced to handle all terrain and snow conditions commonly found on managed ski slopes, with occasional forays into the untracked bowls and trees of "the backside."

Type: All-mountain   *Waist: 76 mm*   *Sidecut: 19 m*

Description: Designed to be skied 50 percent off-trail, 50 percent on-trail. In-between width, sidecut, and flex make for a versatile ski. Edge grip and quickness are traded for stability in ungroomed snow.

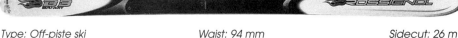

Type: Off-piste ski   *Waist: 94 mm*   *Sidecut: 26 m*

Description: "Off-piste" means "off the beaten track." Width underfoot provides calm, predictable behavior in varying unpacked snow conditions. Soft flex allows ski to bend into deep arc, even with a relatively straight sidecut.

Skis

Type: All-around recreational   *Waist: 67 mm*   *Sidecut: 16 m*

Description: A ski with modern dimensions for intermediate skiers. Narrow waist and moderately deep sidecut combined with soft torsional flex provide a forgiving ski that can still carve.

Type: Women-specific carving   *Waist: 67 mm*   *Sidecut: 14 m*

Description: Flex pattern and binding placement are tuned to work well with the relative lengths and masses of a woman's limbs and body segments. Female-specific models are available in many performance categories.

Type: Mogul   *Waist: 66 mm*   *Sidecut: 24 m*

Description: Relatively straight sidecut facilitates pivoting. Narrow waist allows for quickness edge to edge.

Type: Freestyle/Terrain park   *Waist: 80 mm*   *Sidecut: 24 m*

Description: Wide waist and straight sidecut reduce likelihood of catching edges when landing jumps. Tail has almost as much roll-up as tip so skiing backward is no problem.

Type: Skier-cross competition   *Waist: 68 mm*   *Sidecut: 21 m*

Description: A beefed-up all-mountain ski with extra vibration-absorption components. Designed for edge grip and stability at speed and in rough conditions.

Type: Junior all-mountain   *Waist: 65 mm*   *Sidecut: 13 m*

Description: Dimensions and flex are scaled to a child's weight and size. Junior skis are available in all categories, from beginning to racing skis.

Skis

Design Terms

BASE: *n.* The bottom surface of the ski. All bases are made of polyethylene.

BEVEL: *n.* The angle at which a ski's edge is tuned when compared to the base of the ski. If the bottom side of an edge is not flat and level with the plastic base, it is said to have bottom bevel. If the side of the edge is not tuned to a 90-degree angle to its bottom surface, the variance from 90 degrees is said to be its side bevel.

CAMBER: *n.* The arch described by the ski when viewed from the side. If the ski is laid on a flat surface with no weight on it, the middle of the ski will be off the surface, supported by the tip and tail. The height of the ski off the surface is its camber. Camber helps distribute the skier's weight properly along the length of the ski. Today's skis have less camber than traditional designs.

CONTACT LENGTH: *n.* The length of the ski from its widest point at the tip to its widest point at the tail. This is the important length measurement of a ski with regard to its skiing characteristics. Note that different models or brands of ski may have the same length marked on them, but have different contact lengths. See MATERIAL LENGTH.

FLEX: *n.* The stiffness of the ski when bent from tip to tail. Stiff skis track better and sometimes have more edge grip. Soft skis are easier to turn and perform better in soft snow.

FOREBODY: *n.* The portion of the ski ahead of the binding.

REVERSE CAMBER: *n.* The curved shape a ski takes on when it's edged and bent in a turn. Reverse camber is essential to carved turns. See CAMBER.

MATERIAL LENGTH: *n.* The length of the material used to build a ski as it lays flat on the workbench, prior to being molded to shape. This is the measurement used by the manufacturer when declaring the length of a particular ski. See CONTACT LENGTH.

PARABOLIC: *adj.* A marketing term coined by the Elan ski company to describe their early shaped skis. The term's pseudoscientific sound made it popular, and it was often used to describe all shaped skis. Technically speaking, there is nothing parabolic about skis today, but the term lives on.

P-TEX: *n.* The generic name often used for the plastic material from which ski bases are made. P-Tex was a particular brand of polyethylene used in the 1960s and for some time later. The bases of modern skis are made from somewhat different material.

RADIUS: *n.* The size of a turn (turn radius) or the shape of the curved sidecut of a ski (sidecut radius). Note that although they are related, these are not the same

Skis

number. That is, a ski with a sidecut radius of 14 meters won't necessarily carve a turn of that size. Big turns have a large radius; small turns, a small radius.

REVERSE CAMBER: n. The curved shape a ski takes on when it's edged and bent in a turn. Reverse camber is essential to carved turns. See *CAMBER*.

SHAPED: adj. A ski with an exaggerated hourglass shape, very wide at the tip and tail compared with the waist. Roughly speaking, a ski with a sidecut radius of 30 meters or less.
Syn.: Super-sidecut.

SIDE CAMBER: n. A dimension used to quantify the depth of a ski's hourglass shape, or sidecut. Determined by drawing a line from the ski's edge at its widest point at the tip to its widest point at the tail, then measuring the distance between that line and the ski's waist. See *SIDECUT*.

SIDECUT: n. The hourglass shape defined by the ski's edge when viewed from above. The first skis with sidecut were made by Sondre Nordheim in 1870, in Norway. Most skis have uniform circular sidecuts. Composite curves may be used on some slalom models. Sidecut helps the tip and tail of the ski bite and makes the ski bend into reverse camber when edged and pressured in a turn. See *SIDE CAMBER*.

SUPER-SIDECUT: n. See *SHAPED*.

TORSION: n. Twisting of the ski along its length, as if it were a garden hose you twisted in your hands. A ski that is stiffer in torsion will bite and hold better at the tip and tail, making it better at carving. A ski softer in torsion will be easier to turn.

TRADITIONAL: adj. Describes skis made prior to the introduction of super-sidecuts. Ant.: Super-sidecut or Shaped.

WAIST: n. The narrowest point on a ski when viewed from above.

Performance Terms

ABSORPTION: n. The ability of a ski to bend smoothly as it contacts a mogul or other irregularity, allowing the skier to maintain good balance. A ski with poor absorption can throw you over the handlebars or back on your heels when you hit a bump.

AGILE: adj. Easy to maneuver and doesn't resist efforts to make quick changes in direction. Syn.: Nimble. Ant.: Sluggish.

BEEFY: adj. Hefty feeling on the snow. May feel heavy and sluggish at slow speeds but often becomes livelier with speed. Unfazed by chunks of snow. Ant.: Noodly.

CARVED TURN: n. A turn in which the ski does not slip sideways, but tracks cleanly along its edge. The skier's sensation is that of riding on curved rails.

CHATTER: n. Intermittent edge grip on hard snow or ice (the edge holds, releases, holds, releases, etc.). Gives the sensation of the ski skittering or bouncing sideways across the surface. Often accompanied by a condition called "machine-gun leg."

CHATTER MARKS: n. The condition of the snow surface after many skis have chattered over it. Skiing's equivalent of a washboard road.

CRISP: adj. Feels quick and responsive. A ski with crisp performance is like a tightly sprung sports car; it responds instantly to your every command and inclination. Syn.: Precise.

CRUISER: n. A ski with lots of stability at high speeds and a preference for making big turns instead of small ones. Think "Mercedes sedan on the autobahn."

DAMP: adj. Absorbs vibration well. Feels calm, smooth, and comfortable at high speeds or on hard, rough snow. A ski that is too damp feels dead. One that is not damp enough feels nervous and skittish. A ski that has the right damping for hard snow and ice may have too much for soft snow and vice versa. Ant.: Nervous, squirrely.

EASE OF TURNING: n. This describes how easy it is to start or initiate a turn on a particular pair of skis. Often traded off against stability and edge grip in a ski's design.

EDGE RELEASE: n. See RELEASE.

ENERGETIC: adj. Returns the energy you put into it, much like a spring. Syn.: Lively, Snappy, Responsive. Ant.: Damp.

FORGIVING: adj. Allows a skier to make many technique mistakes without penalty. For example, standing with your weight too far back on a forgiving ski probably won't adversely affect your ability to control it.

GRIPPY: adj. Holds well on hard snow and ice.

HEAVY: adj. Slow to turn. May also be heavy in weight, but not necessarily. Sometimes skis that are overly damp feel heavy, even if they are not.

LIGHT: adj. Feels quick in turns or feels as if it doesn't weigh much. This is desirable in situations where quick turning is needed but not necessarily where stability is required.

LIVELY: adj. See ENERGETIC.

MUSCULAR: adj. Has an infinite supply of power. Combines energy with beefiness, and stability at speed. A muscular ski tends to demand good technique. Syn.: Powerful.

NERVOUS: adj. Exhibits excessive vibration and instability.

NIMBLE: adj. See AGILE.

NOODLY: adj. Marked by excessive instability. Not powerful. Ant.: Beefy.

PLATFORM: n. The feeling of stability underfoot. A ski with a solid platform grips

Skis

and holds its line even when pushed hard by aggressive or heavy skiers.

POP: n. See *REBOUND.*

POWERFUL: adj. See *MUSCULAR.*

PRECISE: adj. See *CRISP.*

PULL: v. To draw the skier easily into and through the turn. Refers to the sensation that the tip of the ski wants to turn, reducing the need for you to actively steer it.

QUICK: n. Turns smartly and sharply, with a minimum of effort on the part of the skier.

REBOUND: n. The feeling that the ski catapults you out of one turn and into the next. It's the result of the ski carving a tight arc at the end of a turn and releasing quickly, or its edge being set sharply. Syn.: Pop.

RELEASE: v. The ski coming off its edge at the end of a turn and allowing the skier to start a new turn. Some skis release smoothly, some quickly, some like to hang on to the turn.

RESPONSIVE: adj. See *ENERGETIC.*

ROLL: v. To tip your ski on edge. A gentle way to start a turn, requiring little effort.

SILKY: adj. Glides smoothly over the snow. A silky ski often exhibits excellent absorption in the bumps.

SNAPPY: adj. See *ENERGETIC.*

STABLE: adj. Feels solid and unwavering underfoot and doesn't vibrate at high speeds. A stable ski usually inspires confidence to ski fast.

SWEET SPOT: n. The optimum balance point on the ski that results in optimum turning. Skis with big sweet spots allow you to stand wherever—fore or aft—and they still deliver good performance. Skis with small sweet spots are less forgiving, because you have less room for error. The sweet spot of such a ski may vary from turn to turn, and even within a turn. A ski with a big sweet spot may not be able to do as many things as well as one with a smaller sweet spot and may require bigger edging and pressuring movements to make adjustments in a turn.

Skis

First Elan and Kneissl shocked the ski world with short, odd-looking skis having narrow waists and clownishly wide tips and tails. They were viewed skeptically by everyone except those who tried them. K2 and Head followed soon with their own models.

It was the K2 Four that finally turned the industry on its ear. Bode Miller, then a young ski racer at the Carrabassett Valley Ski Academy in Maine, astounded everyone who was paying attention by dominating the slalom and GS races at the 1996 U.S. Junior Olympics on a pair of K2 Four factory seconds. These were not designed to be racing skis; they were engineered for advanced recreational use. But Bode, never a person to be hemmed in by convention, recognized their carving abilities and put them to good use.

The next season, K2 Fours were everywhere, and those who switched to them and understood carving became visibly better skiers in a matter of days. There were holdouts, but within a few years, nearly everyone had gotten the message and straight sticks became passé. Things have continued to evolve rapidly, and today a pair of K2 Fours looks quaintly straight and old-school.

If you are interested in the subject of ski design, I highly recommend *The New Skiing Mechanics* by John Howe (McIntyre Publishing, 2001). Howe was the chief engineer at Head through much of the 1970s and 1980s and certainly knows whereof he speaks. The book is also an excellent reference on the fundamental physical mechanics of the sport for those with a taste for vectors and forces.

A note about special-purpose mogul skis: You might think that moguls, demanding quick, short turns, would favor a ski with a short sidecut radius. Ultrahigh-end mogul skiing doesn't, however, involve much carving. Rather, the turns incorporate a lot of quick, precise pivoting, thus favoring a straighter ski.

Your Ability and Taste

Be a straight shooter with the salesperson. Don't oversell yourself. If you will be best off with an easy-turning ski, don't put yourself on a race board with monster edge grip. Don't underrate yourself, either. Pick a ski based on where you are and where you're going as a skier, not where you've been.

I think aesthetics are important, too. If you are repulsed by the graphics on the ski that the salesman says is functionally perfect for you, don't be afraid to say that the skis look repulsive, in your opinion. With so many good skis out there, someone else is bound to make one that fits the bill in all respects.

Pick a Length

You will now have things nailed down to a couple of makes and models. It's time to choose a length.

Since the advent of shaped skis, this part of the process has become trickier. For the first few years that shaped skis were around, people commonly bought them too long, sometimes way too long. People discovered that not only did shaped skis work better in shorter lengths, but that these skis were also much more length-sensitive: The difference between a shaped ski in the 180-cm length and the 185-cm length was much bigger than the

Skis

difference between a traditional ski in 195 cm and 200 cm.

I wish I could give you a table or formula for determining ski length here, but I can't. This is where buying at a specialty shop with knowledgeable salespeople and a good demo policy can make all the difference. A seasoned salesperson will know the right length of each ski in the store for each customer; a guy who just cycled over from the gun department at the end of the hunting season won't.

These days, every manufacturer measures skis the same way: They measure the length of the materials used to make the ski when they are lying flat on the table, before being molded into shape. This is not the measurement that is important to the skier, though. You are interested in the *contact length* of the ski: the length of running surface that is in contact with the snow. This can vary from brand to brand and model to model, depending on how much the tip and tail roll up and certain other details.

Every dimensional parameter that goes into the design of a ski has at least one positive effect on the ski's performance, and most have at least one negative effect, too. Designing a ski well is an exercise in balancing those parameters. When it comes to length, a shorter ski is easier to turn, and a longer ski is more stable. What the new designs have given us is a short shaped ski that is as stable as a much longer traditional ski. A modern slalom-racing ski of 165-cm length, for example, is as stable as a 205-cm slalom ski of ten years ago.

Why is a shaped ski more stable than a traditional ski of the same length? First, much of a ski's character is determined by the way it vibrates. In the past, short

skis tended to vibrate in ways that made them squirrely at speed. Ski designers have simply figured out how to make a short ski vibrate like a longer ski of the past. This is, in some ways, like tuning the suspension of a VW Beetle so it rides like a Ford Crown Victoria.

Second, think of what happens when you put a ski on edge. It grips the snow best in the middle, under your foot. The more it bites at the tip and tail, the more the tip and tail will determine the ski's trajectory. This gives the ski a feeling of authority and stability when it's on its

The long and the short of it. On the right, the cream of the crop of traditional slalom skis for an average male. On the left, its modern, shaped successor.

Skis

edge and is why stiff skis track better than soft ones. Since shaped skis have so much more flare at the tip and tail than traditional skis, they get much more bite at their extremities. As a result, a short shaped ski has the same directional stability as a long traditional design.

Based on that brief tutorial on ski design, it should come as no surprise that the four principal determinants of proper ski length are:

- Your weight. The heavier you are, the longer a ski you should use. The lighter you are, the shorter.
- The ski's stiffness. If the ski is stiff, ski it in a shorter length. If it is soft, ski it longer.
- The ski's sidecut. The more sidecut a ski has, the shorter a length you should be on and vice versa. And finally . . .
- You owe it to yourself to demo each model on your short list in at least two lengths. Before I settled on my last pair, I tried three different models in two lengths each. It was like sampling ice cream. I liked them all, but when I tried the Rocky Road, the decision was easy.

If you are moving to your first pair of shaped skis, your skiing skills have outgrown your current skis, or your old boards are just plain worn out, don't be surprised if the first pair or two you try seem odd and a little ungainly. In particular, they might feel a bit edgy and hard to get started into the turn. Part of your transition to new skis will involve less skidding and more carving, which might take a little getting used to.

If you don't like the first pair you try, give them another chance after you have tried a few more. Your initial dislike may have been due more to unfamiliarity than a poor ski. On the flip side, if the first

pair you tried were an eye-opening revelation that you loved, try them again after you've tried some others.

WOMEN'S SKIS

In the past, "women's skis" were differentiated from the rest principally by their graphics or maybe by a softer flex. But in recent years, the ski industry has stepped

HOW TO TEST SKIS

Salespeople and magazine buyer's guides are intended to assist you in buying skis—not to make your final choice for you. To make that personal decision, the best thing you can do is get out and test some skis. Better ski shops will credit the price of renting demo skis toward the purchase of a pair. Demo centers exist at many major destination ski resorts, and ski manufacturers frequently send demo vans around to resorts and ski areas of all sizes. Your local specialty shop should be able to tell you when these events are taking place. So use the salespeople and the magazines to narrow your choices to a few, then keep the following points in mind as you do your testing.

Take notes. Jotting things down will help you remember what you liked and didn't like about specific skis. It'll also help you think critically about what's going on under your feet.

Be scientific. To glean valid comparative insights, you need to eliminate variables. Ski the same few runs, ones that provide a mix of pitch, terrain, and snow conditions. Make turns of different sizes and at different speeds. Choose both terrain you currently ski well and terrain you'd like to ski better.

But not too scientific. Keep the process enjoyable. One of the best ways to assess skis is by simply noting which ones you had the most fun on.

Skis

up and provided women with skis that are better suited to female physiology. If the category of ski you are seeking is available in a female-specific model, you are likely to ski better on it than its unisex (i.e., male-designed) counterpart. Assuming, of course, you're a woman.

WARRANTIES

Think about gluing steel, aluminum, wood, and three kinds of plastic together, then jumping up and down on the whole shebang to bend it a few thousand times. Such is the life of a ski. They are subjected to considerable physical stress, so their warranties are to be taken seriously.

Most manufacturers now authorize dealers to replace skis on the spot rather than requiring them to be shipped in for evaluation first. Even better, if your skis and bindings come from the same manufacturer, the lengths of their warranties are usually doubled.

TUNING NEW SKIS

There was a time when you couldn't trust a brand-new pair of skis to come from the factory in skiable condition. You would always have to have them tuned before skiing on them. Matt Carroll says those days are over, and few skis need more than a bit of dulling at the tip and tail to prepare them for use. Still, every new pair of skis should be checked for its tune, and some may need to be worked on a bit before you take them to the hill. Make sure your ski shop dulls the edges at the tip and tail, checks that the bases are perfectly flat, and that the edges are beveled to the manufacturer's suggested specifications. This should be included in the price of the skis, bindings, and mounting.

If you find yourself in a shop that doesn't do this as a matter of course or wants to charge you for it, you're in the wrong shop.

IS THERE A LEFT AND A RIGHT SKI?

Yes and no. As far as their design and manufacture go and the way the bindings are mounted, there is no left or right. (Footnote: There have, over the years, been a few models designed with specific left and right skis, but none have been commercially successful.) However, you tend to dull and damage the inside edges of your skis much more quickly than the outside edges. Most experts use one pair of edges for softer snow or rockier conditions, then switch skis when they need the utmost edge performance from their boards. Simply writing "L" and "R" on the tops of your skis with a permanent marker is a good way to keep track. If you need to remove the marks later, acetone will do the trick.

To keep track of your best pair of edges, mark the skis "L" and "R" with a permanent marker. You can remove the marks with nail polish remover if you need to.

Skis

MAINTENANCE AND TUNING

You should be able to get something like 60 to 100 days of skiing out of a pair of skis, depending on your size, strength, the conditions you ski in, and the particular skis themselves. During that time you'll need to subject them to regular maintenance. If they feel tired and old before that age, a $30 overhaul will breathe new life into them.

It pains me to see the bases of most people's skis. Most skiers seem to think that skis require about the same amount of maintenance as a car: every three years or 3,000 runs, whichever comes first. The nicks and burrs in most people's edges make the skis catchy, skittish, and unpredictable on hard snow. The divots in the plastic bases from hitting rocks make them slow and hard to turn. Most have a chalky, white look to the bases, often along the edges under the foot. This shows that they haven't been waxed for a long time. Such mistreatment often causes the plastic base to shrink, which makes the skis excruciatingly hard to turn. These changes happen slowly, so their owners don't notice. They just wonder why they don't ski any better as time goes on.

Skis that are well tuned simply make you a better skier, and so are more fun to ski on. They turn better, grip better, and just feel better under your feet. I seldom put more than two days on a pair of skis without waxing them and trimming up the edges. It takes me about 10 to 15 minutes.

I'm not suggesting that everyone learn how to wax and file a pair of skis. But I am suggesting that every 10 or so days you ski, you get them waxed and sharpened. (If you ski a lot on hard snow, shorten the schedule to every 3 to 5 days.) This will cost about $15, or half the price of a

Trim up your edges regularly with a pocket stone, especially after hitting rocks.

discounted lift ticket, thus increasing your average lift ticket cost by one-twentieth. You'll find it money well spent.

Get your skis a major overhaul every season. Have the bases stone-ground, filled, and waxed, and have the edges tuned to the correct bevel. This should cost you somewhere around $25 to $30. If you keep your skis in good shape, they won't seem that much different. If they feel a lot better after being tuned, you waited too long.

Keeping Track of Your Skis Day to Day

After every day of skiing, run your fingers along the edges of your skis, feeling for nicks and burrs (those little spurs that get pushed up when you hit a rock,

CARVING AND THE
EVOLUTION OF SKIING

Carving has become the *ne plus ultra* of skiing. Magazines shout it from their covers, and instructors shout it at their students. In truth, there is a lot more to skiing than carving, and while carving is a great thing to be able to do, a skier who can only make carved turns is sadly limited.

So what is carving, and how did it get to be so important to everyone? If skidding a turn on skis is like doing a powerslide around a dirt road switchback in a jeep, carving one is like tracking around a banked asphalt curve in a formula 1 race car. Instead of going sideways, the ski follows its edge as it slices the snow. The sensation is intense, magical, and addictive. Once you've felt a good carved turn, you want to feel a lot more of them.

Long ago, when skis were long, stiff, and made of wood, turning was pretty difficult, even when the snow was soft. If the snow was icy, the best you could hope for was a controlled skid. As the introduction of metal and fiberglass in the early 1960s provided racing skis that were more limber and held reasonably well

on hard snow, racers sought to carve their turns as much as possible. Slowly, this goal found its way into the ranks of experts, advanced, and even intermediate skiers.

Short, soft, shaped skis now make carving turns easy for people who couldn't buy a turn ten years ago. In my mid-50s now, I can carve better arcs than I could when I was in my 20s. Some systems of instruction now even seek to teach carving to beginners.

American Kirsten Clark, silver medalist in the 2002 World Championships, carves a near-perfect arc in Val d'Isere, France. Modern skis have brought such turns within the reach of recreational skiers.

Skis

even a small one). Using a pocket stone (see page 103), remove the burrs.

Noticing your edges getting dull is like noticing your hair grow. Because it happens progressively, you may not notice it until it's long overdue.

Look at the plastic bases. If you see whitish areas, they are becoming oxidized and are long overdue for wax.

To prevent the edges from rusting, dry your skis off before putting them away for the day, especially if you put them in a ski bag or cartop box. If you find rust on your edges, a pocket stone will help clean it up.

At the end of the season, have your skis waxed at a shop or do it yourself. This will prevent the bases from oxidizing and the edges from rusting. Store them in a dry place, resting on their tails or flat on the floor. Don't hang your skis in a rack by their tips. This will stress them in a manner for which they are not designed. Such long-term stress can alter the ski or even compromise its integrity.

Having Someone Else Tune Them

The place where the guys with drills and files work on your skis and boots is called the *back shop*. Not all back shops are created equal. Ask for recommendations from as many pros and avid skiers as you can, and go for the shop that gets the most votes. Also be aware that a shop may have one or two exceptionally good servicemen. Ask for them by name. When you find a good serviceman who treats you right or does you a favor, tip him with a six-pack of his favorite beer. (Ask other people in the shop what he likes.) Then the next time you need your skis tuned in a hurry, they might just find their way to the head of the line.

Doing It Yourself

It's really gratifying to whiz past your buddies on a wax job you laid down yourself. Waxing skis is pretty simple and painless. All it takes is a used clothes iron from the Salvation Army, a plastic scraper, and some general-purpose ski wax, both available at ski shops. If you don't have a place you can get away with dripping wax on the floor, you'll also need a painter's drop-cloth. (Get a cloth one, not plastic.)

Lay the skis with their bases up. Set the iron at a very low setting (hot enough to melt wax, but not so hot that the wax smokes). Hold the iron over the base of the ski, point down, and press the wax against the iron's base so that the melting wax drips onto the ski. Move the iron from the tip of the ski to the tail, then back up to the tip. This will leave two ribbons of melted wax on the bottom of the ski.

How to wax a pair of skis. Step 1: Holding a bar of wax against the bottom of the iron, a few inches above the ski, drip a couple lines of wax onto the ski's base from the tip to the tail.

Step 2: Iron out the drips so they flow across the entire base of the ski.

Step 3: After the wax has cooled for five minutes or more, remove the excess with a plastic wax scraper, leaving a smooth, thin film.

Now iron the bottom of the ski like you were ironing a shirt. The wax will melt and spread out over the ski's base and soak into it.

After letting the wax cool for five minutes or more (the longer the better), scrape the excess off with a plastic wax scraper, leaving a smooth, thin film on the ski. (Note that the wax that has penetrated the base is more important to the ski's performance than whatever layer you leave on top of the base, so scraping it thin is preferred.)

You're done and ready to rip! And in ten minutes or less, once you've had a little practice.

Sharpening skis and repairing the bases is more involved than waxing, and takes more tools and tutoring than many people are likely to undertake.

But if you like working with tools and want to get in closer touch with your skis, I encourage you to do it yourself. Your skis and your skiing will be better for it. I recommend the following book: *Alpine Ski Maintenance and Repair* by Seth Masia (McGraw-Hill, 1989). Seth is one of the leading experts in the ski industry on equipment of all stripes. This book covers it all, including working on boots.

Tune Parameters

The new breed of skis are more sensitive to tuning than the planks of yore. In particular, the bottom and side bevels of the edges and the flatness of the base (explained below) can all have dramatic effects on how a ski behaves. Each year the major manufacturers publish charts with the recommended bevels for each of their models, often stated as ranges rather than exact numbers. A good back shop will have these charts tacked to the wall and will follow them. Ask the shop what the recommended parameters are and feel free to experiment within and around the recommended bounds.

Base Flatness

The plastic base of a ski must be flat from edge to edge. If it is not, the ski won't behave properly. If the base is higher in the center than at the edges, the edges will not engage properly. Think "skiing on a hot dog." If the base is dished and lower in the center, or lower than the steel edges all the way across, you've got real trouble. Skis in this condition are very hard to turn. Either condition can develop if the ski isn't waxed often enough.

Fixing such problems yourself is difficult and time consuming. Fortunately, it's easy for a good shop. It's also easy for them to

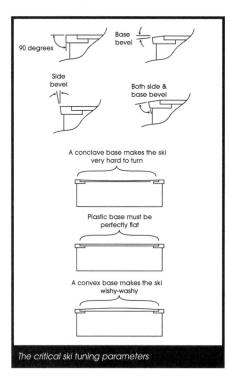

The critical ski tuning parameters

evaluate your skis' flatness—easy enough that they should not charge you for it.

Bottom Bevel

Many skis work best when the bottom side of the edge, the one that sits flush on the snow, is beveled with respect to the plastic base, usually by a degree or two. This makes the ski release more easily and smoothly from one turn into another.

Side Bevel

The surface of the edge that is on the side of the ski must be filed or ground so that it makes an angle of 90 degrees or less with the bottom side of the edge. The degree to which that angle is less than 90 degrees is called side bevel. More side bevel makes a ski grip better. On the other hand, it also makes a ski grabbier, harder to turn, and generally less forgiving. The more an edge is beveled, the more quickly it gets dull, too. Experts typically ski with skis beveled one or two degrees on the side. Some use no bevel. Presently, skis used for World Cup slalom races are tuned with around 5 degrees of side bevel. Don't try this at home.

Base Structure

The plastic base of the ski will run fastest when its surface is not perfectly smooth, but rather has a structure to it consisting of tiny grooves. The depth, spacing, and angle to the ski's direction of travel of these grooves are the subject of intense experimentation in the world of big-time ski racing and vary with the type of snow on which the ski will be sliding. The best way for most of us to have our bases structured is by getting them stone-ground occasionally by a knowledgeable ski shop.

Skis

Bindings

The first release ski binding was introduced by Hjalmar Hvam in 1938. In his magazine ads, Hvam said he invented it because he got tired of hurting himself. Prior to that, bindings held the boots as firmly as they could and only let go if something broke (other than the skier's leg). Release bindings improved the situation, but it wasn't until plastic boots and bindings with antifriction devices (AFDs) became common that things started to get really safe. Until then, the dimensional instability of leather and rubber boot soles, and their nonstandardized nature, made the design and production of a reliable release binding an uphill battle.

Bindings today are so good that broken legs and torn Achilles tendons, the two injuries best prevented by release bindings, are rare. Even so, the industry is reluctant, for legal reasons, to refer to them as "safety bindings."

Most of the major ski manufacturers now produce bindings as well. Those who don't generally align themselves with a specific binding manufacturer. Völkl, for example, is aligned with Marker.

If you buy skis from one of these manufacturers, your best bet is to use their brand of binding. I recommend this for two reasons. First, ski manufacturers usually extend the warranties on their skis if you use the recommended binding. Second, as Jim Vandergrift, an engineer at K2, once explained to me, each manufacturer tests its ski designs with a specific binding. Their testers, who are very good at sensing how a ski performs, work with the engineers to get each ski to behave just so. Every

binding has its own effect on the behavior of the ski, and some of the effects are big. If you stick to the binding the ski company used when testing the ski, you know the ski will be performing the way the designers intended. If you use a different binding, you might not get the best ride from the ski.

Soon, this point may be moot. Manufacturers are migrating toward integrated ski/binding systems that will not accommodate mixing and matching. Some makers are making systems like these right now. They are a positive step because they simplify the mounting

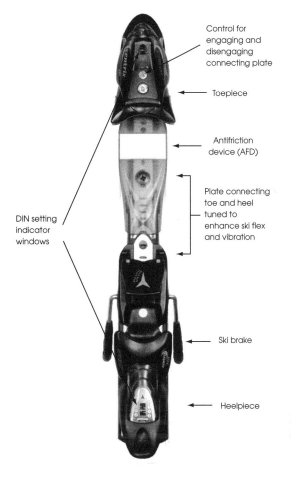

Control for engaging and disengaging connecting plate

Toepiece

Antifriction device (AFD)

Plate connecting toe and heel tuned to enhance ski flex and vibration

DIN setting indicator windows

Ski brake

Heelpiece

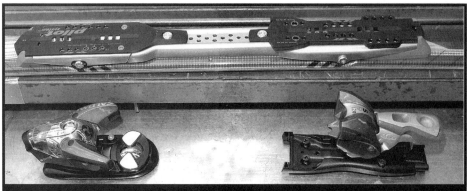

Many skis now have integrated plates for mounting bindings. They typically improve the ski's performance and simplify the mounting process.

process, leaving less room for error and ensuring the bindings will work properly. I expect that in a few years this will be the rule rather than the exception.

The integrated systems either have special holes predrilled in the ski that mate with special screens or special pins on the binding, or a special mounting plate permanently attached to the ski with predrilled holes that match the screw patterns of the companies' bindings. Salomon's Pilot skis and bindings are examples of the first approach, while Rossignol and Atomic produce examples of the latter.

WHICH MODEL?

Don't think that just because you are a lower-level skier, you don't deserve an upper-level binding. These are your legs we're talking about here; bindings are no place to pinch pennies. The only characteristic of a high-performance binding that could make it unsuitable for you is the range of release settings that the binding covers. Your weight, age, and ability are the parameters that determine the proper

release setting for your bindings, as specified by a number on an industry-standard scale (the so-called DIN scale). Every binding is adjustable through a range of these settings. Ideally, you want your DIN number to fall around the middle of the range covered by your bindings.

LIFTERS AND CONNECTING DEVICES

Many of the more advanced bindings now come with devices that couple the toepieces and heelpieces. They do not improve the safety characteristics of the binding but rather serve to enhance the performance of the ski to which they are mated. Most are designed to tune the ski's stiffness and filter its vibrations under the foot. They also improve edge grip in the same way as simple lifters, which I describe next.

Solid plastic lifters that sit under the bindings, raising them an additional 10 millimeters or so off the skis is another common binding accessory. Lifting the binding improves edge grip. Earlier I explained that ice skates hold much

Bindings

better than skis because the edge of the blade is directly below the skater's ankle. A binding lifter, by raising the skier's ankle, moves it closer to being directly over the edge of the ski when the skier makes an edging movement, making the ski behave more like a skate.

Ski racers are well aware of this, and since the mid-1980s have devised ways of lifting their boots higher off their skis. In response, and citing safety concerns, the International Ski Federation (FIS) has placed strict limits on the maximum height the heel of the racer's foot can be above the base of the ski. And they mean business: In 2002 American Thomas Vonn was disqualified from a major race, in which he had placed exceptionally well, for being 1 millimeter over the limit.

BINDING ADJUSTMENTS

Bindings typically have three or four adjustments. The two most visible ones, shown by indicators in small windows on the bindings, are the so-called *release tension* or *DIN setting*. These are the tensions on the springs in the toepieces and heelpieces that determine how much force must be applied to them to make them release.

The third setting is the amount of force with which the heelpiece pushes the boot forward into the toepiece, called the *forward pressure*. This setting must be correct in order for the binding to function properly. Different bindings are designed to work with different amounts of forward pressure, so you should never mix and match toes and heels from different manufacturers. Look and Rossignol bindings, at one end of the scale, are designed to

The bindings on this World Cup racer's skis are mounted on special plates. The plates help tune the vibration and stiffness of the ski. Notice, also, how high the sole of the boot is off the ski. This improves edge grip considerably.

Bindings

ANTIFRICTION DEVICE, or AFD: n. The slippery surface or sliding mechanism under the boot toe. Aids lateral release when necessary.

DAMPING: n. The absorption of shocks and vibrations.

DIN: n. A scale that measures the amount of force needed to cause a binding to release. Every binding has a DIN range. Children's bindings go as low as .75; downhill racers often crank it up to 20. Most recreational skiers fall into the 5–10 range. DIN is an acronym for Deutsche Industrial Norms, the name of a German standards agency.

ELASTICITY: n. The amount of movement or play the binding is designed to provide before it releases. Some elasticity is desirable to prevent prerelease under normal loads.

FLAT SPOT: n. The area in the middle of the ski where the flexed ski's round arc is inhibited by the rigid boot sole being clamped in the binding. Impedes smooth carving.

FORWARD PRESSURE: n. The force with which the heelpiece pushes the boot forward into the toepiece. Correct forward pressure is critical for the binding to function properly.

LIFTER: n. A spacer used to raise both the boot and binding off the ski, offering increased leverage.

PLATE: n. A performance-enhancing lifter designed to stiffen the ski, dampen vibrations, and improve edging leverage.

PRERELEASE: n. A binding releasing prematurely.

RELEASE: n. This occurs when the binding opens due to twisting or excessive force, as in a fall.

RETENTION: n. When the boot is fastened to the ski by the binding.

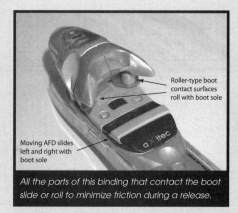

Roller-type boot contact surfaces roll with boot sole

Moving AFD slides left and right with boot sole

All the parts of this binding that contact the boot slide or roll to minimize friction during a release.

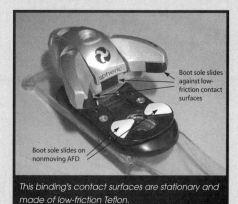

Boot sole slides against low-friction contact surfaces

Boot sole slides on nonmoving AFD

This binding's contact surfaces are stationary and made of low-friction Teflon.

Bindings

work with very little forward pressure. At the other extreme are Marker bindings, which require much more.

The fourth setting, which is not present on all bindings, is the height of the part of the toepiece that fits over the boot's sole. If it is too tight, significant friction can develop under the sole of the boot as it tries to release from the binding. Too loose and the binding does not hold the boot securely.

You should keep an eye on your bindings' settings. A good approach is to write your correct DIN numbers on the ski with grease pencil or permanent marker, somewhere between the toepieces and heelpieces where it won't wear off.

It's a good idea to have these settings checked once a year to see that nothing has changed.

Don't Touch That Dial!

Bindings are not perfect. Sometimes they don't release when you wish they would, and sometimes they release when you wish they wouldn't. The latter incident is called a *prerelease* and most commonly happens in one of the following situations:

- You have snow stuck to the bottom of your boot when you put your ski on, thus preloading the binding,
- You ski into a sharp dip that bends the ski dramatically,
- Your ski tip rams a mogul,
- You lean too far into a turn, putting all your weight on your inside ski and slap your outside ski on the snow,
- The heel binding has slipped in its track and the forward pressure is not right.

Regardless of what caused the prerelease, don't adjust your bindings tighter than the recommended DIN setting. Some people seem to think that skiing with their bindings cranked down tight marks them as hot skiers. This is misinformed machismo that looks silly when you're being ushered down the slope in a toboggan by a patroller. Trust the binding designers: They know what they are doing.

ANTIFRICTION DEVICES

All toe bindings have antifriction devices, or AFDs, on which the sole of your boot rests. Some are small, fixed Teflon plates, and some are mechanisms that allow one piece to slide freely over another. In all cases, their purpose is the same: to provide a low-friction surface under the boot sole so that the force required to make the boot move to one side or the other is very consistent, regardless of the dynamics of a particular fall.

The other surfaces of the toe binding that contact your boot are also critical for consistent release and may have small Teflon pads bonded to them. Any dirt or gravel your boot soles may have picked up while you walked to the snow will wreak havoc on your AFDs. So it's a good idea to scuff your boots a couple of times on the snow before you step into your bindings. Keep an eye on the condition of your bindings' AFDs, and replace them if they get chipped or pitted.

SKI BRAKES

Probably the last great safety advance in bindings was the widespread availability of bindings with integrated ski brakes. Prior to that, we all used safety straps—short leather or nylon leashes that tethered our skis to our ankles. They kept a ski from running off down the hill and hitting other skiers or disappearing into the woods after coming off in a fall, but they also allowed the ski to whip around and hit you. This happened a lot, and ski brakes have almost entirely eliminated the danger.

Ski brakes can get bent, though. If one gets bent outward, it will catch on the snow, sending up a rooster tail. If it bends inward, it can catch on the side of the ski as the brake opens, preventing it from grabbing the snow and stopping the ski. If your skis get banged in a hard tumble or while falling off your car, check that the brakes are working properly.

MOUNTING BINDINGS

Regardless of how handy you are with shop tools, don't mount your bindings yourself! Without very specific tools and training, you stand a good chance of ruining your skis or mounting the bindings in such a way that their release characteristics are inconsistent, releasing more easily in one direction than the other. Leave this to a trained professional.

When you get your new skis mounted, check them to see that the shop did it right. First, check that the bindings are mounted in the right place along the length of the ski. Each boot has a mark molded into the shell along the side of the sole, at its midpoint. Each ski has a corresponding mark printed on it. Click the boots into the bindings and see how the marks line up. Unless you have specifically arranged for your skis to be mounted otherwise, the mark on the boot should line up with the one on the ski. I've seen more than one pair of skis mismounted in this respect.

This is not a catastrophe for some skis. Skis with integrated binding systems make it very easy to reposition the bindings fore and aft. The shop can do this for you in a matter of minutes.

If your skis are not of this sort, and the shop has mismounted them, demand that they give you a new pair of skis. Don't accept any excuses. A shop will sometimes say it knows the right place to mount your bindings, not the manufacturer. Don't believe it.

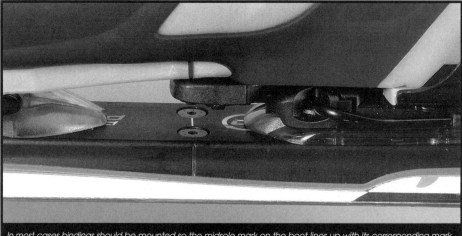

In most cases bindings should be mounted so the midsole mark on the boot lines up with its corresponding mark on the ski. Some women may want to have their bindings mounted slightly forward of this mark on some skis.

Bindings

MOUNTING BINDINGS FOR WOMEN

A number of authorities believe that women should have their bindings mounted farther forward on a unisex ski than the mark indicated by the manufacturer. This is based on much empirical evidence. How far forward the bindings should be mounted is determined by how much different your mass distribution and relative limb lengths are when compared to an average male. One centimeter forward is a good bet for a Rubenesque woman.

Note that this adjustment should _not_ be made on women-specific model skis.

Next, look at the skis from the top and make sure that the toepieces and heelpieces of the bindings are centered on the skis, left and right. I've seen bindings mounted off-center or skewed.

Finally, look at the side and base of the ski where the bindings are screwed down. Look carefully for any bulges in the top or bottom of the ski (where a binding screw may be popping through). Either indicates a serious error in the mounting of the bindings. The skis could be ruined (there is no good way to tell for sure), and you should demand a new pair.

MAINTENANCE

Bindings don't require nearly the care and attention of skis or even boots. But don't take them for granted, because the proper functioning of your bindings is more important than that of any other piece of your equipment.

Have a certified ski mechanic perform a functional-release check on your bindings

every year. These checks work. According to Seth Masia, in Europe, where ski shops have not adopted testing standards as of this writing, the incidence of lower leg fractures is roughly three times higher than in the United States.

Check the AFDs, all plastic parts, and all surfaces where your bindings contact your boots, for chips, dents, and embedded grit. If any are in bad shape, get them fixed before you go skiing.

A ski without a good brake becomes a lethal projectile on the hill. Ski brakes are easily bent, so check their function frequently. Do this by working the brake up and down with your hand. You will not be able to tell if there is a problem by simply stepping into the binding. If a brake doesn't project at least an inch and a half below the base of the ski when deployed, it's probably bent.

Occasionally check that the mounting screws are tight. A simple cursory check is to hold the ski by the toe binding and shake it hard. Then shake it by the heel binding. Any looseness or rattling is a sign that they need attention. When you get your skis their yearly overhaul, have the shop check the screws.

At the end of the season, reduce the release tension on the binding springs. First, write their DIN setting on the ski with a grease pencil or on a piece of paper that you tape to the skis, so you can reset the binding in the fall. Loosen the screws that control the DIN settings until the release-tension indicators on the heels and toes are at the bottom of their ranges.

If you transport your skis in a roof rack, exposed to the elements, clean the bindings occasionally with warm water. Or better yet, protect them with binding covers.

Bindings

Poles

The requirements for a ski pole seem simple enough: It's got to be sharp on one end, you've got to be able to hold on to the other end, and something has to stop the sharp end from going down into the snow more than a few inches. But, of course, there's a bit more to it than that.

STRAPS AND GRIPS

Find a grip that matches the size and shape of your hand. When you try poles in the shop, test the grip using the same type of gloves or mittens you ski with.

This pole has a convenient detachable strap. This is especially helpful for those who ski with puffy mittens.

The strap should be easy to adjust, especially if you tend to switch between winter gloves, mittens, and light spring gloves through the course of the season. It's nice if you can make adjustments without taking your gloves off, and even nicer if you can do it without taking your poles off.

Some manufacturers make strap systems that clip easily in and out of the handle. Some use a special glove from the manufacturer, while one system provides a special strap you secure to your own glove or mitten. When you take your poles off, you unclip the glove or strap from the handle, rather than taking your hand out of the strap. This works particularly well for puffy mittens or gloves that are hard to get in and out of pole straps. The systems also release the strap from the handle if the pole should snag on something and tug hard on your arm.

Avoid strapless poles. Over the years, different designs of this sort have come and gone. None has survived. Although their cause is noble—they seek to reduce the incidence of thumb and wrist injuries that might be caused by straps—every design has problems that are worse than the ones it attempts to address.

Poles for Women

What, you may ask, could be different about a woman's ski pole? The answer is simple: thinner grips. When you shop for poles, ask about female-specific models. Wear the gloves or mittens you ski in on the coldest days, and get a pair that fit your hands.

SHAFT MATERIALS

Poles are made either of aluminum or carbon fiber (also known as graphite).

The baskets on many poles can be interchanged for different snow conditions. The small basket is for packed snow. The large one is for powder.

Aluminum poles are less expensive and more durable, but heavier than carbon fiber. The more you pay for poles, including aluminum ones, the lighter they are, and the less durable. If you fall more than occasionally, go for durability.

BASKETS

The term *basket* refers to the plastic disk at the bottom end of the pole that keeps it from sinking into the snow. The name comes from a time when baskets were large wooden or plastic rings attached to the pole by a web of leather strips.

Although pole baskets look nothing like that today, the name endures.

I have two sets of baskets for my poles. One set is small, light, and suitable for packed snow conditions. The other set is larger for skiing in powder. If you aren't picky about the swing weight of your poles, the inertia you feel when you flick them forward and back, buy poles with larger-diameter baskets and use them all the time. If you are picky, get a spare pair of baskets of the other type and have the shop show you how to swap them for different conditions. Keep the spare pair in your boot bag.

Poles

LENGTH

How long should your poles be? I could paraphrase Abraham Lincoln and say, "Long enough to reach the snow." But that would sound half-witted and would only be half-true.

A pole should be long enough to reach the snow *when you are in a proper posture to plant it.* If your pole is too long, you will have to raise your hand to plant it. This usually results in your shoulders tipping into the hill, which is not good. If your poles are too short, you have to drop your hand to plant them. This may make you stoop forward at the waist, which is also not good, and you will be more likely to miss pole plants on steep slopes.

To determine the best pole length for you, hold the pole upside down with the handle against the floor, grasping the shaft just below the basket. If the pole is the correct length, your forearm should be parallel to the ground. Note: Big-time mogul skiers use somewhat shorter poles, because they are usually planting them from a very low stance.

BENT POLES

If you happen to bend a pole, don't try to straighten it out on the hill. You stand a good chance of snapping it. Your best bet is to take the pole to a ski shop where someone will heat it with a torch before trying to straighten it. This will greatly increase the likelihood of a successful and long-lasting repair.

To check a ski pole for proper length, grasp it upside down as shown. As a general rule, your forearm should be parallel with the ground.

Buying Used Equipment

Just like cars, new ski equipment depreciates the moment you buy it. And as with cars, used gear is plentiful and can be had for good prices. The trick is knowing what to look for and how to evaluate what you find.

USED SKIS

A pair of skis should be good for around sixty to one hundred days of serious skiing. Considering that most folks don't ski more than ten days a season, a two-year-old pair of skis ought to have some real spunk left in it. Don't be concerned about their cosmetic condition. Remember the old saying: "You don't ski on the tops." Even if the bases and edges are somewhat chewed up, they can be rejuvenated with a good $30 tune-up.

You may need to have the bindings remounted to fit your ski boots, but that is seldom a problem. To be sure, have them checked by a ski shop before you buy. Just about any ski can be drilled a second time, as long as the new holes are not closer than a half-inch or so to the old ones. If the skis are of the new breed that have predrilled mounting plates, you've got no worries at all.

As I said previously, don't buy old-fashioned straight skis, even if they seem

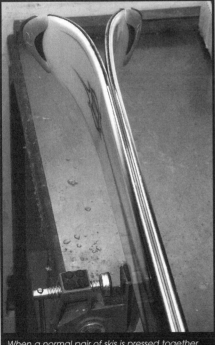

When a normal pair of skis is pressed together at the waist, they stay in contact almost all the way to the tip.

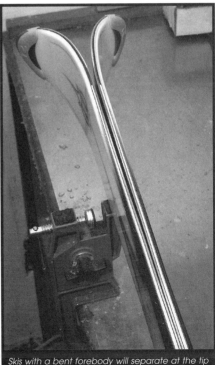

Skis with a bent forebody will separate at the tip when pressed together at the waist.

to be the deal of the century. Good used shaped skis are not hard to find, and with a little coaching, you should feel confident about shopping for a pair.

Things to Watch Out For

Bent skis and broken edges. These are the two biggest problems to look for. Skis are most commonly bent in the forebody between the tip and the binding toe piece. To determine if a ski is bent, hold the pair base to base lightly, so they only touch at the tip and tail, and identify the point where the bases meet at the tip. Next, squeeze the skis together in the middle and see how far the point of contact at the tip moves. If it is more than a few inches, one of the skis is probably bent or was bent and then straightened (which is never completely successful).

Skis can be bent in the tail, too, and sometimes even in the middle. To find such problems, squeeze the skis together and look down the edge.

If the skis are true, they will be mirror images of each other and will meet in a straight line. If one of the skis is amiss, the two won't match up and their meeting line will curve.

To find a broken edge, carefully inspect the skis' edges looking for crimps, cracks, or bends. Also, look carefully at the bases along the edges. If you see any places where the plastic base is raised, look carefully at the edge for a crack. If you find any of these problems, check that pair off your list. The ski is broken and not repairable. The only sort of ski I would buy under such conditions would be one exclusively for powder and junk snow, where edge grip and precise flex are not an issue.

Used Powder Skis

If you are looking for a powder or junk-snow ski, base and edge condition are not very important. This is a place you can save a lot of money by going used. Used intermediate-level shaped skis make good powder skis, too, and can be found at bargain prices.

USED BOOTS

Buying used ski boots can be a good way to go. In contrast to skis, which have improved dramatically since 1995, boots have changed in only minor ways since the 1980s.

There are a few things to watch out for in a pair of used boots, however. Beware of soles that are heavily worn. These will not work reliably with ski bindings and are potentially unsafe. If you find a model with replaceable strike plates under the toes and heels, you should have no worries, as long as you can find replacements.

This ski has a broken edge and is useless for skiing on packed snow. Note the bend in the edge and the "bubble" in the plastic base. Oftentimes the latter is the only visible evidence you will find.

The sole of this boot is worn to the point where it will not release from a binding consistently and is therefore unsafe to ski in.

Broken buckles can almost always be repaired and should not prevent you from buying a pair of used boots that are otherwise well suited to you.

Take the liners out and inspect them carefully. Rips or tears in the liner are cause for dismissal. So, too, are cracks or tears in the shell, particularly inside the cuff, and where parts are attached with rivets or screws.

USED BINDINGS

Before you buy used bindings, ask a ski shop if they are *indemnifiable* and safe. If the answer is no, then the bindings are useless because no ski shop will mount or adjust them. The word indemnify means "to make compensation to for incurred hurt, loss, or damage." Each year the binding manufacturers publish lists indicating which of their older models they still indemnify. The bottom line is that you don't want to go skiing on any bindings that aren't on the list.

Next, check all the surfaces where the boot contacts the binding, especially the toe pieces. These surfaces are usually covered with a slippery material such as Teflon. If any of them are torn, nicked, or pitted, the bindings may be unreliable. Also check the condition of the antifriction devices, or AFDs, on the toe pieces. If they are in bad shape and can't be replaced, move on.

USED POLES

This should be an easy place to save the cost of a lift ticket. Poles are easy to evaluate. If they are aluminum, sight carefully down their length to make sure they haven't been bent, or bent and then straightened. If the poles are made of carbon fiber, check for deep nicks. A good-sized nick is a likely point of failure for a composite ski pole. Nicks are most likely to appear down near the baskets, caused by the edges of skis. ◆◆◆

Buying Used Equipment

A wide selection of ski clothes are available, giving you an opportunity to look good and feel good at the same time.

ACCESSORIES AND SOFT GOODS

In the jargon of the ski industry, ski apparel, including underwear, socks, vests, sweaters, shells, parkas, pants, and hats are known as "soft goods." Everything else skiers use, such as goggles, sunglasses, sunscreen, lip balm, footbeds, helmets, ski waxes, hand warmers, ski-tuning tools, and boot dryers are called "accessories."

Apparel

Some of my most vivid memories of skiing as a child in the '50s are of being cold. Miserably, painfully cold. I remember my fingers getting so cold that they stung like crazy when they warmed up. My toes, too. It's a wonder I liked the sport.

The problem was the clothing. We wore poplin anoraks over sweaters and cotton shirts. We wore wool pants over cotton long underwear. We wore mittens that had barely any insulation. We wore low leather boots that got snow in them in the winter and got soaked in the spring. Sometimes it seemed the only way to stay warm was put on so many clothes that you couldn't bend over to get your skis on.

Skiers today have it easy. (Pardon me for being a crusty old galoot, but I've earned it.) With modern skiwear, you can stay warm and comfortable all day long, even when the temperature, wind, and humidity fluctuate wildly. These days you can look good, feel good, and ski good at the same time.

THE ESSENTIAL SKI OUTFIT

Before getting into the details of ski clothing, I will cut to the chase and describe what I believe to be the most practical and economical outfit for skiing.

- Close-fitting shirt of a wicking synthetic fiber (polyester, polyolefin, polypropylene, or one of their variants), silk, or Merino wool with a zip-up mock turtleneck
- Long underwear, also made of a wicking fiber or light polyester fleece pants
- Polyester fleece or wool sweater
- Light jacket of fleece or insulated nylon
- Nylon shell or lightly insulated jacket, cut loosely enough that you can wear it comfortably over all the above
- Socks of wool, polyolefin, polyester, or silk, blended with nylon and Spandex (or similar synthetic)
- Lightly insulated or shell nylon ski pants cut loosely enough to fit comfortably over the long underwear or light fleece pants
- Knit wool hat with inner headband of fleece
- Insulated leather or nylon gloves or mittens, designed specifically for skiing
- Goggles and sunglasses

By mixing and matching the items in the above list, you should be able to enjoy skiing in all but the most severe conditions. If you ski in a particularly cold part of the continent, you can replace "lightly insulated" with "moderately insulated."

TEMPERATURE RANGE

Every combination of garments you have is comfortable through a particular range of temperatures. Each element of the ensemble that contributes to that range has its own range, too. Over the years, new fabrics and clever features have extended the scope of many garments so that you can now get through a ski season with fewer pieces, and you are less likely to get caught in clothing that is too warm or not warm enough for the situation.

When you shop for a piece of ski clothing, look for features that will extend its range. A good hood on a jacket, for example, will extend its range downward into colder temperatures because of added protection, while zippers under the armpits ("pit zips") will extend its range upward because of added ventilation.

LAYERING FOR COMFORT

To work effectively, your clothes must do three things:

1. Pull moisture away from your body,
2. Trap air near your body, and
3. Prevent cool ambient air from replacing the warm, trapped air.

Structure your wardrobe in layers that serve each of these purposes.

Base Layer: Controlling Moisture

The job of the clothing you wear against your skin is not to provide insulation, per se, but to transport moisture away from your body.

Water is a crummy insulator. If it touches something warm and something cold at the same time, it will suck heat from the warm side and give to the other. Worse yet, the process of evaporation uses up a great deal of heat. That's why you feel colder when you get out of a swimming pool than you do when you're in it: The water on your skin is evaporating, sucking great gobs of heat from your body. Once you're dry, you feel warm again.

You may think that you are always dry when you ski, but that's not necessarily so. When you exercise, you perspire. Even when your feet are so cold they feel like blocks of granite, they sweat. Optimal base-layer clothing for sports quickly pulls any perspiration away from your skin. Wool, silk, polyester, polyolefin, and polypropylene are champs at this. Cotton traps moisture and keeps you damp and cold. Never wear cotton against your skin if you can avoid it.

Middle Layers: Trapping Air

It is the task of your next layer of clothing to trap air in tiny pockets near your body. Air is a great insulator, and when trapped like this, it keeps the heat your body generates from escaping to the world at large. Bulk is the key here. You want fibers and fabrics with loft. Knit wool and polyester fleece are excellent. Loose synthetic fibers inside quilted nylon are good, too. If you wear too much, though, you will overheat, causing your body to perspire. And you should know by now what *that* means.

WHAT IS "TECHNICAL" SKIWEAR?

The term *technical* is commonly applied to more sophisticated skiwear these days. What does that mean? I'll be honest with you: I don't exactly know. But I don't think you want to invest in ski clothing that is not classified as technical. This indefinite term seems to encompass base-layer garments that wick moisture well, insulation-layer garments that are made of synthetic fibers, and outer garments that are waterproof/breathable (see page 75), have lots of zippers, drawstrings with little clamps on them, and one or more useless pockets and pseudo-functional fashion accents. I have one ski jacket that has stylish bits of reflective tape sewn on it—the kind that bicyclists and runners have on their clothes so they can be seen at night. I have another that has a large grommet prominently staked to it. I thought it might be for a walkie-talkie antenna, until I realized that there was fabric in the middle of the hole.

Although some of what qualifies as "technical" seems to be marketing fluff, much of it, such as fabric finishes and liberal use of fleece in clever places, like inside jacket cuffs and collars, is useful.

My advice: Go technical!

The essential outfit. At the base, moisture-wicking synthetic zippered T-neck shirt (1), long underwear or light fleece pants (2), and socks (3). Next up comes a wool or fleece sweater (4). On cold days, layer a fleece vest (5) or light insulated or fleece jacket (6). Facing the elements on the outside are a full-featured shell or lightly insulated jacket (7) and pants (8), hat (9), and gloves (10). Goggles (11) or glasses (12) are absolutely essential, too.

Apparel

Apparel

Outer Layer: Shedding Ambient Air

Your outer garment must keep cold ambient air from replacing the warm air near your skin. If a breeze can blow through your sweater, it's like leaving the windows open on a cold night. That's why your outer layer must always be wind-proof. Different fabrics protect you from the wind to different degrees. To evaluate a garment's usefulness as an outer layer, simply hold a piece of the fabric against your lips and try to blow through it. A knit ski hat, for example, does a lousy job. Fleece is just as bad, if not worse, unless it has a special wind-blocking layer within it. What you want is a tightly woven fabric that also stands up well to abrasion, like nylon or a nylon blend.

Regular fleece jackets just don't cut it as an outer layer on any but the warmest of days because wind goes right through them. But if you simply put a nylon wind-breaker over that fleece jacket, you've got something that will keep you comfort-able on a winter day.

FIBERS AND FABRICS

How to Read a Hangtag

When you're sizing up a particular piece of clothing, take a look at the bouquet of little paper tags and pamphlets hanging from it. While some will be shear mar-keting hype and snake oil advertising, some will contain real information. Look for information about fabric treatments and laminated layers that may not be vis-ible but contribute to the performance of the garment. See if there are special care instructions. You may want to think twice about a jacket that can't be machine washed or requires special detergent.

Check out the fiber-content tag, too. This is a cloth tag sewn into the garment that will have the generic name of the fibers, rather than the brand name you find on the hangtag. Patagonia's Capilene®, for example, is a polyester fiber. So are Thermax® and ThermaStat®. But the hangtags don't necessarily tell you this. If you know from experience that a half day spent in any polyester gives you the aroma of a landfill, the fiber con-tent will be your red flag.

Synthetics

Polyester, polypropylene, and polyolefin are the main synthetic fibers used in base

Polyester, polyolefin, and polypropylene are the leading fibers for base-layer garments. Merino wool and silk are the top picks for natural fibers.

layers today. Woven into fabrics for base layers, they all do a good job of wicking moisture, are easy to wash and dry, and are available in a range of weights, from very light to very heavy. The heaviest are "brushed" to give them some nap, which helps trap air. Proprietary versions of these fibers have special features. Thermax®, for example, is hollow, which adds an insulating feature to its wicking capabilities. Polypropylene and polyester have the unfortunate distinction of retaining salts and fats from sweat that cause body odors. Polypropylene or "polypro" also tends to get hard and scratchy if dried repeatedly at a high heat. The fabric used in most ski boot liners today is a polyolefin blend, which helps to keep your feet dry and warm.

Polyester fleece has become the great utility insulator for ski clothing. Inexpensive and easy to care for, it is extremely popular, for good reason.

Polyester Fleece

Polyester fleece is the most practical of winter insulating fabrics, and the most popular. Fleece sweaters, jackets, vests, neck gaiters, and hats are everywhere. The inside surfaces of ski jacket collars and cuffs are often lined with the stuff. You can even buy fleece ski socks, although I don't recommend them.

"Fleece" is polyester that has been brushed to raise up a thick nap. It's sort of an industrial version of teasing your hair with a comb, something my sister did in the '60s. This makes the fabric a labyrinth of tiny air pockets that trap heat and keep you warm, while the polyester itself wicks moisture.

Fleece is inexpensive and easy to care for. You can wash it out in your hotel sink, hang it up overnight, and blow away the residual dampness in the morning with a hair dryer. Its main drawback when com-

pared to wool is that it can't be given the great colors and patterns of a wool sweater, and it inevitably develops little clumps and pills.

Because air passes through it so easily, conventional polyester fleece does not make a good outer-layer garment. In this regard, it's no better than knit wool. There are varieties of fleece available, however, that have windproof layers laminated within them. These are fabulous at blocking the wind and remarkably warm considering their light weight and low bulk. They cost significantly more than conventional fleece, though, and are generally available in only a few, solid colors.

Nylon

It's hard to find a ski jacket whose outer shell is not made of nylon or one of its

Apparel

close relatives. They are simply the best fibers for the application. They can be woven tightly to block wind, blended to provide incredible durability, yet finished to provide a feel and draping quality that is fabulous. Blends are available that feel like broken-in cotton poplin, while others are rugged and husky in appearance and feel. They all wear like iron and hold their colors after years of wear, exposure to the sun, and repeated washing. You toss them in the washing machine and they come out looking like new.

I've got nylon jackets that are fifteen years old that look and feel the same as the day I bought them.

Natural Fibers

Silk

Silk is a great base-layer fiber. It wicks very well, provides a modicum of insulation, and makes good long underwear, both tops and bottoms. It is not quite as easy to care for as synthetic fibers, but many silk garments are machine washable and dryable. Silk falls short of synthetic fibers, unfortunately, on a few counts. It is not as durable, it is only available in light and medium-light weights, is harder to find, and is more expensive.

One of my favorite characteristics of silk is that it does not develop an offensive odor when you wear it. So I can ski all day in a silk undershirt or turtleneck under a sweater, then go directly to an après-ski gathering, or even to dinner, without hoping that my companions are suffering from nasal congestion. You can also wash silk base layers in the sink and dry them in your room.

I always travel with a pair of light silk long johns and a long-sleeve silk undershirt. They're perfect for wearing under jeans and a shirt when I'm walking around in the mountains at night, making a huge difference in warmth, and adding almost no bulk.

Wool

Wool is nature's great insulator. It traps air and transports moisture like nothing else, and it makes beautiful sweaters. The downside of wool is that it can be itchy for some folks, and those beautiful sweaters are a job to wash.

Things have improved a lot for wool, however, in recent years. Fine-fiber wools, like those from New Zealand's Merino sheep, are itch free for most people. It feels so good against your skin that manufactures are making base-layer garments from it, and it doesn't retain the fats and salts from perspiration that make synthetics stink after a day of skiing. To put icing on the cake, many new wool garments are machine washable.

Cotton

In the words of Nancy Reagan, "Just say no." Cotton's big problem is that it does not wick moisture away from your skin. Instead, it holds the moisture there, where it chills you. A cotton turtleneck feels great when you first put it on, but once you perspire in it, you will be uncomfortable until you change clothes. Cotton socks should never be used for skiing.

In terms of temperature range, a cotton base-layer garment will have, at best, half the range of a garment made of a comparable synthetic.

Apparel

Waterproof/Breathable Materials

Waterproof/breathable is an industry term that applies to a range of fabric laminates and treatments that give a garment a unique characteristic: Moisture that comes off your body as water vapor when you exercise can pass through the material, but liquid water that lands on the outside of the garment, such as rain or wet snow, cannot pass through to the inside. In practical terms, this means you can ski all day in a wet Sierra snowstorm without getting soaked by either the snow or your own sweat.

Waterproof/breathable garments have been a boon to skiers, particularly those on the west and east coasts of North America. I can't imagine living in the Pacific Northwest and not owning a top-quality waterproof/breathable jacket and pants. These garments' fabrics are also more windproof than ones made of the same fibers without the waterproof/breathable qualities. But be aware that they are not as breathable as conventional nylon blends, so you may not feel as dry inside them. In dry winter climates, such as the Rocky Mountains, their reduced ability to let moisture out may not be a good trade-off for their waterproof qualities.

There are two principle ways to achieve waterproof/breathable performance. One is with a sheet of special material that is laminated between the outer fabric and liner of the jacket. Gore-Tex is such a material. (Since W. L. Gore and Associates' patent expired in 1997, others have become available.) The other is to apply a durable water repellent (DWR) finish to a conventional fabric such as nylon. The laminated-membrane approach tends to be more waterproof and lasts indefinitely. The DWR approach tends to be slightly less waterproof, but is less expensive. So if waterproofness is really important to you, go with laminated-membrane garments. In addition, make sure the garment's seams are *taped* or *welded*. This means that a waterproof tape has been applied to the jacket's seams so that no water can enter where the stitches go through the waterproof/breathable membrane. This is very important. The DWR approach is less expensive, tends to be slightly less waterproof, and eventually loses its effectiveness. DWR can be reapplied at home, however, or reactivated by heating the fabric in a clothes dryer.

SPECIFIC GARMENTS

Socks

It's hard to enjoy yourself when your feet are cold. And it's hard to ski very well when the only sensation you have at the end of your legs is pain or no sensation at

Your ski socks should come higher up the calf than your boots. Many have extra padding in critical areas.

Apparel

all. So select your socks with care. No other article of ski clothing has such a small cost differential between the very best and the very mediocre.

Always buy ski socks that come at least halfway up your calves. You want them to extend well past the tops of your ski boots. Many of the better socks are thicker in specific areas to enhance boot fit. Examples are the front of the shin, the heel, and the ball of the foot.

A sock's capacity to keep your tootsies toasty is directly proportional to its capacity to absorb perspiration. Even on the coldest days, your feet will perspire, and it's your socks' job to suck up the moisture and pull it away from your skin. This is more important for your feet than any other part of your body because they're encased in waterproof boots that don't breathe.

Always wear a fresh pair of socks when it's cold. A sock that has been skied in for a day has expended much of its capacity to suck up sweat and so will not be able to keep you as warm as a clean pair. To further maximize your socks' effectiveness, don't put them on until you are ready to go out on the hill.

Take the time to look closely at the fiber content of socks before you buy them. The fibers that do the best job of wicking and insulating are wool, silk, and certain synthetics like Thermax and Thermalite. Good socks will also have a modicum of nylon for durability and Lycra, Spandex, or other stretchy synthetic fiber to give it resiliency and elasticity.

All the wicking and insulating fibers I've mentioned are relatively expensive. A manufacturer can control the price of its sock by increasing the amount of other fibers, like nylon, to fill things out. From a performance standpoint, the less of these filler fibers, the better. You may save some money by buying a less expensive sock, but unless you have feet that never ever get cold, it is false economy.

Just which of the good insulating fabrics you should look for is a matter of personal preference. While I like synthetic fibers in undershirts, I don't like the way they feel in socks. My favorite fiber for socks is Merino wool. It doesn't itch, wears well, and can be machine washed. A mixture of 75 percent wool, 18 percent nylon, and 7 percent Spandex makes my feet very happy.

To find out what works best for you, I suggest the following procedure. Buy or

THIN SOCKS OR THICK SOCKS?

You may have heard this bit of advice: "In a ski boot, a thinner sock will keep your feet warmer than a thicker one." My own experiments have led me to conclude just the opposite. Most boot fitters would not agree with me, but none of the ones I've talked to have ever run *The Experiment*: skiing with a thin sock on one foot and a thicker sock of similar fiber content on the other. I have done this several times, and the foot in the thicker sock has always been warmer. And I ski in a very close-fitting boot.

If the "thinner sock is warmer" theory were true, then you would expect that a thin sweater would keep you warmer than a thick one, wouldn't you? I don't know anyone who believes that.

Try The Experiment yourself and draw your own conclusions.

Apparel

borrow a few different pairs of socks of different compositions. Ski with a different sock on each foot for a few days to see which type keeps you most comfortable.

Long Underwear—Bottom to Top

The vast majority of long johns on the market today are synthetic. Silk is a nice option, as is very fine-fiber wool.

In my experience, the place to be careful when fitting long johns is the crotch. This is where they always seem to come apart, so I recommend pairs that are not too snug at the inside top of the leg.

Lightweight fleece pants under ski pants are an excellent alternative to traditional long johns. This arrangement has a distinct advantage. You can wear the fleece pants to the hill in the morning and slip on your wind pants once you get there. When you leave the hill at the end of the day, you can just take off your wind pants and head off for your chosen après-ski endeavors in those soft, comfortable fleece trousers. They usually have pockets, too. And stick to *lightweight* fleece. Medium-weight fleece pants are too warm under nylon ski pants for anything other than very cold conditions.

Traditional turtlenecks have given way over the last decade to turtlenecks with zip-up collars. These are much more practical. A lot of blood flows through your neck, close to the surface, so you can regulate your temperature through the day by zipping them up and opening them.

Polyester and polyolefin fabrics make great base-layer garments that cover a wide range of temperatures because they wick so well. Outdoor sports stores of all sorts sell them. Ultralightweight brushed polyester fleece turtlenecks are very

THE CURSE OF LUMPY LONG JOHNS

Ankle and shin discomfort in ski boots is frequently caused by wrinkles and lumps in long johns when you pull your ski socks over them. Here are three possible solutions to this problem:
1) Pull your socks up all the way, then pull your long underwear down over your socks;
2) *Roll* your ski socks up and over your long johns;
3) Put your socks on *first*, then pull your long johns on over them, making sure the cuffs of your long johns are snug against your ankles/calves.

warm and have a cuddly feel—sort of like your old flannel "jammies" but without the teddy bears printed on them.

Sweaters

I've got wool sweaters that I love. They're warm. They're great looking. They bring back memories of great days of skiing. They last forever. But the workhorses in my wardrobe are the polyester fleece sweaters. They look okay for awhile, until they develop pills. They're either solid colors or slightly hokey-looking prints. I don't miss them when they're gone. But they have pockets. They have stand-up collars to keep my neck warm. They have front closures that can be snapped up when it's cold or opened when it's warm. I wad them up and toss them in my boot bag, and they don't seem to mind at all. They can be washed in the washer and dried in the dryer. They bounce back from coffee and ketchup spills like nothing ever happened. They last forever. They are half the price of a decent wool sweater. You pick.

Apparel

Regular wool and fleece sweaters are not good as outer layers, except on warm, sunny spring days. They don't block any wind, snow sticks to them, and they are prone to getting wet. There are, however, wool sweaters available with Gore-Tex liners and other wind barriers available, and fleece sweaters with wind-blocking layers, too. These are suitable as outer layers during warmer parts of the season.

Fleece Vests and Jackets

A must-have adjunct to your sweater and jacket, a fleece vest will extend either's range downward a good 10 to 15 degrees. In many parts of the country, a sweater, vest, and shell will get you through much of the winter. Layer a vest between your sweater and a heavy jacket and you're ready for Vermont in January. A fleece jacket turns an appropriately roomy shell into midwinter clothing. Both fleece vests and jackets have the added attraction of giving you a couple more pockets. Some shells are now made with pass-through zippers that give you access to those pockets.

Like wool sweaters, however, conventional fleece vests and jackets do not make sense as a general-purpose outer layer, because they are so porous to wind.

Jackets

The most expensive and complicated garment you will buy is your jacket or

Drawstring and clamps for hood opening

Sleeve pocket

Pit zip

parka. Buy the right one and it could be the only one you need.

When you try on a jacket, pay close attention to the details. While it's important that the cut of your clothes reflect your personal style, don't buy a jacket unless it passes muster on the small but essential stuff that nobody sees. That could make the difference between comfort and misery.

COLLAR

There are major blood vessels running up and down your neck right near the surface. So a ski jacket's collar is one of its most important features. Wind blowing across your neck and face can suck a lot of heat away from your body, even on a sunny spring day.

Before you buy, zip the collar up all the way and see how it fits and feels around your neck. It should not be so tight that it strangles you and should be tall and roomy enough that it covers your chin and lower cheeks when zipped up all the way. Unless the collar covers your chin, the jacket will only be suitable for spring skiing. Try the jacket on with a fleece vest underneath, to make sure there is enough room for the vest's collar, too.

There should be a fabric flap behind the zipper so that the zipper won't scrape your chin raw when the zipper is all the way up. Look for a collar that's lined with a soft material such as fleece. Collars lined with dark-colored fabrics are best. Sunscreen and oils from your face will

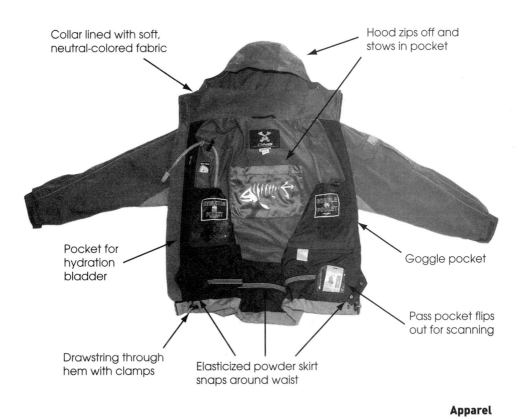

Collar lined with soft, neutral-colored fabric

Hood zips off and stows in pocket

Pocket for hydration bladder

Goggle pocket

Pass pocket flips out for scanning

Drawstring through hem with clamps

Elasticized powder skirt snaps around waist

Apparel

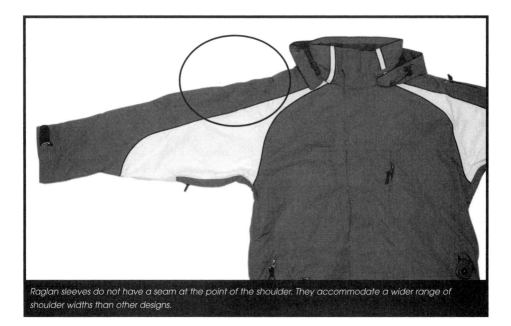

Raglan sleeves do not have a seam at the point of the shoulder. They accommodate a wider range of shoulder widths than other designs.

make a light fabric look disgustingly grubby after only a couple of days.

ZIPPERS

The main zipper on a jacket must have a flap, or *placket*, that lies over it or behind it to keep wind from getting through. Some jackets have both. If the jacket has an outside placket, it should have snaps or Velcro to hold it down over the zipper. If snaps are used, try operating them with gloves on before you buy the jacket. Don't expect to find two-way zippers on better parkas. The bottom zipper pull tends to rise unbidden as you ski, flapping around and letting in cold air.

All the other zippers on the outside of the jacket should have flaps over them to keep snow from icing them up and getting whatever is behind them wet.

All outside zipper pulls should have nylon tabs or cords attached to them so you can manipulate them without taking your gloves off. If you lose a tab, you can make a fine replacement with a short piece of 2-mm utility cord, available in a range of colors from climbing and mountaineering stores.

Pocket zippers are sewn so that when they are up, they are closed. According to Trey Harris at Descente North America, this is done so that if the zipper is half open, the pocket is still half closed. If the zipper were put in the other way, any opening at all would allow things to fall out of the pocket.

SLEEVES

Wear a sweater and gloves when you try the jacket on for fit. Zip it up, crouch low, and reach as far forward as you can. The sleeves must be long enough that no gaps open up between them and your

Apparel

gloves, and the shoulders must be cut so that the jacket does not constrain your arm movement. If you have very broad or narrow shoulders, you might look for a jacket with *raglan* sleeves. This is a type of shoulder-and-sleeve design that accommodates a wide range of shoulder sizes without binding or appearing ill fitting.

Consider how the cuffs feel against your wrists. Stiff nylon gathered by elastic can be rough on your skin. Cuffs lined with fleece or soft fabric are a bonus. When they get wet, you will still be warm and comfortable, and they will never rub your wrists raw.

Take your gloves or mittens with you when you shop for a jacket to see how they coordinate with its cuffs. If they are both snug fitting or both loose fitting, you are headed for clothing collisions. I look for snug jacket cuffs and longer, gauntlet-style gloves and mittens that will overlap them.

POCKETS

You'll need at least three or four of them, and their placement is as important as their number. When you try the jacket on, stick a bunch of stuff in the pockets to see how they take loading. You want at least a couple of large pockets on the outside and one or two smaller ones. A jacket should have at least one inside pocket, too. This is where I keep my keys and wallet. I have never found pockets on sleeves very useful, but I know people who like to use them for lip balm. All outside pockets should have zippers. Velcro alone won't cut it. Some inside pockets, such as those for goggles, can get away without zippers, but zippers are still

required for any inside pocket that will hold small valuables.

If you ski with a cell phone, look for an outside pocket that you can get in and out of easily and that won't muffle the ring.

Many jackets these days have a big inside pocket for goggles—one of the great collateral benefits of the evolution toward looser-fitting ski clothes over the past decade. The best goggle pockets hold your goggles horizontally so they wrap around your torso. Pockets in which your goggles fit vertically are not nearly as comfortable.

Some jackets now have inside pockets for hydration systems like CamelBak, which is a great feature.

Once you get a jacket, adopt a system for what you put in which pockets. This will save you a lot of fumbling time. Don't put your most precious cargo—keys, wallet, and so on—in pockets with sunscreen and things you need to get at often; this will reduce the chances of losing the important stuff.

Learn to periodically check the zippers on your pockets, and those of your friends, to make sure they're closed. A lot of loot appears under the chairlifts when the snow melts away in the spring. It all falls out of unzipped pockets. Even if something valuable doesn't drop out when you fall, snow will drop in. In addition, all pockets must have an inner lip that prevents things from falling out if the zipper isn't closed.

HOODS

Go to a World Cup ski race on a nasty day and you'll see lots of coaches with their hoods up. These are people who know how to stay warm. A hood made of any tightly woven fabric will extend the

Apparel

range of a ski jacket a good 10 degrees or more downward. It can turn a cold, snowy day from a miserable ordeal into the best powder day of the year.

Take a look at how the hood closes in front. It's got to work in sync with the collar and have some way of snugging down so it doesn't blow back when you're skiing fast. It's also a big help if you can manipulate it without taking your gloves off. Can you pull the hood up over your head and adjust the drawstrings with gloves on? By their nature, hoods limit your peripheral vision. Some are worse than others. In any case, you can improve the situation by putting your goggles on over your hood. The strap will hold the hood close against

your head, improving your peripheral view and keeping the hood from ballooning up with air when you ski.

Drawstrings that must be tied in a bow are worse than useless. They should have clamps. If they don't, you can buy a couple at an outdoor sports store and add them yourself.

You don't have to pull it all the way up to benefit from a hood. Pulling it up a bit so it covers the gap between your hat and jacket collar will help a lot on many days. You can hold it in place with your goggle strap.

A hood doesn't have to be insulated to be effective, but if it is, you'll get another 5 degrees of temperature range out of your parka.

PIT ZIPS

This is the name for the zippers that many jackets have under the armpits. They are strictly for ventilation, and will extend the range of a jacket upward a good 5 or 10 degrees. Open them up and lower your main zipper a bit, and the airflow will cool you right down.

POWDER SKIRTS

Many jackets have an elasticized inner cuff inside that closes around your waist and keeps snow from billowing into your jacket from underneath on big powder days. And if your jacket doesn't have a goggle pocket, you can turn the whole inside of the jacket into one by snapping up the powder cuff. Many jackets have instead a drawstring that circles the jacket through the bottom hem or a few inches higher. When snugged up, it acts like a powder skirt.

The snaps that secure this jacket's placket have a special design that makes them easy to close without taking off your gloves.

Apparel

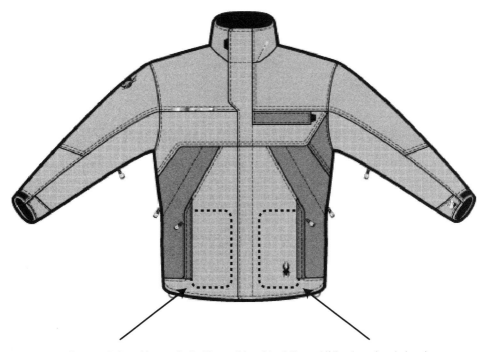

Every pocket must have a lip that keeps things from falling out if the zipper is not closed.

How Heavy a Jacket Do You Need?

If you have a good layering system, you can get by with one jacket. If you live in a particularly cold part of the country or you get cold easily, make it a moderately insulated jacket. Otherwise, a shell or lightly insulated jacket should do the job. Add a good sweater and a fleece vest (or light fleece jacket) under the jacket and you'll have a versatile outfit that should handle just about any conditions, especially if the outer jacket has a good hood and collar. When it gets warmer, you can wear the jacket without a sweater.

Bill McCollum of *Ski Racing* magazine and a Vermonter who skis almost daily (read: person who is often outside in a *cold* place), skis in a lightly insulated parka over a fleece jacket.

If you have the budget for a second jacket, get a full-featured uninsulated shell. You'll be surprised how warm they can be, especially with a sweater and vest underneath. If you are considering a pullover shell, go for one that has a long, navel-length zipper. This will make putting it on and taking it off much easier. Make sure you try doing this a few times in the store, with a sweater and vest on.

Some jackets have zip-out insulated liners, making them extremely versatile. I have one that is comfortable on the nastiest of days when the liner is in it and makes a good spring jacket when the liner is out. And the liner itself makes a nice around-town jacket.

Apparel

On warm spring days, the weather can change quickly. Be prepared with a light nylon windbreaker tied around your waist.

For spring skiing, pick up a simple, inexpensive nylon windbreaker. When things really warm up midday, you can roll it up and tie it around your waist.

PANTS

Ski filmmaker Warren Miller says that skiing's phenomenal growth in the 1960s was fueled by the widespread use of tight stretch ski pants. Spandex shorts have probably done a lot for the health club business, too. But tight, stretchy pants have fallen out of favor for most skiers, and for good reason. They're just not as warm or comfortable as the looser sorts of pants that are now the norm. They don't have usable pockets and your bum gets damp every time you sit on a wet chairlift.

If you like stretch pants, get the type that fit over the outside of your boots. Don't get the inside-the-boot type. They seriously compromise boot fit around the ankles, and on powder days they allow snow to get inside your boots, resulting in wet, cold, miserable feet.

If you prefer loose-fitting nylon pants, you're in good company. Ninety-nine percent of serious skiers wear them. Because you will often be sitting on wet chairlift seats and snow will pile on your thighs when it's storming, it's important that they have either a waterproof/breathable membrane or durable water-repellent finish.

Suspenders

I can't keep a pair of ski pants up without suspenders, and I suspect this is true for many other skiers. The pants may feel like they are hanging fine on your hips while you're walking around in the store, but after an hour or two of athletic skiing they can start to hang a little low. I've clamped regular suspenders onto a lot of ski pants, but I'll always pay a bit more for a pair that has the suspenders built in. Most pants with built-in suspenders come up high in the back to cover your kidneys, too, which helps keep you warmer.

Cuffs

Ski pants must have some sort of elastic cuffs to hold them fast around the top of your boot. Without them, you will get snow in your boots, your socks will get wet, and your mood will turn grumpy.

There are two main varieties of snow-proof cuffs. With one, the bottom of the pant leg has elastic sewn into it and it grips the cuff of your boot. With the other, the pant leg is cut straight and hemmed, and there is a second, inner cuff with elastic that grips the boot cuff. Either works fine, as long as the pants are long enough that when you sit on the chairlift or flex to absorb a mogul, the cuffs stay down on your boots.

Insulation

Unless you ski in a particularly frigid part of the country, you don't need much insulation built into your pants, if any. Shell pants and long underwear will do fine most of the season in Colorado and California. Add a pair of light fleece pants to your wardrobe and you are set for almost any conditions. With medium-weight fleece pants under shells you can ski at night in Minnesota in January.

One-Piece Suits

One-piece suits are like anchovies. Either you like them or you don't. On the plus side, they don't need as much insulation as a two-piece outfit to provide the same level of warmth, and snow can't get into your clothes on a powder day or if you fall. On the minus side, they are less versatile because you can't mix and match the jacket and pants, they are trickier to fit, and you can't take the jacket off when you go inside. The best you can do is pull the top off your shoulders and tie the arms around your waist or let them hang.

Built-in suspenders and coverage for your kidneys are desirable features for ski pants. The patches on the bottom of each pant leg resist cuts from the ski's edges. All ski pants need such protection.

Apparel

GLOVES AND MITTENS

Not all gloves and mittens are created equal. If your hands are prone to getting uncomfortably cold, this is one place where paying attention to detail and spending a little more money will pay big dividends.

If you ski a lot, you'll want one pair for cold days, another for warm ones.

Gloves or Mittens?

Only a fool or a charlatan would claim that gloves are as warm as mittens. On the other hand, mittens are a bit clumsy and must be removed to do some things that you could accomplish with gloves on. If you live in a cold part of the country or your hands get cold easily, then mittens are your best bet. To get really toasty, look for a pair that has fingerlets—little "socks" for each of your fingers inside

A three-fingered glove provides almost all the warmth of a mitten and the dexterity of a glove.

the mitten. They trap air very close to your skin, increasing warmth.

Don't let anyone tell you that mittens aren't hip, either. Two of the undisputedly best ski racers in the world, Bode Miller of the United States and Janica Kostelic of Croatia, routinely race in mittens.

An alternative to both is a mitten that has a free index finger. I have found that these sorts of mittens keep my hands warmer than the conventional variety and give me 80 percent of gloves' dexterity.

Ultimately, the choice between gloves and mittens is immaterial if you don't pay heed to the following considerations.

Insulation Material

Both synthetic fiber and synthetic fur work well. Beware of down. It is good in the back of a glove but not in the palm, where it gets crushed and loses its insulating properties. The feathers slide around on each other, too, giving them a slippery feeling and poor grip. The other big problem with down is that it's worthless when it gets wet.

Fit

This is a case where bigger is better. Tight-fitting gloves and mittens will never keep you as warm as roomy ones, and people often buy them too small.

When trying on a glove, put one on your dominant hand and extend your fingers. The crotches between the fingers of the glove should come down to the ones between your fingers. If they aren't at least very close, the gloves are too small. Next, make a fist and see if the glove is snug around the back and palm of your hand. If it is, the insulation will be compressed when you grip your ski pole,

Apparel

squeezing out whatever warm air was trapped in the fibers.

Don't worry if the gloves feel a bit big and bulky in the store. After you ski in them for a day or two, they will take on the curve of your hands and fingers, and instead of feeling ungainly, they will feel comfy.

The Cuff

The gloves' or mittens' cuffs and the sleeves of your jacket have to mate properly to keep your wrists covered, and do it without a lot of fussing on your part when you slip them on your hands. The blood vessels that go to and from your hand are routed along the front of your wrist, not far from the surface. If your wrists are exposed to cold air, a lot of heat will be lost that would otherwise go to your fingers. The style of cuff is less important in warm weather.

So when you go shopping for gloves and mittens, wear your ski jacket. Make sure that the ensemble works together. My preferences for cold weather are gloves and mittens that have what is called a *gauntlet* cuff.

These cuffs, being long and loose-fitting, slide easily over the cuff and sleeve of your jacket so that your wrist is never exposed. Gauntlet cuffs with zippers that snug the cuff down on the jacket sleeve are the best. Many gloves and mittens have knit cuffs that fit snugly around the wrist. I don't care for them because they always seem to fight with the sleeves of my jacket.

Material

Should the primary glove material be leather or fabric? I've had both, and I've been happy with both. I've got to say,

A glove with a gauntlet-style cuff works best with most ski jackets.

however, that there is something endearing about the way leather forms to your hand and leather's quality of grip—assuring but not aggressive. While I'm happy with synthetics on the backs of my hands, I want something bovine or ungulate in origin on the fronts of my fingers and palms.

Be aware, however, that leather-palmed mittens and gloves will not stand up long to the rigors of snowboarding. For that, go synthetic.

If you ski in a wet climate, I recommend synthetic gloves with a waterproof-breathable layer. Leather will not hold up well in wet conditions, even with such a layer. Be aware, however, that there are so many seams on a glove that staying completely dry is difficult.

Liners

If your hands get cold easily, consider getting light silk or synthetic glove liners. Hollow synthetic fibers such as Thermax are quite effective. I don't use them myself, but I know many instructors who swear by them.

Apparel

HEADGEAR

The traditional single-layer knit ski hat has a certain jaunty alpine flair and works well in many weather conditions. They are available in an incredible range of styles, patterns, and colors, allowing you to express yourself with your head. They are relatively inexpensive, too, so you can afford to humor yourself with several.

The best hats for most conditions are wool or fleece (fleece works out better in wet climates). Unfortunately, both types are sieves against the wind, and wool can be itchy. The itch problem can be addressed by finding a hat with an inner headband of acrylic yarn or polyester fleece. The best have wind-blocking fleece, which solves the wind problem. They are more expensive, but I can't think of any other part of your ski wardrobe that can be elevated to the top echelon of alpine fashion and function with as small an incremental expenditure.

If you ski in extreme-cold country, do yourself a favor and get a hat covered with a tightly woven fabric, such as nylon, and earflaps you can cinch down with a string under your chin, *à la* Elmer Fudd. You will be amazed by how much warmer this sort of hat will keep your whole body.

Helmets are pretty warm all by themselves, but for really cold weather you may need adjunct insulation. Light synthetic skullcaps and balaclavas (fabric hoods that cover your head, neck, and chin) work well under helmets. If you buy a helmet big enough to fit over a knit ski hat, it will be too big to be safe without the hat.

Maintaining Hat Performance

If your hat gets wet when you're skiing, you can dry it out under the hand dryer in the restroom. Rub it between your hands under the dryer, just as if you were drying your hands. This will get it to dry more quickly.

To dry your hat at home, turn it inside out and stand it up in a warm, dry place. Good candidates are on top of the refrigerator or the water heater. Stuff it with a wadded up page of the newspaper to make it stand up.

For cold weather and wind, a hat with a nylon shell and earflaps will keep you much warmer than a conventional knit one.

Apparel

Most ski garments can be thrown in the washing machine. Many can even be put in the clothes dryer. (Wool hats and sweaters, which should be dry-cleaned or hand washed, are the main exceptions.) You should, however, observe a few procedures unique to cleaning these "technical" types of clothing. When in doubt, follow the instructions on the apparel's care label.

Don't use liquid detergents or liquid fabric softeners. They leave residues that prevent synthetic fibers and waterproof/breathable membranes and fabric treatments from properly doing their microscopic chores of wicking, insulating, and passing water vapor. Use only powdered detergents or so-called "sports washes" made specifically for these types of garments. Rinse them twice to thoroughly remove soap residue.

Turn fleece garments inside out before washing and drying. This will keep the outside from pilling.

Most often, if a waterproof/breathable garment is leaking or damp, it is because the manufacturer's durable water repellent (DWR) finish is matted or dirty. To keep your fabric performing like new, adhere to the guidelines on the care label inside every garment. Wash your garment periodically in warm water with no detergent.

DWR finishes can often be rejuvenated by simply running the garment through a low-heat cycle in the dryer.

Repeated washings and wear eventually break down DWR finishes. (This is not an issue with Gore-Tex or similar waterproof/breathable membranes.) They can be touched up with refinishing treatments, available in outdoor sports stores. Spray-on treatments are usually better than wash-in treatments, because they only affect the outer surface of the garment. If the garment has a lining that is intended to wick moisture, its performance will be degraded by a wash-in treatment.

The waterproof/breathable finish of ski jackets and pants can be easily rejuvenated with special treatments available at most outdoor equipment stores. Such treatments also work on some garments that are not already waterproof.

Apparel

Coordinate a neck gaiter with your hat and goggle strap to provide extra protection.

NECK AND FACE

Neck Gaiters

Neck gaiters are useful, inexpensive, and effective. Made of polyester or acrylic fleece, they stay warm when wet, dry fast, and don't chafe. Whoever invented these things should have filed for a patent.

I know lots of ski instructors who wear neck gaiters half the season. On really cold days, they pull the neck gaiter up over the back of their hats and keep them in place with their goggle straps.

I have one big complaint with most neck gaiters: You can't take them off and put them on without messing with your hat and goggles, too. I've seen a few that look more like bandannas with Velcro closures at the back, and these work much better. Personally, I find that with a good collar and a hood on my jacket, I don't need a neck gaiter.

Scarves

Scarves are a good retro alternative to the ubiquitous fleece neck gaiter. I like them better because they are easier to take off when you get too hot. It is a simple matter to wrap a scarf around your neck and chin when you want protection, then unwrap it when your radiator starts to overheat halfway down the back bowls. And nothing, but nothing, feels as good against your jowls on a cold day as cashmere.

One caution about scarves: They are not suitable for children. Stories have circulated for decades about choking incidents on chairlifts and rope tows. Isadora Duncan, the infamous Victorian dancer, was strangled by her scarf when it got caught and wrapped around the axle of the convertible car she was riding in. While this was not a skiing accident, it points to the potential for lethal mishap.

Masks

The Seirus company markets face masks for extreme weather that cover everything from your nose down and back, and close with Velcro behind your head. They definitely work. And when you're not skiing, you can use them for professional wrestling or holding up liquor stores.

Goggles and Glasses

SELECTING GOGGLES

People are funny about goggles. I know people who wear them all the time, even in the spring when everyone else is wearing sunglasses, and I know people who wouldn't wear them if they were skiing underwater. Unless you are in the second camp, you're going to need a pair.

Double Lenses

Don't even consider getting anything that doesn't have a double lens. This *thermopane* system for ski goggles was invented in 1962 in Sun Valley by Dr. Bob Smith, a dentist who liked to ski. Smith started making double-lens goggles for himself and his buddies and then began peddling them to shops in resort towns. The lenses were very bulbous and odd-looking, and made of hard plastic. The frame was just a few struts around the circumference of the lens, wrapped with a thin sheet of porous foam that let lots of air through, but no snow. It was immediately obvious that these were the way to go in deep powder.

I remember riding the tram at Jackson Hole in 1968 and seeing cadres of locals with these slightly goofy-looking but obviously effective (and very cool) goggles on. I wanted a pair.

So did millions of other skiers. Smith became one of the great names in ski goggles—and still is today. Now, any decent goggle has a double lens. The only exceptions are some high-level racing goggles, which have single lenses made of a plastic that is very sturdy and pliable and unlikely to shatter or splinter if

it hits the deck at 70 miles per hour. You don't need or want them.

Antifog Coatings

Quality goggle lenses have a coating on the inner surface that helps prevent fogging. These coatings are fragile. They scratch easily and smear if they're rubbed when wet. Only dab the inside surface to dry it; never rub it. The coating can be restored somewhat with special cloths provided by the goggle manufacturer.

Extreme Antifog

Even a double lens doesn't cut the mustard if things get humid enough in your goggles. For that, the ultimate solution to fogging goggles is to buy a pair with a fan that blows air across the inside of the lens. They always work (as long as the

HOW DO DOUBLE LENSES WORK?

A goggle lens fogs when it is colder than the air with which it is in contact, and when that air is humid. When the moisture in the air comes into contact with the cold lens, it condenses, just like it does on the outside of a glass of iced tea on a hot day. The fog on your goggles is really just a bunch of very small water drops, condensed on the cold surface of the lens.

The surface of the lens closest to your face is exposed to air that is humidified by your face and breath. If the other side of the lens is in contact with the outside air, it gets cold, and fog forms on the inner surface. The second, outer lens insulates the inner lens from the cold outside air with an intermediate layer of air. As a result, the inner lens seldom gets cold enough to make the moisture condense. Voila! Visibility!

Goggles and Glasses

batteries aren't dead). If you live in a humid area like the Pacific Northwest or western British Columbia, or do a lot of powder skiing, they could be worth the investment ($190 for a pair of Smith Cascade Turbo Cams, for example).

Keeping Goggles Clear of Fog

So you've just spent $80 on a pair of goggles with super ventilation, a double lens, and an exotic antifog coating. Still, they fog up when you pull them down onto your face at the top of the lift. What's wrong?

Even the best goggles will get steamed when the conditions are right and the goggles are handled wrong. Here are a few tips to help any pair of goggles perform their best:

- Don't put your goggles up on your forehead while you ride the lift or stand around, particularly if there is snow on your hat. The moisture and heat rising from your head will fog even the best of them. Once you've stepped outside and put them on your face, keep them there. If you want to take them off for the lift ride or switch to your sunglasses, put the goggles inside your jacket.

- If your goggles get fog, snow, or water drops on the inside of the lens, do not rub it with anything. Instead, blot the offending moisture with a chamois, a paper napkin, or special goggle cloth. Modern antifog coatings smear and scratch very easily when wet.

- You can dry your goggles under a restroom hand dryer, but be careful. The air can sometimes get hot enough to warp the goggle lens.

- Be careful putting on your goggles when there is snow on your hat. Keep snow out of them by holding the goggles against your face with one hand while pulling the strap into position on the back of your head with the other.

- If you are so unlucky as to get frost on the inside of the lens, the best you can hope for is that the warmth of your face will melt the ice, or that they clear if you put your goggles inside your parka for the lift ride. The only alternative is to go in and warm up. If it's that cold outside, you probably need a hot drink anyway.

- Your goggles are likely to get wet inside and fog up if they come off in a fall, especially on a powder day. Tightening

These goggles have a fan that clears the lens quickly in even the worst of conditions. Note the battery pack on the strap.

Photo courtesy Smith

Goggles and Glasses

When there's snow on your hat, it's easy to get some in your goggles when you put them on. The trick to keeping it out is first holding the goggles against your face, then pulling the strap back over your head.

your goggle strap will reduce the chances of this happening.

- If you get snow in your goggles, knock as much out as you can by smacking them against your hand. Blowing in your goggles will dispel snow but will also fog the lens.

Be nice to your goggles. Carry them in a soft bag, treat the lenses right, and they will help you enjoy more time on the slopes.

CHAMOIS AND NO-FOG CLOTHS

I always carry a piece of chamois in my pocket. As far as I can tell, man has yet to produce a better material for soaking up moisture from optical surfaces than the stuff that covers the butt of a European mountain antelope. Professional ski photographers the world over carry pieces of chamois with them to mop their Nikon and Canon lenses. If it's good enough for a $5,000 300 mm

f2.8 lens, it's good enough for your goggles.

Get a large piece of chamois at your local auto parts store and cut it up into eight-inch-diameter circular pieces. Put one in each of your ski jackets and pants, and give the rest to your family and friends for Christmas. They'll never forget you. When the chamois gets dirty, simply wash it by squeezing some soapy water through it then rinsing it well. After it dries out, pull it gently back to shape.

No-fog cloths are good for restoring the coating on the inside of your lens, but they aren't nearly as effective as chamois for cleaning your lenses or drying them out after they get wet.

Goggle Squeegee

When the snow is coming down like oatmeal or you find yourself skiing in the rain, one of these little wonders is worth its weight in titanium. They do a remarkably good job of improving visibility and work far better than anything else. You wear

The ingenious goggle squeegee is an indispensable accessory for skiing in wet conditions.

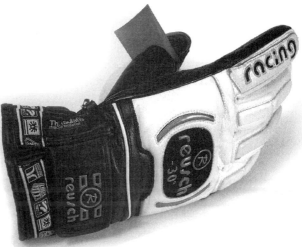

Goggles and Glasses

the thing on your thumb. This seems a bit odd at first, but you quickly realize that it's perfectly poised to do its job.

This is one of those gizmos that's so simple and effective that it makes you smile when you use it.

Lens Color

This is probably the most important consideration in a pair of goggles, after double lenses. Brownish orange is good for most conditions. If you like to ski with goggles a lot of the time, you might get a gray lens, too, for sunny days. If you ski at night under the lights, use a clear lens. These can be hard to find but are definitely worth the search.

Everyone wears goggles on snowy days, and most seasoned skiers wear them when it's cold to protect their faces. The common denominator about most such days is that the light is cloudy, diffuse, or shady—what skiers call *flat light*. The light turns "flat" when it shows no visual detail in the snow, which is mostly a matter of contrast. If there are a lot of distinct little shadows and shades of color, your brain infers relief in the surface. If the shading is uniform, the surface looks smooth, even if it isn't. Shading becomes uniform when the light is coming from all directions at the same intensity. Think "fog bank." The light is getting bounced around by the snow, the clouds above you, and if it is snowing, the snow in the air. Consequently, there is no contrast on the surface of the snow.

The best lens colors in these conditions fall somewhere between yellow and vermilion. Just where is mostly a matter of taste. I find vermilion, or rose, provides the very best visibility in the very worst light,

but it is annoying in moderate to good light. For me, brownish orange is the best all-around choice.

How does a colored lens improve the situation? Although we think of snow as white, it is really somewhat blue. So the light that the snow scatters is a little heavy on the blue side. A yellow, orange, or vermilion lens filters out more blue light than it does other colors, and so it filters out a lot of that scattered light. This adds some contrast to the snow and helps you see.

FIT

Shape

Just as ski boots are designed to fit certain feet, goggles are designed to fit certain faces. When viewed from above, my head is more oval than many people's, while some folks' heads are quite round. A pair of goggles with a soft, compliant frame and lens will fit a wide range of noggins, but many very good goggles are not simpatico to a wide variety of heads. Try on a bunch.

The Nose Knows

If the nose you sport is on the large side, as is mine, make sure the goggles you buy don't restrict your ability to breathe. If, on the other hand, you have a small nose, look for goggles that fit close over your bridge or you'll get air leaks that make your eyes water.

Clip on the Strap

I won't buy a pair of goggles that doesn't have a buckle or clasp in the middle of the strap, behind my head. This simple feature enables me to put my goggles on and take them off without ever pulling them over my forehead,

A strap that separates in the back makes it much easier to put on and take off your goggles without getting snow in them.

where they invariably pick up snow on powder days. I'm amazed that some manufacturers of otherwise fine goggles don't employ this simple device, even on their most expensive models.

"Helmet helpers" are often available for such goggle straps, too. These are extra sections that clip into the strap so it fits well on a helmet.

CONTACT LENSES AND EYEGLASSES

I've worn eyeglasses since the third grade. Without some sort of corrective lenses I'd have to use my hands to tell the tip of my ski from the tail. I've skied both with eyeglasses and contact lenses. If you have eyes like mine, you've got my sympathy.

Contact Lenses

Fortunately, contact lenses work well for me, and that's what I wear when I ski. I use disposable lenses and always carry a spare pair in my boot bag, in case I lose one on the hill.

If you wear contacts, be careful when you're putting on sunscreen. I have on a number of occasions inadvertently pushed a lens into the corner of my eye while slathering my face. While I accept that I might be more clumsy or careless than many people, I'm guessing that there are a lot of other contact lens wearers out there who are at least as clumsy and careless as I am and will suffer the same problem.

Eyeglasses

Eyeglasses and goggles are a tough combination. Fit and fogging are the main problems. Get a pair of glasses with small plastic lenses and minimalist frames, and get so-called over-the-glasses (OTG) goggles if you can. They have recesses in the frame for the temples of your glasses to pass through and hold the lens farther from your face than other goggles.

The other big problem with glasses under goggles is that they fog easily. To combat this, try rubbing them with an antifog cloth or antifog goop, both available in ski shops. Soap works, too. Dampen your finger, rub it on a bar of soap, then on the lenses of your glasses. Or use a drop of liquid dish soap.

Some manufacturers, Bollé and Smith for example, make special inserts for their goggles that hold prescription lenses. This

Goggles and Glasses

is an excellent alternative to OTG goggles. The only issue with them is that you have to carry a pair of eyeglasses with you for when you take your goggles off.

Dry Eyes

Some folks' eyes get dry when they ski, especially those who wear contact lenses. If you have this problem, carry a small bottle of artificial tears. These are the safest and most effective type of eye-drops for frequent use.

If Your Lenses Get Trashed

Goggle lenses get scratched. There is simply no way around it. By the time your goggles have kicked around in your boot bag, on your face, and across lunch tables for a season or two, they have enough little dings in them to significantly reduce the clarity of your view. And the days when you wear goggles are, almost by definition, the days when you need the clearest view you can get.

Years ago, a good ski shop would carry replacement lenses for the goggles it sold. They cost a couple of bucks. No more. There are, however, a number of Internet-based vendors of replacement lenses and a phone-order company, 1-800-PRO-LENS, that can supply you with just about any replacement lens, for a price. Expect one to cost one-third to one-half what you paid for the goggles in the first place.

There is an alternative. Get a bottle of Maguiar's (pronounced *McGuire's*) plastic polish. It is made for polishing jet fighter canopies, motorcycle-helmet face shields, and the like—items that are even more costly to replace than a goggle lens. Polish the outside surface

(never the inner surface) with this stuff and I guarantee you will see a big difference. It works on sunglasses, too.

Plastic polish is available in stores that sell serious automobile polishing supplies, and I'm sure there are other brands of the same sort of stuff. A lifetime supply will cost you less than $10.

Sunglasses

Fashion and function meet, right there on your face, in your sunglasses. I can't advise you on the former, but I can on the latter.

SAFETY

Glasses for skiing protect you in several ways. First and foremost they protect your eyes from ultraviolet light (UV). You can't see UV, but it's the stuff that causes snow blindness and skin cancer. Skiing deals you to a double dose of UV. The sun bombards the earth constantly with a lot of UV, but most of it is filtered by the atmosphere. At skiing altitudes, there is less air, so there is more UV. Snow compounds the problem because it reflects a lot of those harmful UV rays at you.

Fortunately, just about any plastic lens absorbs a great deal of UV, so a $10 pair of plastic shades from the local gas station will give you pretty good UV protection. Even clear, colorless plastic lenses will protect your eyes from UV.

Some manufacturers will also tell you that their glasses protect you from infrared light (IR), but the medical jury is out on whether there is any significant safety issue with IR in the first place.

Another safety consideration with sunglasses for skiing is that they must be able to take a good wallop without breaking. If you happen to take a header, you don't want pieces of lens getting rammed into your face. For this reason, glass lenses are inappropriate for skiing, unless they are safety lenses of tempered glass. Former Olympian Billy Kidd told me that he skied for years in classic aviator-style Ray Ban sunglasses with wire frames and glass lenses. Then he took a fall that broke a lens, cutting his face just below the eye. He switched to plastic lenses.

Finally, a well-designed pair of glasses will shield your eyes from the wind, so they don't fill with tears at speed. For this reason, I recommend glasses with larger lenses. Small ones may be chic, but they don't cut the mustard for skiing. Along the same lines, my experience is that if a frame doesn't fit closely across the bridge of your nose or has a gap designed into the frame in that area, it will let a lot of wind hit your eyes.

INTERCHANGEABLE LENSES

If, like me, you prefer to ski in glasses rather than goggles, look for sport sunglasses that come with two or more pairs of lenses in different tints. There are a lot of them out there. You can switch lenses as the light changes and get replacements if they get scratched.

If you have nothing else in which to carry your glasses, use an unmatched sock. If you want to get fancy, you can cut the sock off at the right length for your glasses. (Because of the way socks are knit, it won't unravel.) The sock will also make a passable cloth for cleaning the lenses.

Sport glasses with interchangeable lenses are far more versatile than regular sunglasses. A piece of chamois, as shown in the photo, is the best thing to use for drying and cleaning your glasses and goggles.

Goggles and Glasses

Carrying and Caring for Glasses and Goggles

Weather is unpredictable in the mountains, so it's a good idea to ski with both sunglasses and goggles much of the time. Some jackets have special inside pockets for goggles. If yours does not, but it has a powder cuff inside, snap the cuff together and you can just drop your goggles inside your jacket without fear of losing them. If the jacket has a drawstring around the hem, as many do, tightening that will provide the same service.

Never throw your glasses or goggles in your boot bag without putting them in something else first. They will get scratched. Use the bag they came in or buy one at the ski shop. For real panache, find yourself an old Crown Royal bag. Seagrams packs its high-end Canadian whiskey in purple velvet bags with gold embroidery and drawstrings that are the perfect size for goggles.

Cleaning Glasses and Goggles

It is easy to scratch plastic lenses if you clean them improperly. Dust and dirt are plenty hard enough to mar the plastic. The best way to clean sunglasses is to rub the lenses between your fingers with a little soap under running water. Then dry them with a chamois or soft clean cotton cloth. If soap isn't available, you should still get them wet if at all possible. Microfiber cloths, such as those sold for prescription eyeglasses and camera lenses, are excellent at removing oils and smudges from lenses, but won't dry them as well as chamois. Avoid paper napkins and Kleenex if you can: they often have hard fibers and tiny grit in them that can scratch plastic lenses.

When cleaning goggles, only wet the outer lens surface. Wetting the inner lens will likely ruin the antifog coating.

A great bag for storing goggles. This company provides a fifth of Canadian whiskey as a bonus.

Goggles and Glasses

Helmets

Helmets have become quite popular in recent years. A lot of good skiers I know wear them all the time, and I haven't heard a good logical argument yet against wearing one. The only reasons I can give are aesthetic. Still, I don't wear mine all that much. I do wear it when I ski at crowded ski areas, when I snowboard (because I fall a lot), and on powder days when I'll be skiing in the trees.

Fit is critical. A hat that's too tight or too loose may be a mild annoyance, but an ill-fitting helmet is either unsafe (if it's too loose) or a literal headache if it's too tight. Don't try on a helmet with a hat underneath. You won't need the hat for warmth, and the helmet will be too big.

Not only is size important, so is shape. Just as with goggles, some helmets fit round heads well, while others fit best on oval heads. Take your time and try on as many as you can find.

A full-coverage helmet. Note the soft padded sleeve on the chinstrap and the vents over the forehead. The small holes in front of the ears are attachment points for a face guard.

HOW SAFE IS A HELMET?

To begin with, any ski helmet you consider should be certified. The trouble is, there is more than one organization that certifies them. The most common, in descending order of the toughness of their standards, are the Snell Foundation, the American Society of Testing and Materials (ASTM), and Common European Norm (CEN). You can read the standards yourself, but they are couched in terms of dropping a pointed metal object on the helmet from such and such a height. You'll have a hard time translating them into how fast you can hit a tree and expect to walk away in a coherent state.

A "shortie" helmet. The hard shell does not extend completely over the ears, making the helmet a bit lighter and improving hearing.

Helmets

- How well can you hear with the helmet on? Some helmets are like pillows on your ears. Find one that affects your hearing as little as possible.
- How well ventilated is it? Helmets can be plenty warm. On the other hand, you will need a good array of vents to keep from getting hot on warm days. Look for vents that can be opened and closed.
- As long as the helmet is safety certified (see below), lighter is better.
- Can you manipulate the strap with gloves on? How does it feel under your chin? Is it easy to adjust?
- How does it work with goggles? The helmet must have some way of securing a goggle strap on the back so it doesn't slip (see "How safe is a Helmet?" on page 99).

The helmet should cover your forehead and temples. It should never sit on the back of your head.

When buying a helmet for a child, do not buy one that he or she will grow into. Buy one that fits now.

Almost all modern ski helmets are lined with a plastic material similar to styrofoam. It absorbs a blow to your noggin by being crushed itself. Even if you can't see any damage to it, the helmet should be replaced after having intercepted a blow that would have injured you.

Because they are lighter, better ventilated, and have less effect on your hearing, three-quarter-length helmets, which don't come down as far over the ears and the back of the neck as full-coverage models, are becoming more popular.

This ski helmet, based on bicycle helmet technology, is notably lighter and better ventilated than traditional ski helmets. The helmet has plugs that can be inserted in and removed from the ventilation ports and earflaps, and an optional visor. Such helmets are gaining in popularity.

Helmets

These goggles have extensions on the sides of the frame and an auxiliary "helmet helper" strap to make them compatible with just about any helmet.

Spending more money on a helmet will not usually buy you more safety. You can figure that two helmets with the same certification will provide your melon with just about the same protection. What the extra bucks get you is lighter weight, better ventilation, better hearing, and maybe a fancier paint job.

Regardless of the testing standard your helmet has passed, consider carefully these words from the Snell Foundation: "As with other Snell standards (our standards for ski helmets) do not specify all the helmet an individual might need but merely as much helmet as one might reasonably be expected to wear." As a rule of thumb, you should figure that if you hit a stationary object while going 15 miles per hour, you've exceeded the ability of any certified ski helmet to protect you.

For more information, check out www.skihelmets.com. This Web site has reviews of many brands and models and a good fit guide.

Goggles and Helmets

This is a gear combination that must be carefully coordinated if it is to work well.

Not all goggle straps work with all helmets, and some goggle frames don't fit with some helmets. If you are buying both a helmet and goggles, pick the helmet first. If you already own goggles, take them with you when you shop for a helmet.

Put both the helmet and goggles on and look in a mirror. How much of a gap is there between the goggles and the helmet? Exposed skin, especially on your forehead, will get cold on a chilly day. An overly tight fit, on the other hand, may prevent air from circulating through your goggles, increasing the likelihood of their fogging. Some points to pay attention to:

- Does the helmet hold the goggles off your face at the edges? If so, look for a pair of goggles with straps that are positioned farther away from the sides of your head.
- Does the adjustment clip on the strap collide with the helmet's strap retainer?
- Does the strap adjust to a long enough length to fit comfortably on the helmet? The straps on some goggles separate with a clip in the back. For most of these, there are extender straps available.

Helmets

Miscellaneous Essentials

SUNSCREEN

This is an absolute necessity. Keep a tube or tin in the pocket of your ski pants. That way, regardless of which jacket you're wearing, you'll always have it.

My personal favorite, Dermatone, comes in a small round tin about two inches across and a half-inch thick. The tin fits neatly in a pocket and never leaks. The stuff works on my skin and lips and makes darn good waterproofing for my gloves, too.

A SKIING KEY RING AND SAFETY KEY

Keep a small key ring in your boot bag that has just the one or two keys you really need on it, and take it with you on the hill rather than your regular key ring. If there's one place you're most likely to lose your keys, it's skiing. And besides, why carry any more junk than you have to? All I carry are the keys to my car and rooftop box, or a key to my hotel room, depending on the situation.

Because it's so easy for things to fall out of your pockets when you ski, I strongly recommend keeping a spare key stashed under the bodywork of your car. I recommend the type that attach with a big piece of Velcro. They never budge.

A SKIING WALLET

For the same reasons you should have a key ring just for skiing, you should keep a nice, thin, simple wallet in your boot bag just for skiing. All you need is a bit of cash and a credit or debit card, your medical insurance card, and a list of emergency

Always carry a small container of sunscreen and use it! A pocket stone for trimming up your edges is a good idea, too.

phone numbers. I carry a separate credit card in my skiing wallet so I can easily track my skiing expenses. (You may not have the stomach for this.)

POCKET STONE

This is for trimming up your edges on the hill, particularly after you hit a rock. Such close encounters of the geological kind can put a jagged spur on your edge, called a burr, that makes the ski grabby and inconsistent. When this happens, a few quick strokes with the stone will smooth it right out. If you don't have a pocket stone, a rock will do.

A good sharpening stone can be had for a few dollars in any hardware store. You will need a sheath to carry the stone in, too. If the stone doesn't come with one, or the one it comes with is bulky, you can make a great slim one out of duct tape. Slap two pieces together, sticky side to sticky side. Wrap them loosely around the stone, then wrap the whole thing with another, larger piece of duct tape to bind it up. Trim the package to size.

LIFT TICKET REEL

These little spring-loaded gadgets are fabulous. They make life a lot easier for both you and the ticket scanner and can be moved from garment to garment when the weather changes. A testament to their durability and tenacity: the Breckenridge Ski School gave every instructor one of these a number of years ago, and the last I heard, not one season pass has been lost. They have become ubiquitous in Europe, where they are commonly given away as promotional items.

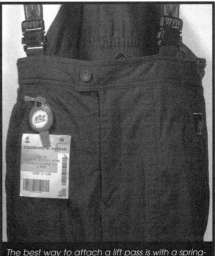

The best way to attach a lift pass is with a spring-loaded reel, clipped to your pants.

A lift ticket reel makes life nicer for both you and the ticket scanner.

Miscellaneous Essentials

A BIG BOOT BAG, WELL STOCKED

Have you ever arrived at the slopes on a snowy day, only to find that you left your goggles at home? Or worse, your boots?

Relieve yourself of the burden of organizing your stuff every time you go skiing. Get yourself a large ski-gear bag with a big central compartment, compartments on the ends for your boots, a smaller outside pocket, and a good shoulder strap.

Keep it stocked with the stuff you need for skiing in all conditions, but remember to take your boots out when you get back to your home, condo, or lodge. Otherwise they'll be damp and cold the next day. Following is a list of things to toss in the bag:

- Several pair of clean ski socks
- Sunscreen and lip balm
- Goggles
- Sunglasses
- Chamois for cleaning goggles and glasses
- A hat or two
- Helmet (if you wear one)

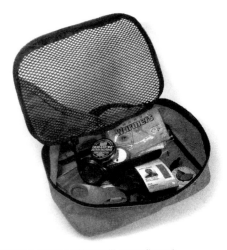

A small zippered travel bag with a see-through mesh top is a good place to put small items in a big gear bag. Get one in a bright color so you can find it easily amidst your gloves, hats, and clothes.

- Midwinter gloves or mittens
- Spring gloves
- Antiperspirant (for your feet)
- A neck gaiter or scarf
- A minimal set of keys just for skiing (see page 102)
- A small wallet just for skiing (see page 102)

A good general-purpose gear bag has a big central compartment and separate pockets for your boots.

Miscellaneous Essentials

- Ibuprofen (required sports equipment for the mature skier)
- Boot-fitting materials
- Alternate pair of pole baskets (for powder or hard snow, depending on what's on your poles at the time)
- Toenail clippers

Because you can't go skiing without them, I carry an extra pair of glasses, goggles, and gloves and an extra hat. These are to cover friends who forget them.

Many such boot bags have one, single big compartment for everything other than your boots. For the little stuff, get yourself a small zippered bag like the ones sold in travel stores. It will save you digging endlessly through the dark pit of your bag for your Ibuprofen.

For longer trips, I recommend a big boot and cargo bag with wheels, an internal frame, and a handle. These behemoths will hold everything you need for a week of skiing and après-skiing, other than your skis and poles, and are infinitely more schleppable than a conventional gear bag. ♦♦♦

For big trips you need a big, rugged bag with wheels and a handle. Boots go in the lower compartment with tools and other hardware.

"Neither rain, nor heat, nor gloom of night . . ." You know the drill. We skiers travel often and far to indulge our passion. You've got to know how to get there safely, with all your gear intact, and in a good mood.

GETTING *THERE*

For much of my life, I have had a recurring dream about skiing. I am on my way to the mountain. Sometimes my dream is taking me to a mountain I know well, sometimes to some mountain I cannot name. Always, the sky is blue, the snow beckons, and I am anxious to get on the hill.

As usually happens in recurring dreams, however, things turn sour. I realize halfway there that I've left my boots at home. My car breaks down. The person I'm traveling with has to stop to rent equipment. The rental shop is run by Franz Kafka's insane grandson. In short, I simply can't get to the hill. Soon I'm singing "Stuck Inside of Mobile with the Memphis Blues Again."

Some people actually live parts of this dream when they go skiing. But it needn't be like that. With a bit of planning and forethought, getting to the mountain can be hassle free.

Planning
CHOOSING A RESORT

Once you have a general idea where you want to go, log onto the Internet. Researching, planning, and booking a ski vacation online gets easier every year. All the major ski resorts have their own Web sites (though only the largest resorts allow you to actually book a trip and pay for it online). Some of these sites link to an online-booking distributor (WorldRes) that allows you to book packages that include lodging, lifts, rental equipment, and ground transportation. You can customize your search by clicking on specific dates and amenities. If the exact property you want isn't available online, call the lodge or property directly. In some cases, you can buy your vacation à la carte, purchasing lift tickets, rentals, and lessons separately.

The pleasures of a ski vacation extend well beyond skiing. Pick a resort whose off-slope ambience suits you.

PACKING

Everyone has his or her own way of packing. Some prefer suitcases with zippered pockets and compartments to keep their things organized. I always pack a couple of plastic trash bags for my dirty clothes. In contrast, Jesse Hunt, the Alpine Program Director of the U.S. Ski Team, has spent years traveling constantly all over the world with one large, formless duffel bag known affectionately as "The Sausage."

The unfortunate fact is that ski clothing is bulky, so you need a lot of room. I believe you are best off with one big bag for everything other than your skis, rather than two smaller ones. You'll have your hands full as it is.

Some items you may not have thought of but are worth taking:
- A spare pair of contact lenses, if you wear them.
- A copy of your health insurance documents related to receiving out-of-network care.
- If you are going to Canada, take your passport. The airline will ask for it when you check in for your outbound flight.
- A small folding hair dryer with a cool setting. This can be used to dry your boots in a pinch, or clothes that have not dried overnight.
- When driving in unfamiliar territory, carry a small compass and flashlight. This could save your bacon, especially at night. If you are going to Europe, get good road maps and look them over well before you leave.

VACATION COUNTDOWN

Don't procrastinate! Start planning your ski vacation at least six months in advance. If you don't, you may end up spending more and skiing less. Here's a timetable to follow.

SIX MONTHS

Now's the time to decide where you're going to ski. Write or call for ski resort brochures. Read the resort reviews in last year's magazines (which you should have held on to, because the ones for next season will come too late). Talk to friends and travel agents.

Now is also the time to start talking up your trip with whatever friends you want to go with you and to get verbal commitments from them.

Pick a date. Remember that the cheapest parts of the winter are also the least crowded, meaning more snow for less money.

Check airfares. If the fare is less than $400 to a major ski destination, you're not going to do much better by waiting. And it is possible that the reasonably priced seats will sell out. If you are willing to make a connection you can often save quite a bit of money.

Look into packages, also known as tours, which are usually the cheapest way to ski. Some packages are available from the resort itself, some from independent tour operators. Some tour operators specialize in ski vacations and are extremely knowledgeable. Others wouldn't know

snow from grits. The downside is that you sacrifice some flexibility (you fly their choice of airline, stay in their choice of hotel or condo, etc.).

FOUR MONTHS

If your vacation will be during high season, book your hotel and air travel now. You can wait another month or two to book a slow season trip.

Investigate cancellation insurance, especially if you are dropping significant money on your ski vacation.

If you plan to take a private lesson with a ski instructor, book it now.

TWO MONTHS

If you're going to Canada or Europe, check your passport to see if you need it renewed. If you don't have one, get moving on it.

If you want to have a special dinner at a special restaurant, make a reservation now. Likewise, if you want to do something special, like a dogsled trip, a guided snowshoe tour, or a day of snow-cat skiing, book it.

Take a good look in the mirror and assess your physical condition. How far out of shape are you? What's a realistic plan for getting ready to ski? If you don't exercise regularly and you're over the age of 40, that plan should start with a visit to your doctor. Then get yourself to a health club and get a trainer to write you up the rest of the plan.

Planning

ONE MONTH

Reserve a rental car if one isn't included in your package and if you really need one (at many areas, airport and town shuttles eliminate the need for a car). Remember that sometimes the rental car company's 800-number folks don't know what the local rental office has available. For instance, the Denver Avis office might have a specific brand of SUV that you like, but the folks at the national reservations office might not know about it.

If you need a refill on prescription medication for your trip or a new set of contact lenses, get the ball rolling now.

Now that you've seen the doctor and have a plan, you should get cracking on it if you haven't already; It's not too late.

TWO WEEKS

Make a list of all the ski gear and duds you want to bring and start packing. If you find out now that you left your goggles in Sun Valley last year and your long underwear doesn't fit you anymore, you'll have a chance of getting things together by the time you leave. If you're shepherding a family across the country, two weeks is barely enough time.

If you're taking your own skis, get them tuned and waxed. The wax will protect the bases during travel and is especially important if you are driving. During the month prior to Christmas, it may take your local ski shop a full week or more to get to them.

If you'll be renting skis, call ahead and make a reservation.

If you're not renting a car, make reservations for the airport shuttle.

If you are staying in a condo, get a grocery list together.

ONE WEEK

If you're driving, put the rack on your car now. That way you'll have time to react if some part is missing or broken, and your neighbors will know that you're going to have a better time than they are.

Make an extra copy of your insurance card, pack it in a safe place, get some cash, and make sure your credit card is paid down. If you're going somewhere where you'll need your passport, make a couple of copies of it.

ONE DAY

If driving, remember that it is imprudent to bombard your bindings with road grit and salt at 65 miles an hour if you want them to save your sorry ass when you hit the first mogul. Put on binding covers.

Start drinking a lot of water.

TRAVEL DAY

If you are flying, this is the worst part of your trip. But stay calm. Almost everyone in the history of ski travel has made his or her connection and received his or her luggage. Your vacation has at this point begun, so roll with the punches.

Upon arrival at your lodging, do not get

Older hotels often have an alpine character that can't be found elsewhere.

lazy and leave your boots in the car. You will be very angry in the morning if you do.

Get everything you can now that you will need tomorrow, your first day on the hill. This includes:

- Buying lift tickets
- Renting ski equipment
- Getting registered for ski school
- Picking up any odds and ends you don't own or left at home, like gloves, goggles, and such.

Keep drinking water. Don't drink any alcohol (there will be plenty of time for that later). Get to bed early.

—Adapted from *SKIING* Magazine

Planning

Driving There

Until the 1970s, when front-wheel drive cars started to become common, we had to negotiate snowpacked and icy mountain roads with classic Detroit rear-wheel drive automobiles, which were often ill suited to the task. Fortunately, we now have all manner of snow-worthy vehicles available to us. Still, piloting a four-wheel drive sport utility vehicle (SUV) in a wet spring snowstorm is not the same as driving to work.

Types of Drivetrains

REAR-WHEEL DRIVE

Rear-wheel drive is the Rodney Dangerfield of drivetrains. It gets no respect from skiers.

However, rear-wheel drive cars corner and stop just as well as anything else, as long as they have the right tires. The thing they don't do well is go forward on slippery roads, especially uphill. You can help the situation by putting the very best studded snow tires you can get on all four wheels and keep some sandbags in your trunk to provide extra weight to the driving wheels.

FRONT-WHEEL DRIVE

Prior to the 1970s, few front-wheel drive cars were available in the United States Saab, made in Sweden, was one of the few. While Detroit engineers were preoccupied with tail fins and chrome trim, the Swedes were thinking about snow. The Japanese were the next to catch on, and once their front-wheel drive cars started to make big inroads into the American market, Detroit finally woke up.

Front-wheel drive is superior to rear-wheel drive in most winter conditions, but you must put the same sort of tires on the rear wheels that you have on the front. Putting grippy snow tires on the front and leaving your summer highway tires on the back is an invitation to disaster.

FOUR-WHEEL DRIVE

Four-wheel drive will get you moving more reliably than anything else. In addition SUVs have more ground clearance than other cars. This could keep you from getting high-centered if you have to drive through really deep snow, like the sort you see in the TV ads.

Four-wheel drive won't corner or stop any better, though. Unfortunately, some drivers feel invincible driving a big, heavy SUV and end up off the road because of it when conditions are slick. Four-wheel drive SUVs are generally *less safe* than other cars in some important respects. Government safety tests show that SUVs are almost categorically more prone to rollover accidents than other cars. At the time of this writing, more than 60 percent of fatalities in SUVs involve rollovers, compared to 22 percent in deaths involving passenger cars. Bigger and heavier does not mean safer.

Always take a four-wheel drive car out of four-wheel drive on dry pavement. Operating such a vehicle in four-wheel drive on a dry road is hard on the drivetrain, wears your tires much more quickly, and reduces your gas mileage considerably.

ALL-WHEEL DRIVE

"All-wheel drive" is something of a misnomer. "Any-wheel drive" is a better description. This type of drivetrain senses the amount of grip each wheel has and delivers power accordingly. If both tires on the right side of the car are off the shoulder and in soft snow, for example, most of the power will be delivered to the left wheels. Power is parceled similarly to the front and rear wheels.

As opposed to four-wheel drive, which must be manually engaged and disengaged by the driver, all the power-distribution decisions in an all-wheel drive car are made automatically by the vehicle itself, leaving you to concentrate on other things, like steering and braking. And with these drivetrains you don't have to worry about putting the car into two-wheel drive when you get onto dry pavement.

Going in the Snow

SNOW TIRES, STUDS, AND CHAINS

By far the most important factor in how any car behaves in unsafe conditions is the tires. According to Mark Cox of the Bridgestone Winter Driving School in Steamboat Springs, Colorado, you should outfit your car with winter-specific tires. All-season tires are only a compromise on any vehicle, including an SUV. You must have the same model tire on each wheel, and the tires must be inflated correctly. If you're like me, you'd like to believe that letting your mechanic check your tires when he changes the oil is good enough, but it's not. Well-treaded tires that direct your car with decisive precision when inflated to the right pressure can become downright dangerous when under- or over-inflated. Tires that are incorrectly inflated also wear out much faster. So do the right thing and check your tire pressures every time you head off for the weekend.

If your state allows their use, get studded snow tires. When it's really slick, they make a big difference.

PARKING IN MOUNTAIN TOWNS

Mountain municipalities take their parking seriously, and so should you. Be observant of the posted parking regulations. The police enforce them ruthlessly, and nothing puts a damper on your après-ski fun like finding that your car has been towed while you were skiing. Likewise, be careful where you leave your car overnight. Ski towns frequently plow their streets at night when it snows and will post that certain areas are off-limits for overnight parking for that reason. If you are lucky and don't get towed, you might get plowed in with a four-foot snowbank around your car.

Chains provide the ultimate in traction for the ultimate in crummy driving conditions, but they also provide the ultimate in outdoor misery. They are a cold, wet hassle to put on and take off, especially in the conditions where you need them most, and you can't drive at normal highway speeds with them. But when all else fails, chains will give you the best chance of getting where you want to go.

Winter-Driving Skills

TESTING THE ROAD

Frequently check your tire grip by using your brakes. On a straight stretch—at a slow speed, making sure that no one is behind you—hit the brakes firmly until the wheels lock up. This will give you a clear indication of the grip you have to work with.

BRAKING

You can only control the direction the car is going when its front wheels are rolling. So in an emergency situation, it's important not

Driving There

to lock up the brakes. If your car does not have an antilock brake system (ABS), you need to know how to *pump the brakes:* Push firmly but slowly on the brake pedal until you feel the tires break loose, let off for a moment so the tires start rolling again, then repeat the sequence. The beauty of ABS is that the system performs this same sequence for you automatically—simply push as hard as you can on the pedal and let the ABS system do its thing.

Don't Lose Your Grip

When roads are slippery, your tires only have so much grip available to them. The three things you need that grip for are braking, turning, and accelerating. Use it wisely—and use it for only one thing at a time.

Braking while the car is turning, an example of using that grip for two things at once, is one of the most common causes of skidding. Another is accelerating before you have finished turning.

When approaching a curve, do all the slowing down you need to do *before you start to turn.* Taking your foot off the brake before you start to turn allows you to use all the grip just for steering. This is not only what the Bridgestone Driving School teaches, it is standard practice in race-car driving. If the tires break loose and skid while you're going straight, it's no big deal. If it happens while you're turning, you could be in trouble.

Once you straighten the steering wheel at the exit of the turn, use the available grip to accelerate.

Intersections and Hills

Be aware that these are typically the slipperiest portions of the road. With

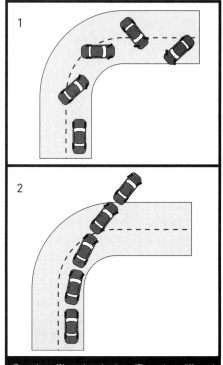

Oversteer (1) and understeer (2) are two different types of trouble that require two different types of response from the driver.

numerous drivers braking in the same area, snow gets burnished into ice. When you approach a hill or intersection, anticipate having reduced traction.

Recovering From a Skid

There are two types of skid, and different types of cars tend to skid in different ways. Regardless of the type of skid, the approach to regaining control is the same: *Do something to transfer more of the car's weight to the wheels that are skidding.* This will give the tires more grip.

Oversteer is the classic "fishtail" skid. If you go into a turn and the rear wheels slide to the outside, threatening to put the car into a spin, you are experiencing oversteer. It is most common in rear-wheel drive cars, but it can happen with any car.

In this situation, your first reaction is often to try to slow down, so you use the brakes. This is definitely the wrong thing to do. Even a light tap on the brake pedal can aggravate the situation dramatically, flinging you hopelessly out of control. The technique taught at the Bridgestone Winter Driving School is to look in the direction you want to go, turn the front wheels so they point in that direction, and accelerate slightly. Accelerating will transfer some of the car's weight to the rear wheels, giving them more purchase on the snow or ice, and hence more grip.

Understeer is more common with front-wheel drive, four-wheel drive, and all-wheel drive cars, although it is also possible in rear-wheel drive vehicles. In this case, the front wheels break loose from the turn and start plowing toward the outside of the turn. You're not spinning, but you are either headed into the other lane or off the road.

In this situation, *let off on the gas*, keep your foot off the brake, and steer the front wheels in the direction the car is going. This will let the car slow down a bit, shifting some of its weight to the skidding front wheels.

If you carry your skis on a roof rack, you should protect your bindings with covers like these. They zip around the center of your skis with elastic that holds them snug in front of and behind the bindings.

HOW TO HAUL SKIS
Ski Racks

You may not have noticed them: car after car heading to the slopes with skis on the roof and their tips pointed in the same direction as the car is heading.

Bad idea.

Always put your skis on the car with the tips pointing back. When the tips are forward, they catch an unsafe amount of air under them at highway speeds. Tales abound of ski racks that have been launched from the roofs of cars like fighter planes from the deck of the USS *Nimitz*, because the skis were positioned that way.

If your rack won't take the skis bottom to bottom, so you have to split them, load them with their tips toward the rear and their bases down, protecting them from dirt and ultraviolet radiation. All the dirt, salt, and other junk that you find on roads in the winter is pretty bad for them, too. The skis will pick up the least of everything if they are facing down.

The best racks are those that hold skis base to base. The ski's bases are better protected, and the rack allows you to put covers over your bindings.

ROSSIGNOL

Photo courtesy Rossignol Ski Company.

Driving There

Get a rack you can lock. It's sad but true: people steal skis.

You can improve the situation further by transporting your skis in a ski bag. I once had a pair of skis come off my rack on an interstate highway at 70 miles an hour. In my rearview mirror I watched them bounce and roll for quite a ways before they skidded to a stop on the shoulder. They were in a bag and were hardly scratched. The bag, on the other hand . . .

A rack that will accept skis paired base to base will most likely be able to carry the skis in a ski bag. Just don't get a bag that's got a lot of padding. You don't need it, anyway. If you have a rack that won't take skis in a bag, you can put them in a bag anyway and tie them down with bungee cords.

A small folding step stool makes getting skis in and out of a ski box or rack a breeze. You can also use it as a stool when putting on or taking off your boots.

Rooftop Boxes

This is far and away the best, but also the costliest, way to carry your skis. It also gives you a way to transport your poles so they're not rattling around behind the backseat. You can leave your skis in there without worry while you stop for a pizza on the drive home. Or even better, while you spend the night in the Best Western in Hays, Kansas. (It's a good idea to take your skis out of the box when you get home though, because the snow that was left on them can rust the edges.) These boxes are four-season accessories, too. Tents. Stoves. Sleeping bags. You can use them to carry tents, stoves, sleeping bags, and clothes so funky you don't want them in the car with you.

If your car's tall, measure the height of your garage door and the height of your car before you go shopping. You may have to search for a low-profile box that will fit in your garage. A couple of years ago my neighbor bought a great box for his minivan and immediately took off for a week of skiing without ever driving into his garage. When he returned, he couldn't get in his garage with the box on top. There's always eBay . . .

If your car is extra tall, get a small two-step ladder and carry it with you. No more floundering around in your ski boots, standing on the top of your rear wheel. And it doubles as a stool for putting on your boots in the parking lot.

Once you've purchased a box and mounted it on your car, measure the height of the whole unit, write the number on a piece of paper, and put it in the glove compartment. The ceilings of many parking garages are too low for minivans or SUVs with ski boxes on top. If

Driving There

The rubber cover on this wiper blade keeps it from getting clogged with snow in a storm.

it comes to a fight between your ski box and the concrete ceiling of a parking garage, the ceiling will win.

Carrying Skis Inside Your Car

According to Carl Ettlinger, one of the ski industry's most knowledgeable safety experts, skis carried inside a car can become lethal projectiles in a crash. You can, however, carry skis safely under the seats of a van or minivan. Be careful not to set the skis down on the snow right after taking them out of the car. Because they will be warm, they will melt the snow, which can then refreeze on the bases in the form of ice. Skis in this condition do not glide at all. It takes a windshield scraper (a credit card will work in a pinch) to get the ice off.

DRIVING TIPS
See Your Way Clear

If you're like me, the morning after a big snowstorm you get so excited about getting to the hill that you don't want to take the time to clean off your windows. Do yourself a favor: calm down and take a minute to clear them all off. You should also sweep off your hood and roof, because a lot of that snow will end up on your front and rear windows once you get going. Clean off all your headlights and taillights, too.

To make the job easier, go out and start your car ten minutes or so before you intend to leave. Put the ventilation control on "recirculate," crank up the windshield defroster, and turn on the rear-window defroster if you have one. Half the work will be done for you by the time you leave. Make sure to set the ventilation control to "fresh air" when you drive off, or your windows will fog on the inside while you are driving.

Put winter blades on your windshield wipers. These have rubber shrouds that cover the wiper-blade frame, preventing it from getting clogged with snow. This is a real lifesaver in a wet snowstorm.

Put a new pair of winter blades on every season. You'll be glad you did. In addition to a snow brush, pick up a wind-shield scraper that has a brass blade.

A windshield scraper with a brass blade is the tool of choice for getting ice off a car's windows.

Driving There

These are far superior to the plastic variety, particularly if there is any ice on your windshield. If you find yourself with ice on your windshield and no scraper at all, blast it for a while with the defroster, then scrape it with a credit card.

If you drive an SUV or minivan, get yourself a snow brush with a telescoping handle.

Keep your windshield-washer reservoir filled and carry a jug of washer fluid in your trunk. There is nothing worse than running dry on one of those sloppy days when you need to wash the windshield every twenty seconds.

Defogging Your Windows

If your windows get foggy after driving for a few minutes, check to see if your car's ventilation system is set to "recirculate." This traps the humidity from your breath, perspiration, and snow melting off your clothes inside your car. Set the system to bring in fresh air.

If this doesn't help, turn on your air conditioner. Part of its function is to dry out the air in your car. So turn the defroster on with the temperature set high, then kick in the air conditioner. You should soon be fog free.

If your windshield is still fogged and you smell antifreeze, you have a leaky heater core. Turn off the heat and defroster and drive your car to a repair shop.

Headlights and Snowstorms

When it's snowing hard, keep your headlights on their low-beam setting. Your high beams will bounce back off the flakes right into your eyes, making visibility worse.

Repairing Rear-window Defrosters

Those brown lines on your rear window are actually little wires painted on the glass. The rear-window defroster system runs electrical current through them, heating them up a little and thereby defrosting your rear window. If one of those wires gets nicked, it will no longer work. This can happen easily when things you are carrying in the back of your car knock against the rear window, especially in station wagons and SUVs. If you find that your rear-window defroster only works on part of the window, buy a repair kit at an auto supply store or better hardware store. It is an easy job and it works great.

Driving There

Flying There

The airlines and airports that serve ski destinations do a great job with ski equipment. But just as with any other baggage, it is entirely possible for you to arrive in Reno only to discover your gear is shaped differently than it was when you checked it in Los Angeles. Or that it is two time zones away. Such are the perils of air travel.

FLYING WITH YOUR SKIS

First of all, get yourself a ski bag. The sort of clear plastic bags that the airlines offer for your skis may be adequate protection for produce from the supermarket, but won't protect your skis in the belly of a jumbo jet from Cleveland to Salt Lake City.

Now that short skis are popular, ski bags come in different lengths. Get one that is appropriate for your skis. There is no need for a 210-cm bag if your skis are 170 cm long.

Get a bag that will carry two pairs of skis. They don't cost much more than single-pair bags, and they provide a great place to stash extra ski clothes, especially dirty ones on the return trip home. I pack my camera tripod in mine. And if you happen to pick up a new pair of skis on your trip, you'll have something to ship them in.

Prepare your skis for packing by binding them at the tip and tail with the inexpensive nylon-and-Velcro straps that many ski shops give you when you have your skis tuned. To make the package really solid, wrap a third strap tightly around the skis just ahead of the binding toe piece. This is how World Cup ski technicians tie skis together for transport.

Get a ski bag big enough for two pairs of skis, and you can use it to carry bulky ski jackets and pants, too.

Secure your skis for travel with three Velcro straps made for the purpose.

FLYING WITH YOUR BOOTS

Consider carrying your ski boots onto the plane with you rather than checking them. Arriving at the Vancouver airport on your way to Whistler without your skis is one thing; you can easily rent a good pair. Arriving without your boots is quite another. I know a number of professional skiers who never check their boots as baggage. They take them as carry-on baggage and stow them in the overhead compartment.

FROM THE AIRPORT TO THE MOUNTAIN
Shuttles and Vans

You can get by just fine without a car at many ski resorts. Once you're there, you can get everywhere you need to go on foot or shuttle bus. You can rent a car to get from the airport to the resort, but it will just sit around accruing charges on your credit card while you ski, or you may pay a hefty drop charge to leave it at the rental company's local office.

Fortunately, most destination resorts have convenient and economical van service to and from the airport. You can get their names from the resort's central information office. If you're traveling during high season, book your ride as soon as you've booked your plane tickets. Never fly in without a prearranged ride, if you can help it.

Rental Cars

When you make a reservation for a rental car, make it clear that you will be taking the car into the mountains for skiing. Tell them you want a car with snow tires and a ski rack. Before you leave the parking lot, check the windshield washer fluid level and make sure there is a windshield scraper in the car.

Arriving

Wouldn't it be great to have a locker at the base of the mountain where you could store your ski clothes and equipment between visits? You'd never have to put your boots on in the parking lot or grapple with your skis and poles as you clomp through rows of cars. If you decided at noon that you were a little overdressed, you could swoop down to the bottom and swap that thick parka for a shell and fleece vest.

Unfortunately, few of us have that luxury. Instead, we schlep our gear from parking lot to lifts. Sometimes that can feel like more work than skiing itself. While modern ski equipment excels at swooping and darting down the mountain, it's heavy, clumsy, and annoying in any other setting.

Here are some approaches to easing the pain.

PARKING LOTS

It's obvious: the best way to get a close-in parking space is to arrive early. Look for little ways to accelerate your arrival: gas up the day before. Load the car the night before. Postpone breakfast until you get to the mountain. These simple tactics can get you there up to an hour earlier, putting you in the fourth row of the parking lot rather than the fortieth. I love getting to the mountain well before the crowds and relaxing with a cup of coffee, a bowl of oatmeal, and some fruit. Then I stretch a bit, put on my boots, and amble over to the lift.

If you don't get a parking space close to the lifts, you face a trek across the

A small folding chair and doormat (or carpet remnant) make it easier to get into your boots in a muddy or snowy parking lot.

parking lot in your ski boots, grappling with skis, poles, and other awkward gear. Rather than making everyone in your car share the same misery, drop everyone off at the spot closest to the lifts with all the gear, including your ski boots. Then you, gallant person that you are, drive to the far reaches of the parking lot, park the car, and walk back to meet your friends in your comfortable sneakers or hiking

Never lean your skis against the side of your car bases-in. You are inviting big scratches when your skis fall over—a common occurrence. Swinging a door shut is often all it takes to send skis sliding down across the side of your car, scratching the car's paint and clattering onto the gravel and gunk on the ground.

The best thing to do is prop them on the rear bumper, as shown in the photo. At a low angle like this, they are very unlikely to fall over, and even if they do, they won't harm your car.

boots. Change into your boots in the base lodge and stash your shoes in a corner or rent a locker for them.

If you must walk across the parking lot with your boots, carry them instead of wearing them. Walk in your shoes. Walking in ski boots on asphalt or gravel damages the soles of your boots, which can adversely affect binding release in a fall, a potentially dangerous situation.

For those times when you must put your boots on at the car, carry a small folding chair in your trunk. This makes the task a lot easier than doing it inside the car or standing up with one hand on the bumper for balance.

WHAT TO DO WITH ALL THIS STUFF?

Boots. Sunscreen. Goggles. Sunglasses. Skis. Wallet. Hat. Gloves. Neck gaiter. MP3 player. Lip balm. Poles. All-purpose multi-tool. Car keys. Cell phone. Hand warmers. No-fog cloth. Camera. Candy bar. Trail map. Such is the common equipage for a day of skiing, making you feel as much pack animal as skier. For many, the most challenging part of the ski day is that portion spent on foot.

Carrying Your Boots

Most boots these days have stout nylon straps with Velcro closures, called power straps, for tightening the top of the boot—sort of an extra buckle. These straps are also useful for tying your boots together so you can sling them over your shoulder, making them very easy to carry. If it is snowing, stuff a glove in each boot to keep them dry inside. If your boots don't have power straps, cut off the ends of an old belt and just close the top two

The right way to carry skis: with the tips forward and the toe bindings behind your shoulder. You can use a pole as a walking stick.

buckles of your boots over it. If you want to get fancy, buy a couple of feet of nylon webbing and use that. When you walk in your ski boots, unbuckling the top two buckles will make things a lot easier.

Carrying Your Skis and Poles

Forget the gadgets and gizmos. Not one of the devices I've seen for sale in ski shops for clamping your skis and poles into a tidy package for carrying are worth the money Nor have I ever seen a seasoned expert use one. One good reason is that you have to find a place to stash gizmos while you're on the hill. Likewise, the tactic of weaving your poles together into a handle from which your skis hang by the pole straps (known as the "Texas suitcase" by some ski instructors I know), seems clever, but is a lot of trouble and doesn't work very well.

Here is the best way to carry your skis and poles. Place your skis together base to base, using the ski brakes to clip them together. Hoist them onto your shoulder (right shoulder if you're right-handed, left shoulder if you're left-handed), tips forward, with the binding toe pieces *behind* your shoulder and the flat of the skis

Arriving

resting on your shoulder. Put your hand on the forebody of the skis just behind the tips to balance them. Hold your poles in your other hand.

This is how the pros do it. It is the best way to balance the skis, and if one of them has a bad nick in the edge, it won't snag on your clothing.

While you are walking along, if the ski brakes become disengaged and the upper ski slides forward, flip the skis over so the upper ski is now underneath. The skis won't slide apart now.

If the path is slippery, use one of your poles as a walking stick in your free hand.

Skiing with Stuff

If the stuff you need to carry on the hill won't fit in your pockets, use a small daypack rather than a fanny pack. Fanny packs are cute and tidy, but they don't ride

nearly as well while you ski, bouncing up and down more than a small backpack would. Worse, they limit your cargo. Whichever you choose, I suggest picking one in a color found in nature. Green and brown are good. This way you don't have to ski with the thing all day. Find a good central spot on the mountain, probably near the top and in the vicinity of several lifts, then stash your pack in the trees. It is very easy to hide a forest green pack in a small stand of evergreen trees. Flame red with yellow trim is much easier to spot.

Lockers are usually available at the base of the mountain if you've got things you want ready access to but don't want to hump around the slopes. For a small price, it beats walking back to the car. You will probably need a supply of quarters. I keep an empty tin candy box in my car, into which I regularly toss change for such purposes.

Carry you boots by meshing their Velcro power straps together and slinging them over your shoulder.

Ski brakes hook together to make your skis easier to carry.

Arriving

Dressing for Success

As the bumper sticker says, a bad day of skiing is better than a good day in the office. But only if your clothes match the weather. Dress correctly and you can enjoy almost any day on the slopes. Dress incorrectly and even a beautiful day can be a trial.

PREDICTING THE WEATHER

Information is power. In this case, the information is a good weather forecast. Your best source of information is the most local one. Local radio stations are a good bet. The RSN cable channel, carried in most ski resort markets, runs continuous local weather and snow reports in the morning during the ski season. Be aware that unless stated otherwise, the temperature, humidity, and wind reading you get will usually come from the nearest airport, which may be 20 miles away and a thousand feet lower than the base of the mountain.

The weather in the nearest metropolitan area is not a good indicator of what it's like in the mountains. It is often sunny in Denver when it is dumping in Breckenridge, and vice versa.

All other things being equal, the temperature of the atmosphere drops by a certain amount as you go up in altitude. This is related to the so-called *adiabatic lapse rate*, which you might remember from high school. (Okay, so I was a science nerd.) If the air is dry, the drop in temperature is in the neighborhood of 5 degrees Fahrenheit for every thousand feet you go up. So the air should be about 10 degrees colder at the top of a mountain that has a 2,000-foot vertical

Dress by the numbers: learn to match your clothes to the temperature and wind predicted by the weather report.

rise from the base area. The drop is about half that for very moist air. There are exceptions to this rule, however. Some mountains are known for frequent temperature inversions, when it is colder at the bottom than at the middle or top.

Here is my personal rule of thumb: If I am comfortable, or just a little chilly, standing at the bottom of the mountain at 9 a.m., I will probably be about right up on the mountain throughout the day. If I am toasty warm on that first lift ride at 9 a.m., I'm going to be overdressed, especially if there is no wind.

GETTING TO KNOW YOUR CLOTHES

Most ski areas have thermometers at lift terminals. When you are out skiing, take note of the temperature now and then, and you will soon develop a good idea of what temperature and wind ranges are covered by each combination of your ski clothes. Soon, you'll be able to dress right based on the morning weather forecast.

Lift Tickets

For all the noise people make about the price of a full-day adult lift ticket, only a small percentage of skiers actually pay full price to ski. In the 2002–2003 season, the average list price of an adult lift ticket in this country was $52 and change. The average price paid for a day of skiing was just under $29—just 55 percent of the list price. This figure includes days skied on season passes, which accounted for almost 30 percent of those days skied.

MONEY-SAVING STRATEGIES
Discount Tickets

In an effort to maximize their revenue, ski areas have created all sorts of packages and special tickets. By giving skiers financial incentives to ski, especially when the mountain isn't busy, everyone wins. If there is a sizable metropolitan area near your ski destination, check to see if discount tickets are available in the city. They are often sold at supermarkets.

Some of the best deals on tickets are available only in the fall before the lifts open. Ski areas are willing to do this because they like getting their cash up front. In Colorado, for example, several of the ski areas sell tickets in packs of four for less than $70—if you buy before November. Full-price tickets at these areas are in the $60 range, so this represents a big saving. If you do not live in the area, but have some friends who do, arrange to have them purchase some of these preseason deals for you.

Many areas offer frequent-skier cards. One variant of this is a punch card. Ski nine days and get the tenth free. The Hunter Mountain, New York, version gets

Opportunities abound for saving money on lift tickets. Here's a kiosk for buying discounted lift tickets in a Colorado supermarket.

you a discount on every ticket you buy at the ticket window.

Midweek tickets are often cheaper at areas that cater to weekend skiers.

Season Passes

Saving money is not the only good reason to get a season pass. When you have one, your attitude about skiing changes. Once you've spent the money up front, a day of skiing becomes as inexpensive an entertainment as a day of fishing. You'll ski more, which is bound to make you a happier person. And when you ski, you'll feel more relaxed about it, because you won't be thinking about the money. If the weather turns sour, you'll go in and not worry about it. If you want to get an early start on the drive home to avoid traffic, it's no big deal.

Season passes have gained considerable popularity in recent years. In the three years between the 1999–2000 and 2002–2003 seasons, season-ticket sales increased 60 percent. This has undoubtedly been fueled by the trend of ski areas offering discount season passes. To get the sweetheart price, which runs in the $200–$400 range depending on the ski area, you must buy the pass before a specified date in midfall. This gives the area operator a nice lump of cash before opening day. (Mammoth Mountain, California, sold 32,000 season passes at $400 before the 2002–2003 season; you do the math.) And it gives you a ticket to ride.

This concept was first tried at Kirkwood, California, and soon after at Bogus Basin, Idaho, in an effort to get the local population out skiing and to get cash into the ski area's kitty ahead of the season. It worked and the idea spread. In Colorado, these season tickets are called, for historical reasons, "buddy passes." When they were first offered, you could not buy one by yourself; you had to be one of a group of four people purchasing them together, hence the name. The group constraints were eventually lifted, but the name stuck.

These are fabulous deals on season passes for anyone who skis as few as ten days a season. Some are good at more than one ski area.

Half-Day Tickets

Afternoon half-day tickets are not a good way to save money. They are not usually available until 12:30 or 1 p.m., and you will be lucky to save 20 percent over a full-day ticket. Still, if you really want to go skiing, and it's already 11:30 or 12, you might consider waiting until the half-day tickets go on sale to save some money.

A few ski areas sell morning half-day tickets. These can be a very good deal for the last day of a ski trip, if you have to leave for home midafternoon.

Co-marketing

If you keep your ear to the ground, you might find some good deals where you least expect them. A few years ago Sugar Bowl, California, cut a co-marketing deal with McDonald's that turned Happy Meal© eaters into happy skiers. Keystone, Colorado, ran a breakfast-cereal promotion for a couple of years: with a cereal-box top, you could get a full-day adult lift ticket for $18.

Free Passes

If you live in the mountains or ski at a particular area frequently, there are several possibilities for getting free passes.

RACES AND SPECIAL EVENTS. Ski areas often need help getting set up for races and other events, and their method of payment is often in lift tickets.

MOUNTAIN AMBASSADORS. Many resorts maintain a part-time staff whose job it is to show people around who are unfamiliar with the mountain. The compensation is usually a uniform and a season pass. If you are outgoing, know the mountain well, and have time on your hands, you might try getting such a job.

SKI-TOWN JOBS. Some jobs in ski towns come with a season pass as part of the compensation package. There are many variations on this theme. Sometimes, the employee must pay some portion of the cost up front but is repaid in part or in full by the employer if the employee hangs in there until the end of the season. Some passes have blackout days when they are not valid.

WORKING AT THE AREA. Ski schools and patrols commonly provide their staffs with a certain number of free tickets each year to give to friends and family. The staff of other departments is often eligible for such tickets, too. If you are one of those friends or family members and are not above a little friendly persuasion, you might consider asking.

A common way to carry a season or multiday pass is on a neck strap.

ATTACHING LIFT TICKETS

This may seem like a topic that hardly needs elaboration, but in fact there are a few considerations to keep in mind.

Put your ticket where it can be easily seen by the ticket checker. Unless you are absolutely certain you will ski with your jacket on all day, attach your ticket to your pants. You should not have to unzip your jacket to display your ticket. Any place that requires you to do so is a bad place to attach it. Do not put it on your jacket's main zipper pull. With the zipper up all the way, the ticket will flog your face unmercifully in the wind. Those little clips on your ski gloves are not there for lift tickets, either. For some reason I cannot fathom, some teenagers seem to think that a boot buckle or zipper on the cuff of a pant leg makes a good place to attach a zipper.

If you have small children, attach their tickets for them. They may have no idea how or where to put it.

Lift Tickets

If you make a mistake attaching the ticket and render it unusable, the ticket office should give you a new one.

Season passes and some multiday lift tickets are issued on plastic cards the size of a credit card. The mountain town local chic is to wear it on a strap or cord around your neck. The only problem with this approach is that you end up having to unzip your jacket every time a lift attendant needs to check your ticket. A better idea is to get a spring-loaded pass reel (described on page 103 in chapter 2). Some jackets have special clear plastic pockets on the chest or arm for such passes, and these work well, too.

Some areas issue tickets with a tear-off stub that has a barcode matching the one printed on the ticket itself. Tear it off and put in a safe, well-zipped pocket. If you should happen to lose your lift ticket or decide to ski without the article of clothing to which the ticket is attached, the ticket office will give you a new one if you present them with the stub.

REMOVING OLD TICKETS

For good reason, some lift tickets are hard to remove. The sticky-backed type that fold over a wire bail are the toughest. Forget about trying to take one off with your bare hands. You can cut the ticket itself with a knife or scissors, or you can cut the wire with a pair of wire clippers. Most lift-ticket offices have clippers on hand for just this purpose.

TICKET ETIQUETTE

Finally, when you peel the backing off a sticky-backed lift ticket, throw it in the trash. Throwing any trash on the ground, for that matter, is uncool. Cigarette

Some lift tickets come with detachable stubs. If you lose the ticket, the stub will get you a free replacement.

butts, tissues, candy wrappers, film boxes, spent chemical hand warmers . . . the sheer range and volume of our culture's commercial detritus that litters our mountains is astounding. Some people seem to think they are at a theme park, and the hired help will magically appear to clean up after the rides close. This is not the case. ◆◆◆

I have a hard time traveling light. I tend to carry more stuff with me than I need. There are, however, certain items that just about every professional skier carries when skiing.

A TRAIL MAP: There's a wealth of invaluable information that goes beyond the names of the trails and their difficulty ratings. If you forget to pick one up when you get your lift ticket (maps are always available at the ticket windows), you can sometimes find them at the bottom of the lift.

A SMALL SHARPENING STONE: This will help keep your edges sharp and smooth on the hill. (See page 103.)

SUNGLASS OR GOGGLE CLEANER: The best thing for this purpose is a piece of chamois, about eight inches in diameter (refer to Goggles and Glasses section). Other options are a commercial no-fog cloth or a man's handkerchief.

LIP BALM: Get one with a sun-protection (SPF) rating of 15 or higher.

SUNSCREEN: Again with an SPF of 15 or greater; certain types will double as lip balm.

A SMALL WALLET: Bring just the things you'll need during the day, like money and a credit card. Leave the rest in a locker or in your car.

A KEY RING WITH ONLY A KEY TO YOUR CAR ON IT: (and perhaps the key to your ski rack or cartop box).

MORE USEFUL STUFF

Here are some things that are not universally popular but get a lot of votes.

GOGGLES: even on days when you think you'll be wearing sunglasses. (See Goggles and Glasses, page 91.)

ARTIFICIAL TEARS: Many skiers, especially ones who wear contact lenses, find that their eyes dry out when skiing from the wind and dry air. A small bottle of artificial tears, available in any drugstore, is essential equipment for these folks.

CELL PHONE: If you have kids in ski school and there is mobile phone coverage on the mountain, this is a must-have item.

A SNACK: Pick something that is light, small, and stands up well to cold. Cookies crumble too much; PowerBars get too hard. I like soft cookie-type energy bars and gummy bears. Erik Steinberg, a longtime international coach, swears by beef jerky.

WATER: The most critical nutritional need your body has. Carry a hydration bladder and tube, like a CamelBac®, or just a small bottle that you can fill up when you go inside.

NAIL CLIPPERS: This may sound a bit quirky, but if you ski in very close-fitting boots and have bruised a toenail because you forgot to keep them clipped, you'll understand.

You are here

Everything you've done so far has gotten you to the bottom of the mountain, ready for action.

Lift Tickets

This is what it's all about. Regardless of ability, we all feel the same wonderful sensations and emotions when we ski.

GOING SKIING

Finally. You're ready to head up the hill and have some fun. This is what you came for. Like the proverbial kid in a candy store, you've got lots of choices, and they all look good. Where are the grooviest groomers? The meatiest moguls? The most pristine powder? What follows will help you get the most out of your day on the slopes.

Getting Up the Hill

Call me lazy, but I don't know how much I would ski if I had to climb the hill for every run. Without ski lifts, not many others would ski either, which means nobody would have developed the great terrain, grooming machines, and ski equipment that make our winters so much fun—even if we were willing to slog up the mountain. We wouldn't get very good either, because we'd only be able to make a few runs a day.

LIFT LINE ETIQUETTE

Put your skis on a reasonable distance from the entrance to the lift line. Don't make others walk around you to get to the lift. By the same token, if you've got your skis on and you're waiting for your friends, don't block the front of the line.

When you ski up to the lift, slow down well before you get there. Ripping up to the line and throwing your skis sideways in a spray of snow doesn't make you look cool. It makes you look rude and careless.

Don't crowd the people in front of you in the line. Stepping on their skis with yours won't get you on the lift any sooner. If you see people cutting in line or barging past you, call them on it. If they ignore you, tell one of the lift attendants.

If the line you're in merges with another one, take your turn and alternate.

Don't ride alone if there is a lift line. If the lift attendant doesn't pair you up with someone, do it yourself. Yell "Single!" as soon as you get in line. You may get lucky and pair up with someone at the front.

When you get off the lift, get far away from the unloading area before you stop to put on your poles and decide what to do next.

Other than the rope tow, which was patented in Switzerland in 1931 and quickly imported to the United States, lift technology in this country has its roots in the mining and tropical fruit industries. In the first half of the twentieth century, many of the ski tows and lifts built in this country were based on designs for hauling ore around. The first chairlift, which was built in Sun Valley, Idaho, was inspired by a contraption used to load bunches of bananas onto boats in Honduras.

CHAIRLIFTS

Chairlifts are by far the most common of ski lifts. They are easy to ride, get you up the hill quickly, and are dependable.

Types of Chairlifts

Chairlifts come in two major species: fixed-grip and detachable. A fixed-grip lift has a single moving cable to which the chair is clamped. The chair goes through the loading and unloading zones at the same speed it goes up the hill. A detachable chair, on the other hand, comes off the main cable when it enters the loading and unloading stations. There, it is moved along at a much lower speed by a separate drive mechanism. Once you have loaded onto the chair and it leaves the loading station, the chair grips onto the main cable again. This arrangement allows for much higher cable speeds going up the hill than a fixed-grip chair. It also makes unloading easier because you don't have to have much speed to ski away from the chair. In contrast, the unloading ramp of a fixed-grip lift needs a pretty good pitch to give you enough speed to get away from the chair.

Loading and Unloading

High-speed detachable chairlifts are easier to get on and off of than fixed-grip chairlifts. The one thing that can be tricky is getting lined up properly at the loading station so that everyone ends up in the right place when the chair arrives. It is not hard to squeeze one of your companions off to the edge of the chair, so they are greeted by the armrest rather than the seat. Some quads have an armrest in the middle, which is even easier to get entangled with.

The loading area will have a designated spot, usually a board, to stand over as the chair approaches (think of it as "home plate"). Where you stand on that board will match where you end up sitting on the chair. Eye your spot on the board as soon as you start to shuffle into the loading area. Once you're standing on the board, look back over your shoulder to see how you're lined up with the chair as it comes your way.

If you should happen to get tripped up boarding the lift and fall, hit the deck and keep your head down until the chair is well past you or the lift attendant has stopped it. The last thing you want is to get smacked by a big steel chair.

As chairlift technology has progressed to quads (four passengers) and six-packs (six passengers), getting off the things in a tangle of inexperienced skiers and snowboarders has become problematic. Talk to your chairlift companions on the way up to establish which direction everyone is going before you get to the unloading station at the top. If you sense that some of your companions are a little sketchy skillwise, either push off quickly to get ahead of them, or hang back and let

CHAIRLIFT ETIQUETTE

Chairlifts put you in close proximity to strangers for a period of time. Be nice.

Before you lower the safety bar, ask the others on the chair if they are ready. Simply yelling, "Coming down!" doesn't cut it. I don't know how many times I've been banged in the head, had my arm crushed, my leg mashed, or my ski pole bent because some overzealous person at the other end of the chair felt it was not only his prerogative but also his duty to get that thing down right now! The same thing goes for bringing the bar up at the top of the lift. Ask first, then raise it.

Pay attention to the little things. Don't take up more than your share of the chair. Don't flail when you dig into your pockets.

If you feel chatty and they don't, be civil but quiet. I have a vivid memory of listening to three perfect strangers discuss the extramarital shenanigans and subsequent nasty divorce of some friend of theirs. This was not what I wanted to hear on a nice, sunny day in the mountains.

them sort things out ahead of you. If you end up in front, don't make any quick turns to the left or right that could trip them up.

What To Do with Your Poles

Poles can be an encumbrance on the lift. It is best to take your pole straps off well before you load the chair and leave them off until you have unloaded. This eliminates the chance of them sticking in the snow, tripping you up, and getting bent or broken. To reduce the likelihood of dropping one off the chair when you pull out your sunscreen or high-five your

Getting Up the Hill

A good place to put your poles when riding a chairlift is under your leg. They will be out of the way, and you'll never drop them.

skiing buddies, tuck them under one leg, handle-end first.

If you are riding a lift with footrests, angle your poles away from the footrest. This way, the footrest won't hang up on your poles when it goes up or down.

If you need to take your gloves off on the lift, either put them under your other leg or put them inside your jacket. Putting them anywhere else is inviting them to fall off the lift. This includes handing them to a companion. Remember, even Joe Montana fumbled a few handoffs.

Should you happen to drop a glove or something else from the lift into a closed area or a run that is beyond your abilities, don't try to get it yourself. Get a good description of the spot (the number of the next lift tower makes a good landmark)

and tell the operator at the top of the lift. He or she will call the ski patrol, who will be happy to retrieve it for you.

Warming Up Your Feet

If your feet are cold or hurting from painful ski boots, unbuckle your boots for the lift ride. This will help a lot. If the lift has a footrest, you can do this once you're on the chair. If it doesn't, unbuckle them in the lift line. If you have rear-entry boots, be careful you don't unbuckle them in such a way that they could fall off. (Don't laugh: I've seen this happen.)

Riding Alone

When you ride a chair by yourself, sit on the side nearest the lift towers. If you sit on the other side, you increase the chances the chair will bang into lift towers as you pass them. On a windy day, the lift attendants may not let you ride by yourself at all.

Graduating from the Beginners' Chair

Sometime during your first few days on skis you'll face a potentially terrifying event: graduating from the beginners' chair, where the lift attendants have the demeanor of kindergarten teachers and the other skiers are just as green as you. Now you're thrust into a melee of skiers and machinery where everyone is expected to know what they are sup-posed to do and when to do it.

If you can, plan your first foray up the Big Lift during slack time—first thing in the morning, during lunch, or late in the afternoon.

Tell the lift operators that you're new to

this and ask them to slow the lift down a bit. They'd rather do that than deal with a tangle of lift line carnage. So would the people behind you in line.

If you're taking a lesson, you don't have to worry about anything. Your instructor will tell you just what to do and ask the lift operators to help you.

Most lifts are operated at a speed that runs a chair through the loading area every six seconds. Chairlifts intended specifically for beginners are often run with longer intervals between chairs. So when you graduate to the rest of the mountain, be ready for the chair to come faster than you may be used to.

When you get to the unloading station, expect the ramp to be a little steeper and longer if you're riding a fixed-grip chair. If the lift is of the high-speed detachable sort, the unloading area will be flat and mellow.

GONDOLAS

Gondolas are great on cold, windy, or wet days. You can take off your hat and goggles, even your jacket, and not worry about dropping anything. They are also a very nice way for a nonskier to get a won- derful view of the mountains and skiing. Contrary to what you might think, though, they are generally slower than detach- able chairs.

While you ride inside the gondola, your skis are carried in a rack on the outside of the cabin. If you are unfamiliar with the lift, an attendant will load your skis for you. There will also be someone at the top who will unload them from the rack. Some modern skis have too much roll-up at the tail to fit in the racks as a pair and must be separated.

Gondola cabins have racks on the outside for your skis. Most twin-tip and powder skis must be separated in order to fit in the rack.

TRAMS

While they are common in Europe, only a few places in this country have tramways, or *trams* for short. A tram has two large cabins fixed to a cable, each halfway around from the other. Each cabin generally holds fifty or more people (the famous Snowbird tram in Utah holds 125). When one of them is docked at the lower terminal, the other car is docked at the top. As one car goes up, the other comes down. Some tram cabins load and unload from the same side of the cabin; on others you enter on one side and exit from the other.

I much prefer to be against the win- dow, rather than in the middle of the cabin. And I either try to be one of the first to load, or the last, depending on how the cabin unloads so I can get off quickly.

Getting Up the Hill

SURFACE LIFTS

Conveyances that pull you along the snow are called *surface lifts*. They include T-bars, Poma–lifts, and a few other less common species. Once ubiquitous, they are less common these days than chairlifts, but you still find them at smaller ski areas, on the more exposed parts of larger resorts, on many beginners' slopes, and all over Europe.

Surface lifts are good alternatives to chairlifts on cold or windy days. You are down out of the wind, and because you are standing up and using your legs, you keep yourself warmer.

Ski areas often put surface lifts on beginner terrain. Some think it's so the attendants can have fun watching the novices flail. I think it's because surface lifts are better for short slopes than chairlifts.

Also, because they require you to balance on a pair of moving skis, they help you learn to ski more quickly.

T-bars get their name from their shape. (The first one, at Pico, Vermont, was called the "He-and-She Stick.") Poma-lifts get their name from their inventor, Jean Pomagalski who, back in 1935, developed the first detachable surface lift. From that beginning in the early days of skiing mechanization, the Pomagalski Company of Grenoble, France, has become the largest manufacturer of ski lifts and other cableway transportation in the world, making everything from detachable quad chairlifts to urban-transportation systems to amusement park rides.

A single-rider lift, a Poma-lift pulls you up the hill with a long pole suspended

T-bars handle two skiers at once, but can also be ridden alone.

Getting Up the Hill

The most important thing to remember about riding a T-bar is that you NOT sit on it. Stand and let it pull you up the hill.

At the T-bar unloading area, the riders get off one at a time.

from a moving cable. The pole has a plastic platter, about the size and shape of a Frisbee, attached to the end, which you put between your legs so that the disc pulls against your butt.

There are a few things to be careful about when riding surface lifts.

Resist the temptation to sit on the thing. This is not how they work, and you will fall over. Imagine someone pushing you up the hill from behind. You would lean back a bit, but you would not sit down. This is how T-bars and Pomas are designed to work. Also, you can't do many of the things you can on a chairlift. Putting on sunscreen, eating a candy bar, or making a call on your cell phone can be tricky.

Some of these contraptions can give you a good jerk when they take off, sort

of like popping the clutch on a car. So when you first get on the lift, crouch a bit, and prepare for the possibility of the lift giving you a jerk as it takes up the slack and propels you forward. Bad things ranging from falling over to wrenching your back are possible.

Before you get off a T-bar, come to an agreement with your T-bar companion as to which direction each of you will go when you get off, and which of you will "hang up" the T-bar. Simply letting go of it to flop and writhe chaotically until the spring pulls it up is dangerous and impolite to other skiers.

When you get off a surface lift, let the bar or pole go at the earliest reasonable opportunity. If the unloading area is graded downward so that you ski forward

Getting Up the Hill

faster than the lift is moving, you stand a chance of getting whacked by the T-bar or Poma if you hold on to it too long. On the other hand, don't be rash and fling it away where it might hit other people.

Three other common types of surface lifts are worth mentioning: Pony lifts, Magic Carpets, and rope tows.

Pony lifts are often found on the extra-gentle slopes intended for people who are spending their first day on skis. The lift has a steel cable that runs about belly button height above the snow. Plastic handles are attached to the cable at regular intervals. You simply step up to the cable and grab

the next handle as it passes by. These lifts are great for never-ever skiers because they are very easy to ride, while providing some extra mileage on skis. By contrast, chairlifts are tricky to get on and off and do not supply the bonus of sliding on skis while they are being ridden.

Essentially moving sidewalks on snow, Magic Carpets are also found in places intended for never-ever skiers and are especially popular with children's ski schools. While they are the easiest type of ski conveyance to ride, getting on them can be tricky. Once you have put one foot on the thing, you need to get the

Poma-lifts pull skiers up the hill one at a time. As with a T-bar, stand and let it pull you up the hill.

Getting Up the Hill

First used for children's ski schools, "Magic Carpet" lifts have become popular for beginners of all ages. They are by far the easiest of all lifts to ride.

other one on pretty quickly, or you'll get pulled into a very awkward position.

Fred Rumford, manager of the adult ski school at Beaver Creek, Colorado, gives the following advice for getting on and off a Magic Carpet. To get on, approach the moving carpet from below in small, shuffling steps. When your first ski takes hold, make the small shuffle forward with the other ski to bring it onto the carpet. When you get to the top, do nothing; just let the carpet push you forward onto the snow until you stop.

Rope tows are, fortunately, becoming less common. Much of the ski industry in this country was built on such contrivances, which were often powered by a jacked-up car or truck: a rear wheel was stripped of its tire and given a couple of wraps with a long loop of rope

that extended up to the top of the hill, where another wheel was attached to an old telephone pole. The lift operator would open it for business by firing up the truck's engine and throwing it into gear. Rope tow technology quickly advanced to the use of large electric motors and some safety devices, but to the rider they have always been the same: tiring for the hands and arms and destructive to the gloves.

Rope tows will quickly ravage a pair of good gloves. If you will be riding one, take an old pair of gloves, or a pair of heavy-duty leather work mittens (called "choppers" in the Midwest). Another option is a pair of rawhide glove covers, made specifically for the purpose. These can be found in parts of the country where rope tows are more common.

Getting Up the Hill

Scoping Out the Mountain

Standing at the top of a ski mountain, I feel like someone has taken me into the wine cellar of a fine restaurant and asked me to pick a bottle. I know most anything will be good, but somewhere in there lies a transcendent experience. Over the years, through trial and error, I've learned to find good snow and uncrowded runs while avoiding rocks and long lift lines. Hopefully, this section will help you do the same.

SOURCES OF INFORMATION

Get a Trail Map

Most skiers spend most of their time on trails they already know or can see from the lift. The rest of the time they are, technically speaking, lost. Many shaky marriages have been pushed over the edge by slipups in terrain selection, usually on the part of the husband.

Unless you know the mountain like the back of your hand, carry a trail map. Even if you know a mountain well, pick one up each year to see what new terrain or lifts may have been added since last season. You might be surprised at what you find on the map of an area you've skied for years. Trail maps contain useful information such as the opening and closing times of various lifts, locations of the cafeterias, restaurants, terrain parks, ski patrol cabins and phones, and hours of operation of each of the lifts and on-hill restaurants.

Some trail maps show the trails that have machine-made snow. This will save your skis in early season when natural snow is sketchy. Some also show the easiest way down the mountain—important information for many skiers.

I use trail maps even at mountains I've skied for years. I'm always finding interesting places to ski I didn't know about. Since this terrain is usually off the beaten path, it almost always has the least traffic and the best snow.

Take a Mountain Tour

Many ski areas offer complimentary skiing tours of the mountain. Under the guidance of an employee, someone with a title like 'Mountain Ambassador,' you will learn your way around the area along with a little history and useful tips on traffic and snow conditions known only by people who live there.

Look Around from the Lift

Keep your eyes peeled when you're riding the lift. Turn around and look back from the chair now and then. You will discover things to the sides of trails and on other faces of the mountain that you might otherwise miss.

If you see a shortcut to another run, a slot through the trees, or a good stash of powder, you need a way of finding it again on your way down. Use the technique patrollers use to locate things: note the number painted on the side of the nearest lift tower. If you can't see the number, count down to it from a good landmark such as a road, an island of trees, or a junction with another trail.

Read the Grooming Report

Every night, snowcats prowl the slopes, turning hardpack into packed powder. And every morning, ski areas publicize the trails that were groomed the night before by the mechanical felines. Some print up handouts, post them at the tops of lifts, and make them available at the lift-ticket

The following table appears within the trail map:

ELEVATION TOP:	11,212 ft/3,418 m
VERTICAL RISE:	3,267 ft/996 m
TERRAIN:	673 acres/273 hectares
LONGEST RUN:	3 miles/4.83 km
LIFTS:	Silver Queen Gondola, 1 high-speed quad chair, 1 high-speed double chair, 2 quad chairs, 3 double chairs
LIFT CAPACITY:	10,755 riders per hour
AVERAGE ANNUAL SNOWFALL:	300 inches/762 cm
SNOWMAKING CAPABILITIES:	210 acres/85 hectares (33% of area)
EASIEST TERRAIN:	None
MORE DIFFICULT TERRAIN:	48%
MOST DIFFICULT TERRAIN:	26%
EXPERT TERRAIN:	26%
SEASON DATES:	November 28, 2002 - April 20, 2003

A good trail map has information that is indispensable for even the seasoned veteran.

Scoping Out the Mountain

windows and ski-school desk. Other areas simply write the names of the groomed trails on a chalkboard. Regardless of how they get the information out, you should check out the grooming report every day. If you can't get your own copy, pick up a trail map and mark the groomed runs. If you are looking for some pleasant cruising, follow the cats. If you want powder, moguls, or other sorts of gnarl, you'll know where *not* to go.

Ask Patrollers and Instructors for the Inside Scoop

Want to know the easiest way down the mountain? Where the best moguls are? Where there still may be some powder left from yesterday's storm? How long it will take you to make a run while your

significant other enjoys a cup of coffee by the fireplace? Ask someone in a uniform. Patrollers usually have the best information on snow conditions, especially on the more difficult terrain. If you are interested in the conditions on a certain part of the mountain, stop in the patrol shack nearest it. The ski patrol will be happy to give you the lowdown.

Instructors are another excellent source of mountain information. They are the most knowledgeable about the relative difficulty for various slopes in various snow conditions and states of grooming. And, from coordinating the timing of their lessons over the years, instructors have the lift times down cold.

MOUNTAIN TACTICS
Finding the Easiest Way Down

The easiest route down the mountain is usually along the network of roads that service the lifts and restaurants. It may be identified on the trail map. If the run you're on is just a little more than you feel like dealing with, the snow conditions are bad, or you're just tired and would like to take it easy on the way down, seek out the roads by looking for them on the trail map.

If for any reason you don't feel like skiing down, you can usually ride down on the lift. This is called *downloading*, and you should feel no embarrassment about doing it. Accomplished skiers often do it early and late in the season when the snow is just too thin on the lower slopes of the mountain. As a bonus, you get a great view on the way down.

Finding the Best Snow

For the most part, I pick the run I'm going to ski based on the type of snow I want to ski and where I think I'll find the highest-quality snow of that type.

Most times of the year, the best snow on the mountain will be at or near the top. The snow there will be colder, drier, softer, and lighter than the snow lower on the mountain. There are two exceptions to this rule: First, strong winds can scour the snow and whip it into inconsistent drifts, and this effect will be most noticeable at the top of the mountain, especially on ridges. Second, the morning after a warm spring day, the snow at the top will remain frozen longer than snow lower down.

If you are a novice, look for ski areas that have easy terrain at the top of the mountain. The snow there will be the easiest to ski on.

The other primary determinant of snow quality is its exposure, or *aspect*. This refers to the direction the slope faces and how well it is sheltered from sun and wind. North-facing, tree-lined slopes have the best exposures. When the rest of the runs on the mountain are scraped and hard, their snow is the softest.

As the sun shines on the snow through the day, it warms the snow, melting it a little and increasing the humidity of the air between the crystals. This makes the snow heavier, so it settles a bit. Then at night, that moisture refreezes, making the snow firmer. Finding snow that goes through the least of such cycles will reward you with better skiing.

Because the trees along the side of the trail shade the snow at least part of the day, the snow will be better along there than in the middle of the slope. On a sunny morning after a snowstorm, ski the east side of the trail, because it will have gotten the most shade. On the

The snow on the west side of these north-facing slopes gets good protection from the warm afternoon sun.

second day after a storm, try skiing the west side of the trail. It will have been protected from the warm afternoon sun of the previous day.

Groovin' on the Groomers

Admit it. We all love skiing freshly groomed runs. The snow feels like cream cheese, and the mountain is our bagel. We can make our skis carve at will, and can ski at warp speed with no worries. That's why they call it *ego snow*.

A grooming report and a trail map are your guides to the good skiing. Groomed runs that are visible from the lift, are main thoroughfares, or have great reputations, like Buddy's Run at Steamboat Springs, tend to attract a dangerous crowd:

Scoping Out the Mountain

people who ski too fast for their own good—or your's, either. The premium trails are the ones that aren't as busy. Look at the trail map and the grooming report together to find out-of-the-way stretches of magic carpet snow.

If the conditions are right, these are good places to ski fast. The hill must be empty and your legs must be fresh, so it is best to do this early in the morning. This is when you'll find the best groomed snow, too. But remember the words of the Bard:

Discretion is the better part of valor. It is too easy to go too fast on well-groomed terrain; you might not realize how fast you're going because the snow is so smooth. Keep your head about you, and don't ski fast anywhere near other skiers, the sides of the trail, or lift towers. Slow way down above the blind spots. A close encounter of the wrong kind will ruin your day.

Powder Perfect

The three most important factors affecting the quality of powder snow are exposure, exposure, and exposure. Those big, open sun-drenched bowls look great in the magazines, but there are only a handful of days in a season when the snow isn't better in the shady nooks and crannies. As soon as the sun hits the powder—unless it's a cold, cold day—the snow will start to get heavier. Look for north-facing slopes that are protected by trees, especially ones on the downwind sides of ridges.

Powder can be found, even several days after a dump, if you know where to look. First of all, forget about the terrain you can see from the lift. Everyone else sees it, too. One of the first tricks, then, is to look where others don't. When you're riding the lift, look around at other parts of the mountain. You might see stashes of powder that can't be seen from ground level.

Tree Islands

Look for islands of trees in the middle of runs. Since skiers tend to go more or less straight downhill, in the fall line, tree islands cast sort of a "skier shadow," and the snow just below them does not get skied much. Cut in tight under them and

The glade in the lower left of the picture is much more open than it appears here. The shadows from the trees make it look much tighter than it is. This glade is virtually invisible from the moguled trail next to it and will hold powder snow for several days after a storm.

you are likely to find powder when the rest of the slope is tracked out. If the trail is north facing, the snow below an island will also be shaded from the sun and therefore drier and lighter than the snow out in the middle of the run.

Glades

Glades are great places for powder. The sparse trees give shade and protection from the wind. The problem is finding them, and finding ones where the trees aren't too tightly spaced. Glades are often more open than they appear from the outside, but if you find yourself in something that makes you uncomfortable, just turn around and traverse out. A

glade is often hard to see from the run right next to it. On the other hand, they are easy to see from across the valley.

Shady Sides of Trails, Nooks, and Crannies

Get used to scanning the sides of trails. There are often pockets of powder to be found there. A phenomenon similar to that caused by tree islands occurs at places where the run suddenly widens to one side or the other. Where the tree line angles away from the main direction of the run, you will find good stuff.

To find these stashes you need to look through the trees that line the trail. With a little practice you'll find open groves and

Scoping Out the Mountain

By lunchtime, the powder is gone on the trails. But look! There is a spot just off to the side of the trail . . .

slots separated from the run by only one or two trees where you can pop in, and get a few good powder turns, then cut back out onto the run. Sometimes you find amazing lines that go on and on.

When you are skiing along a road that traverses through the woods between two runs, look up into the trees on the uphill side of the road as you cruise along. You'd be surprised at the number of skiable slots that drop down to the road. Once you've spotted one, you just need to figure out how to traverse into it from one of the runs.

Testing the Snow

So you're standing on the edge of a cat track, wondering if you should jump into the virgin snow below you. Your concern is that it may look great, but you don't know what's below the surface. Is it soft? Is it frozen crud from yesterday that will rip your foot off? Is there a breakable crust four inches below the soft new snow? Before you commit yourself, test the snow by poking it with your ski pole. You'll be able to tell quickly if the snow is good or not.

Beware the Early Season

Skiing early-season powder is a dicey enterprise. Rocks and stumps lurk beneath the fresh snow, waiting to trip the unwary; so be careful, especially in the trees. More than your skis are at stake here. I've known people to get seriously injured when their ski gets stopped short by a submerged log or they fall on a stump or rock. Wait until there is plenty of snow before you venture off the beaten path, or *off-piste*, as they say in Europe.

Scoping Out the Mountain

This is the spot pointed to by the arrow in the preceding picture. There are four or five pristine powder turns hidden here.

Moguls—Mellow to Mighty

Moguls are entirely man-made, caused by lots of skiers turning in the same place. It should come as no surprise, then, that the best moguls are formed by the best skiers—those who make round, smooth turns. The worst moguls are formed by the worst skiers—those who make short, sharp, hacking turns.

While the depth of moguls is the characteristic most fretted over by intermediate skiers, their circumference, shape, and the rhythm of the lines through them have more of an effect on how easy or hard they are to ski. A field of big moguls with smooth, continuous lines running through it is a delight. A file of small, choppy moguls with lines that close out every third turn is a chore.

The most visible and popular bump runs often attract aggressive but technically weak skiers who hack out choppy, annoying moguls. If you find yourself on such a trail, you have two places to look for the most tractable bumps. The first is directly under the chair, if there is one over the run. Few people feel comfortable skiing right under the lift, and so the bumps there get skied less. Also, the people who do feel comfortable there are generally better skiers—who make better moguls. As long as you don't care what the people on the lift think, you'll find some of the best moguls on the hill. (And why should you care? They probably don't care how you ski, anyway.) The other place to look is near the sides of the trail. Again, fewer people ski there. Take it

Scoping Out the Mountain

Because people gravitate toward the middle of the run, the moguls are usually deeper and more difficult there.

A half-groomed, half-moguled run. Notice that the bumps are smaller at the edges of the mogul field.

easy on the sides, though. The last thing you want to do is ski off into the trees.

The moguls on a mountain change from day to day as runs go through the cycle of being groomed and skied. What was mellow yesterday may be gnarly today. Your best sources of information on where to find good moguls are ski instructors, because they know where the best moguls live for skiers of different abilities. Many of those mogul fields will be in out-of-the-way places you wouldn't know about. In my experience, patrollers tend to spend less time in the bumps than instructors and their advanced students.

In the early 1990s ski areas started using an interesting grooming technique that makes it easier to ski moguls without committing yourself or your companions to an entire run of the things. Only one side of certain runs gets groomed, leaving the other

side bumped up. This allows skiers to switch at will between the bumps and the buffed. The moguls on the border with the groomed side of the slope will always be more gentle and rhythmic than those deeper into the bumped-up side of the slope, too.

When the snow is sparse, especially early and late in the season, treat moguls with skepticism. Rocks are likely to lurk in the troughs between them. The steeper runs and those lower on the mountain are the worst. Keep an eye out for bamboo poles stuck in the snow by the ski patrol to mark rocky spots. Test things out by exploring out-of-the-way mogul fields first. For tips on becoming a better mogul skier see the "Moguls" section on page 195.

Terrain Parks
Every ski area of any size now has at least one terrain park where snowcats with

weird mechanical attachments sculpt the snow into jumps, half-pipes, and bizarre features with names known only to people under the age of 30.

Even if you have no intention of trying your luck on the snowy playground equipment, I recommend checking out a terrain park. It's entertaining to ski through them, see what the features look like, and watch young humans fling themselves recklessly through the air. These places are safe for spectators: Just stay well out of the way. But you may have to put up with some loud music you don't like.

Most big ski areas have several terrain parks, each designed for a different level of ability and sanity, and they are usually marked on the trail map.

If you've got the itch to try your luck on some of the hits (park jargon for "jumps"), see "Hangin' and Hunkin' in the Terrain Park" on page 207.

AVOIDING ROCKS

I hate hitting rocks, and I will do everything I can to avoid them. Fortunately, the people who manage and maintain our ski mountains have gotten incredibly good at snowmaking and grooming. So good that in the forty days I ski in an average season, I hardly ever hit a rock anymore. These guys are the unsung heroes of our sport. Still, you need to use some common sense; here is some for you to use when things are bony.

Pick Your Area Wisely

During times of poor snow, ski at areas you know well. You are much less likely to get into bad places. You are also more likely to know people there who can tell you where the skiing is good.

Pick Your Runs Wisely

Early in the season, or whenever the snow is thin, look for terrain that is covered with machine-made snow. These runs are often marked on the trail map. The snow may be bulletproof there at times, but at least it's snow.

If you are bored to death with skiing the runs with man-made snow, seek out trails high on the mountain, on the downwind sides of ridges, or that face north. These will have better coverage than the others. Avoid south- and west-facing runs, steep runs, mogul fields, and lower slopes. Under no circumstances should you ski a lift line.

Stick to runs that have been groomed recently. Grooming sometimes churns up

KNOW WHERE ROCKS LURK

- **In mogul fields:** It stands to reason that the bottoms of troughs are the most likely places to find rocks. They are, after all, troughs because more snow has been carved away. Early in the turn, look at the area where you will be making the last half of the turn. If you see anything suspicious, adjust your turn early to skirt the danger. Finish your turn against the uphill shoulder of a convenient mogul, where the snow is plentiful, and don't put your skis sideways in the trough.
- **On ridges:** The runs that go along ridges are exposed to more sun and scouring by the wind than other trails. Avoid them in times of sparse snow unless they have good man-made snow coverage or they have recently been groomed.
- **Below roads:** Just over the downhill edges of roads lurk some of the nastiest rocks on the mountain. If the snow is thin, always stop before proceeding over them.

Scoping Out the Mountain

some rocks, but these floaters do much less damage to your skis than ones that are stuck in the ground.

Ski on Old Skis

Skiing in rocky conditions is a lot more fun when you're on a pair of skis you can be cavalier about. Professional skiers usually have a pair of "rock skis" they use in such conditions—usually their previous good pair. So, when you head out for early-season skiing, don't start with that hot new pair of skis you just bought. First make a few runs on the old ones to see if the snow is good enough.

Turn for Turn Tactics

If you see a rock in your path, adjust your line so you don't hit it. If you're in the middle of a turn, this usually means standing up, relaxing, and letting your skis run straight for a few feet, then settling down onto them quickly to resume the turn once the danger is past. Occasionally, it means shortening the turn quickly, or flipping your skis sideways for an abrupt stop.

Hopping over rocks is a viable tactic, too. Just be sure that you're not going to get yourself into more trouble on the other side.

When you're in moguls, turn on the rock radar. Early in the turn, look at the area where you will be making the last half of the turn. If you see anything suspicious, adjust your line early to skirt the danger. Finish your turn against the uphill shoulder of a convenient mogul, where the snow is plentiful, and don't put your skis sideways in the trough.

The damage a rock does to your ski depends on how you hit it. Taking a divot out of the plastic base is far more benign than hitting a rock with a metal edge. Hitting a rock at the end of a turn, where there is considerable force on the ski, does more damage than anything else. So, if there is no option but to ski across a rock or two, stand up and put your skis flat on the snow if you can. You're much better off going straight over it than hitting it sideways.

AVOIDING CROWDS

Few of us are blessed with jobs that allow us to ski regularly during the week. Most of us have to ski with everyone else on the weekend. If you're like me and have children, you also get to take your vacations when everyone else with children takes theirs.

I have never liked standing in lift lines, so I've applied myself to the study of ways to avoid them. Here are my best tips.

Ski Small Ski Areas

Seek out ski areas that don't have big names, and you're likely to find smaller crowds. Small ski areas have other endearing qualities: They generally have less expensive lift tickets, and you can let younger children ski on their own without worrying about them getting lost. Last, but not least, people who ski at small ski areas do so because, first and foremost, they love to ski, not because they like to tell their friends about it. This makes them pleasant people with which to share the hill.

Ski at the Right Time of Year

You can save yourself money and time standing in line if you ski the so-called *shoulder seasons*—between Thanksgiving and Christmas, mid-January, and after spring break.

<u>*AFTER THANKSGIVING AND BEFORE*</u> <u>*CHRISTMAS*</u>. The snow is often excellent. Since it is cold, whatever new snow you get will be soft and dry. The locals aren't sick of seeing tourists yet, so you'll be treated well. Instructors are revved up for skiing, and many of the best aren't booked yet. The best deals are to be had during this period, too.

<u>*MID-JANUARY*</u>. After the Christmas crowds have hobbled home and before the fair-weather skiers show up for February and March sunshine come some of the best snow conditions and lightest crowds. I love January because the snow is dry and the skiers are hard-core.

Resorts have for decades run promotions to get people to go skiing and bolster business during this period. It's no accident the traditional winter carnivals in New England are held in January. Similar events are held at ski resorts across the country.

<u>*LATE MARCH AND BEYOND*</u>. Spring skiing is festive, and once the spring break crowds have returned to school, the mountain ambience changes from energized to laid-back. Many skiers have switched to golf, so only the hard-core come to the hill. You can get out on the mountain a little later, waiting for the frozen slush to soften up and leave a little earlier when it gets too mushy. You hang out with your friends, new and old, on the deck at the base lodge in a Hawaiian shirt and grin over a frozen Margarita. You never have trouble finding a deck chair to sit in. Life is good.

Ski on the Right Day

Weekend crowds are bigger on Saturday than Sunday. My explanation for this is twofold. First, some people tire themselves

Spring can bring out a skier's animal instincts.

out skiing or beat themselves up partying on Saturday, and so they opt out of Sunday skiing. Second, a certain percentage of skiers also go to church. If one in ten skiers are also churchgoers (quite possibly a low estimate), the number of skiers on a Sunday will be 22 percent fewer than the number on Saturday. (You can trust me on the percentage: I've done the math.)

Ski at the Right Time of Day

<u>*SHOW UP EARLY*</u>. The bulk of the skiing public gets to the parking lot between 9:30 and 10 in the morning and steps into their skis about a half hour after that. If you arrive at the mountain with them, you will be caught in the crest of this wave and find yourself in the biggest lift lines of the day.

Scoping Out the Mountain

Get yourself on the lift within a half hour of its opening, generally 8:30 or 9, depending on the area and stay away from the bottom of the mountain until after 10:30 a.m. You will enjoy two hours of short or nonexistent lines, uncrowded slopes, and the best snow the day has to offer.

SKI THROUGH LUNCH. From noon to 1 p.m. the on-hill population takes a dip, so this is a good time to ski. Take a snack break at 11:30, then another one at 1:30. Ski in between.

SKI LATE. Around 2:30 things start to thin out. On Sundays, it's even earlier because many people want to get an early start on the drive home. If you ski in a part of the country that has bad Sunday afternoon mountain highway traffic, consider skiing to the end of the day, then having dinner in the mountains before you drive home.

Ski When the Weather Stinks

Crummy weather keeps people off the hill. Dress right, take a few more breaks during the day, and you can have some terrific skiing.

Call up your best buddy who loves to ski more than anything else. Put on that heavy sweater that's been in the back of your closet all year. Add a fleece vest. Pull up your hood. Ride surface lifts. Ski the protected exposures. You'll have a great time, and you'll have the mountain to yourselves.

Ski the Bottom of the Mountain after 10:30

At ski areas with two or more tiers of lifts going up the hill, almost everyone wants to ski on the upper parts of the mountain. Once the morning crowd has taken its first

chairlift ride from the base area, those lifts are usually the least crowded. So, if the lines are long up on the mountain, ski to the bottom. It is usually warmer there, and you often have more options for eating and relaxing.

Study the Trail Map for Out-of-the-way Lifts

Most sizable ski areas have at least one lift that gets little traffic or is only open on very busy days. Either it serves the same terrain as a high-speed quad or it cannot be seen from any other lifts or high-traffic areas. Examples are the Minnie's Mile lift at Vail and the Saint John lift at Keystone. A close look at the trail map will usually reveal them.

High-speed detachable quads (four-person chairlifts) have drawn people away from the old, slow lifts. You are often better off riding the slower lifts, because they have no lines. In addition, on a slow double chair you can have the sort of private conversation with a friend that you could never have on a quad.

Avoid Popular Dead-end Lifts

Some trails leave you no option when you reach the bottom other than to wait in the line for one lift. There are no other lifts there, and no trails down. These are so-called *dead-end lifts*. On busy days, you should avoid them if you can. A classic example is Lift 5 at Vail. This is the chair that services Vail's original Back Bowls, Sunup and Sundown. If you ski to this lift after 9:30 a.m. on a powder day, you are likely to find yourself in a half hour or longer lift line from which there is no escape. Instead, pick routes that take you to lifts with options at the bottom.

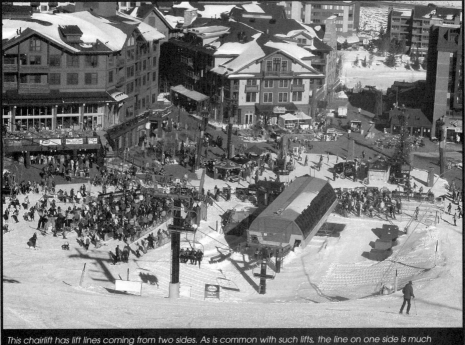

This chairlift has lift lines coming from two sides. As is common with such lifts, the line on one side is much shorter than the one on the other. Which would you rather wait in?

Look Carefully at the Lift Corral

Most busy lifts have a corral with several lanes that funnel people up to the loading point. Often, one side or the other of the corral will have a shorter line. Pick your lane carefully and you might save yourself significant line time.

Many modern chairlifts have two corrals feeding them: one from either side of the lower terminal. In many cases, one of the corrals attracts more skiers than the other. With a little forethought, it is usually easy to get to either corral from any run. The key is to look at the lines on both sides of the lift well before you get there and pick your side carefully. Examples abound, a famous one being the Montezuma lift at Keystone.

In some cases the lines may be the same length on both sides of the chair, but there will be only half as many lanes on one side. That's the side to go to, since fewer lanes mean less alternating between them.

Use the Singles Line

Most ski lifts have a special line for people who are by themselves. It will usually get you on the lift faster than the regular lines. Even if you are skiing with friends, this can be a good option if the lines are long. Just regroup at the top. Your biggest risk is riding with a stranger who wants to annoy you with his or her life story. Sometimes you can do better than the singles line on a quad lift by finding a group of three that needs a fourth.

Scoping Out the Mountain

Because people often ski in pairs, the singles line moves fastest on triple lifts and slowest on doubles.

Study the Flow of the Lift Line

Watch how the lanes merge. Occasionally a lift corral is laid out so that certain lanes merge one or two times more than others before they reach the loading station. Avoid these lanes, unless they are much shorter than the others.

Observe How the Lift Attendants Merge the Lanes

Some lift corrals, especially those for high-speed detachable quads, have four or more straight lanes that all feed into a single transverse lane at the loading station. Sometimes the lift attendant will simply walk along in front of the feeder lanes beckoning anxious skiers forward from one lane at a time. When they get to the end, they turn around and do the same thing going in the other direction. In such cases, avoid the lanes at either end of the corral. They get serviced half as often as the inside lanes.

Gondolas versus Chairlifts

Gondolas are almost always slower than high-speed chairlifts. People seem to prefer riding gondolas, too, so their lines get longer. If you find yourself presented with a choice of standing in line for a gondola or standing in line for a high-speed chair that goes to the same place, you will usually be better off taking the chair. If in doubt, ask an instructor or patroller which is the faster way up the hill.

Other Sources Information

Ask patrollers and instructors if particular lifts are crowded. They will often know.

When you ski by the top of a lift, ask people getting off the lift how long the line is at the bottom.

Some ski areas have light boards positioned at strategic locations on the mountain that give an indication of how long the lines are at various lifts. Check them.

FUELING THE ENGINE

Skiing is a vigorous sport. It taxes your body, sapping energy from your muscles and leaving you depleted by noon if you don't feed yourself properly. And I emphasize the word properly. It can mean the difference between feeling great until the lifts close and wobbling your way down the mountain on shaky legs in the early afternoon.

What to Eat

Human society has elevated the preparation of food to a form of art, and its consumption to a form of entertainment. Ski area operators are well aware of this and do their best to enable the latter by providing the former. As a skier, though, you've got to ask yourself, "Am I an athlete, an enthusiast, or a dabbler?"

If you're a dabbler, you can eat lunch like you're at a baseball game. Go ahead and enjoy that burger and plate of fries. Have a beer while you're at it. Just don't plan on skiing very hard or very well for a couple of hours afterward.

If you're an enthusiast, keep it light. For lunch, have a light sandwich and a soda, and maybe a cookie, candy bar, or piece of fruit. You'll feel a little loaded down for the first couple of runs after lunch, but you'll be ready to ski for the rest of the day.

If you want to take the athlete's

Having a slopeside lunch with friends is almost as nice as skiing. Eating the right foods will insure that you enjoy the rest of your ski day.

Sports drinks are designed to replenish electrolytes you may have lost during exercise. They are basically salty water to which enough sugar and flavoring have been added so that you don't mind the salt. Plain old water is just about as good for a skier, a lot cheaper, more readily available and, I think, tastes better.

Energy bars are great for skiing, but they're not all created equal. Don't go for ones that have a lot of protein. Remember, you want carbohydrates. A little bit of fat is good, too, as it will help smooth out the uptake of sugars into your bloodstream and give you a more measured, long-lasting effect from the carbs. The cake and cookie-like variety work the best for me at skiing temperatures. Unless it's really warm out, I stay away from the energy bars that are extruded, taffylike stuff, such as the original PowerBars. While they may be nutritionally excellent, they become impossible to eat at skiing temperatures. Even keeping one inside your jacket doesn't seem to do the trick. The only approach I know that works is one my friend Gary Cage employs: He cuts one in half, rewraps the two halves, and puts one in the back of each glove. He says this works, but I wonder why you should bother when there are plenty of good alternatives.

Erik Steinberg, a former U.S. Ski Team coach, praises the virtues of jerky for on-the-hill energy. Jerky holds up well to cold and will last for days in your parka. Erik also offers the following advice for traveling, especially in other countries: take peanut butter. A plastic jar of the stuff packs perfectly in a ski boot. Bread and crackers are a snack. Add peanut butter and you've got a meal. And when you're in a foreign land, no other food takes you back to your American roots like peanut butter.

approach, you have to think more carefully about what you eat. Dr. Sue Robson, head physiologist for the U.S. Ski Team, gives the following advice:

First and foremost, you have got to drink a lot of fluids. (See "Hydration" below.) After fluids, pay attention to carbohydrate and protein intake. Your focus from breakfast through the end of the ski day should be on carbohydrates, not protein. At the next level of detail, choose your carbohydrates based on how long you intend to go between food breaks. The more frequently you snack and eat, the more you should slant your intake toward simple sugars and other simple carbohydrates. U.S. Ski Team athletes snack frequently during their training day and are big on gummy bears. If you just eat breakfast, lunch, and have a snack when you get off the mountain, you may do better to steer toward more complex carbohydrates like oatmeal or similar porridge, vegetables, potatoes, and the like.

For a short period of time after you get off the hill, a half hour or so, your body will be in a particularly good position to benefit from carbohydrate intake, so feel free to stop and pick up a cookie at the bottom of the mountain.

The time to take in protein is the evening, when you have dinner. This meal will help your body recover from the exertion of the day and get it ready for another good day of skiing.

The choice of how you eat, and ski, is yours. After all, it's your day to enjoy as you see fit, not mine or anyone else's.

Hydration

The simplest, least expensive thing you can do to ski better, feel stronger, and enjoy your skiing more is to drink lots and lots of water.

The late Dr. Edmund Burke, a well-known sports physiologist, once said, "There are three times when a skier should drink water: when he's thirsty, when he isn't thirsty, and in between." Over the course of a day, you should drink at least two quarts of water and aim for four. It's virtually impossible to drink too much.

It may be hard to believe, but you can easily lose more than a gallon of water in a day of skiing, even on a cold day. Some is lost through perspiration, and some is lost from breathing cold, dry air and exhaling moisture. The rest is lost through excretion.

As little as two hours of hard skiing can dehydrate you to a level that has an immediate impact on your strength and endurance. It also makes you cold, because dehydration results in a lowering of the volume of blood in your body (which is, after all, mostly water). When your blood volume goes down, your body responds by cutting down on the circulation to your skin and extremities. So you get chilly.

Dehydration is cumulative, too. After three days of skiing and not drinking enough, you go deeper and deeper into water debt. Many headaches, ear problems, sleeping difficulties, fatigue, and other ailments that skiers are quick to blame on altitude are really due to dehydration.

Here's a good rule of thumb: If you feel thirsty, you're already dehydrated. Start drinking water early in the day and keep drinking at every opportunity. Drink enough that you have to stop every few runs to urinate. And use that opportunity to drink some more. Sports drinks are good, too, but stay away from caffeine and alcohol: They are diuretics and will promote dehydration by speeding urine production. One more rule of thumb: If you don't have to urinate once an hour or more, or if your urine is deeply colored or strong smelling, you are not drinking enough water.

Unfortunately, there are no water fountains on the ski slopes, so you have to carry water with you, or stop inside now and then. Some skiers carry water bottles on hip belts or in daypacks. Others ski with hydration backpacks, such as those made by CamelBak. Some ski jackets now have special inside pockets with hydration bladders. My personal approach is to stop inside every few runs and drink as much as I can.

OUT TO LUNCH

While we're on the subject of food, here are a few things worth mentioning about lunch on the mountain.

Unless you like crowds, avoid eating lunch between noon and 1:30. I like picking up a light snack around 11 or 11:30, then stopping again around 1:30 or 2. This way, I don't have to wait for a table or jostle for position in the baked potato line, and I get to ski while everyone else is eating and the lift lines are shorter.

Scoring a Table

Have you ever wandered around the lunchroom with all your ski clothes on and a tray full of food, unable to find a place to sit down? I hate it when that happens. I will usually find a table before I go foraging for my meal, reserving a spot with my jacket and accessories. Rather than roam around searching for a seat, I'll stand in a spot that gives me a view of the whole place. From there, I scan for

No room for your lunch because of all your skiing accoutrements?

Stuff your hat, goggles, gloves, and all the rest in the sleeves of your jacket where they will be safe and out of the way.

an empty spot or a party that is getting ready to leave. Once I've located my target, I go claim it. If you are skiing with others, you can split up to cover the entire room more effectively. If it looks like it will take awhile to get a table, one of you can scout for a table while the others go get food for everyone.

MAKING ROOM AT THE TABLE

You need a better place to put your hat, goggles, gloves, and such than the table, where they take up space and become targets for every six-year-old with a cup of hot chocolate.

Stuff your accessories in the arms of your jacket. This keeps them out of harm's way, takes up no table space, and guarantees you will not leave something behind on the table when you leave.

If some of your things are wet, especially your hat, you may not want to stuff them in your jacket sleeve, where they won't dry out. The chairs in some lunchrooms have shelves underneath the seats that make for a good place to put wet accessories. Just make sure things don't fall on the floor and get even wetter.

KEEP YOUR FEET DRY

If your feet are so cold or hurt so badly that you must emancipate them from your boots, don't go walking around in your socks. Chances are good that you'll step on something wet. Then your feet will be *really* cold for the rest of the day.

Once they're out of your boots, put your feet up on a chair. The air there will be warmer than the air down at floor level, and your feet will warm up faster.

Safety

As outdoor sports go, skiing is relatively safe. Gone are the days when seasoned skiers traded stories about their broken legs. Due to improvements in equipment and snow grooming over the years, most skiers never hurt themselves beyond a few bumps and bruises. (Knee sprains are unfortunately all too common, but that's another story.)

The sport is not entirely without its risks, however, and it is incumbent on you to observe some precautions.

The subject of ski safety is not all about *your* safety, by the way. Much of what I have to say is about not endangering others. All but one of the items in the Skier's Responsibility Code (the industry-standard rules of the road, presented in detail later), state your responsibilities vis-à-vis those with whom you share the mountain.

BE RESPONSIBLE FOR YOURSELF

Somewhere along the way, people in America came to regard ski areas as something like theme parks, where the various attractions are engineered and maintained to give the customers con-trolled thrills. This is wrong thinking. Skiing is a vigorous outdoor activity done in an environment that preceded humanity by several million years. If you hit a tree or fall off a cliff, it is not because some engineer didn't design things correctly. It is because you messed up.

CARRYING SKIS IN A CROWD

When I was about 10 years old, I nearly took the nose of someone's face with my skis. I had just taken my skis off at the end of the day and was hoisting them onto my shoulder when someone walked behind me. The tails caught him right under the schnoz.

I learned something important that day: Skis become weapons in a crowd. When you're in one, carry your skis straight up and down in front of you, where you can see them.

CROWDED SLOPES

Sometimes you just can't avoid a crowded hill. Here are some strategies to cope and stay safe.

Ski to the Side of the Trail

Skiers are drawn toward the middle of the slope. If you ski at the sides of the trail, you're

When you're near other people, always carry your skis vertically, like this. Never carry them on your shoulder.

RESPONSIBILITY CODE

Following is the Skier's Responsibility Code, with some annotations. You should read this, understand what each item really means, and imagine situations where each applies.

■ *Always stay in control and be able to stop or avoid other people or objects.*

Comment: Most skiers think that as long as they don't feel in danger of falling, they are in control. This is the sad precursor to many bad and sometimes fatal collisions. Being in control means that you can, as the code says, "stop or avoid other people or objects."

■ *People ahead of you have the right of way. It is your responsibility to avoid them.*

Comment: This is the same as my first safety rule on page 165.

■ *You must not stop where you obstruct a trail or are not visible from above.*

Comment: The safest place to stop on a trail is off to the side. Never stop below a road or drop-off. Snowboarders should be especially careful since they often sit down when they stop, making themselves even less visible.

■ *Whenever starting downhill or merging onto a trail, look uphill and yield to others.*

Comment: This is something of an exception to the second item in the code. It says that people who are already skiing down the hill have the right of way over people who are stopped and getting ready to go down the hill. This is similar to the protocol you follow when entering a highway from an on-ramp.

■ *Always use devices to help prevent runaway equipment.*

Comment: By "devices" this rule refers to ski brakes and leashes for snowboards. Over the years, there have been many horrific injuries, including deaths, caused by runaway skis and snowboards. Don't be the cause of another one. Ski brakes bend and break at times, so keep a close eye on them. If one of your skis comes off in a fall and goes down the hill more than a few feet, carefully inspect its brake to see if it is working properly.

■ *Observe all posted signs and warnings. Keep off closed trails and out of closed areas.*

Comment: If an area is roped off, it's for a good reason. The ski patrol does not close a trail just to keep you from having a good time or to save it for themselves. They do it because the area is unsafe either for your body or your equipment, or both. Ducking under ropes and skiing in closed areas is not cool. It's stupid.

■ *Prior to using any lift, you must have the knowledge and ability to load, ride, and unload safely.*

Comment: There is no shame in asking a lift operator for some guidance about an unfamiliar lift. Having the lift stopped because you fell getting on or off is far more embarrassing. If you are skiing with small children, ask the lift attendant for help loading them.

Safety

Need a safe place to stop and rest on a crowded slope? Stop directly below an island of trees, like the ones on this run, and you'll be out of harm's way.

likely to get both clearer sailing and softer, better snow. If the run has any counterslope to it (or what some call a *double fall line*, where the slope falls off to the left or right) try the uphill edge. Most skiers will gravitate, literally, toward the other side of the slope, leaving you with more breathing room, snow that has seen fewer skiers, has smaller moguls, and less likelihood of rocks.

There is one more advantage to hugging the uphill margin of a sidehill: Most ski slopes face more or less north, to reduce the exposure of the snow to the sun. On a counterslope that faces this direction, the uphill margin will also be the shady side of the trail, meaning the snow will be of higher quality. If the run is concave, skiing up the sides of the gully will keep you out of the thick of things.

Passing Other Skiers

If you find yourself overtaking another skier, you should either slow down, stop, or direct

Skiers gravitate toward the middle of gulleys. Note there is no one skiing the counterslope on the left.

When entering a run from a road, as the skiers on the right of this picture are doing, always look uphill for oncoming skiers. They will assume they have the right of way.

your line well to one side or the other of that skier. Watch the rhythm of the skier's turns and time your pass so it happens when he or she is going away from you.

When overtaking other skiers on a road or flat, call out, "On your left" if you will be passing them on their left side, or, "On your right" if passing on the right. Do it well before you get to them, so they don't panic and turn in the wrong direction.

The Most Dangerous Slopes on the Mountain

You might think that the most likely places on a ski mountain to get seriously injured while skiing are the double black diamond runs with names like "Widowmaker" and "Satan's Playground."

You would be wrong.

The places where people get really hurt are the groomed intermediate runs. Why? Because people ski faster there. Physics tells us that the force it takes to bring you

to a stop is proportional to your speed. In plain English, that means if you hit someone going 20 miles an hour, you will get hurt twice as badly as you would if you were going 10. At 30 miles per hour it would be triple. If you hit something that brings you to a stop—be it the ground, a tree, or another skier—that energy has to go somewhere. If you are wearing a helmet, some of that energy will go into the helmet, but not all of it. Speed kills.

The parallel evolutions of snow grooming and ski equipment have enabled skiers in less-than-perfect control to remain upright at higher speeds, until they finally hit that little ripple in the snow that sends them reeling. At the speeds skiers are going when they finally lose it on groomed slopes, they often have plenty of momentum to toss them 20 or 30 feet into a tree or another skier.

My point is this: Be extra cautious on

those groomed slopes. Don't ski fast near the sides or other people, even if you feel comfortable doing it, and keep an eye uphill for the bozos who do, as they are a danger to both you and themselves.

IF THERE IS AN ACCIDENT . . .

The odds are you will never get hurt skiing. But if it does happen to you, to someone you are skiing with, or to someone you happen upon, you should know what and what not to do. We'll imagine here that you are not the injured party.

The first thing to do is protect the injured party from getting hit by another skier. Take your skis off and stick them in the snow, crossed, uphill of the downed skier. If the snow is too hard to jam a ski into, stand uphill of the injured skier and flag oncoming skiers away.

Send someone to a ski patrol phone to call for help. These red boxes with white crosses are usually easy to find along the sides of runs and may be indicated on the trail map. If one can't be found, have someone ski to the bottom of the closest lift to report the accident. Make sure he or she knows the name of the run the injured skier is on. If you or someone in your party has a cell phone, you can try using it to contact the patrol without leaving the scene.

Don't play doctor. The best thing you can do is keep the injured skier warm and protected from other skiers. Use common sense, however. If the person is bleeding, apply pressure to stop it. If the victim isn't breathing, administer CPR if you know how.

You can ask the injured skier, "Are you okay?" but don't assume he is okay just because he says so. If you think the skier may have injured his neck or back, nothing should move until the ski patrol arrives. If it's a limb injury, ask, "Can you move the (leg, arm)?" If the answer is yes, the next questions are, "Do you think you'd like to get to a safer and warmer place?" "Can you do it under your own steam?" "Can you ski?" But bear in mind that many people, especially men, will underestimate their injuries and overestimate their ability to take care of themselves.

Don't let the injured skier get up and move around unless you are very sure he or she is okay.

Don't let machismo get in the way of prudence. If you are hurt, wait for the patrol to take you down in a sled. If the injured party is someone else, give them the same advice.

MY TWO MOST IMPORTANT SAFETY RULES

1) People Downhill of You Have the Right of Way

When people are skiing, they look where they are going: down the hill. They cannot be expected to see you if you are uphill of them. *You must give them the right of way!* If you hit someone downhill of you who suddenly cuts across the hill into your line, they are not at fault! You are.

2) Don't Count on Anyone to Adhere to Rule #1

There will always be people who ski too fast in traffic. Watch out for them, especially when your line takes you across the hill. Whenever you traverse onto a slope or complete a turn that takes you across the hill, glance uphill as you complete the turn. Your well-being could depend on it.

Safety

Enjoying Yourself in Challenging Weather

Although my parents tell me I loved to ski as a child and always jumped at the chance to get on the hill, my most vivid memories center around not being able to see where I was going and being painfully cold. I remember being stuck above tree line in a whiteout at Arapahoe Basin with my father. The visibility was so bad that we could barely move. My fingers and toes were so chilled that when I finally got inside, they stung like they'd been slammed in a car door. The problem was a combination of 1950s equipment and clothing and a lack of knowledge about how to deal with bad light and keeping warm.

If I'd only known then what I know now.

Pick the right clothes, the right goggles, and the right slopes, and you can have a great day of skiing in horrible weather.

THINGS TO AVOID

- **Alcohol.** If you are cold, stay away from beer, wine, and the like. It may make you feel better momentarily, but alcohol is guaranteed to make you colder.
- **Cigarettes.** Another warmth killer. Its other health risks aside, tobacco is a *vasoconstrictor* that will chill you down.
- **Coffee.** Yes, coffee. The hot liquid is great, but coffee is a *vasodilator*. This means it widens your blood vessels, allowing them to dissipate more heat.

FLAT LIGHT AND FOG

To someone who has never seen it, the idea of *flat light* must seem strange. To a skier caught in it, however, the name makes perfect sense. Flat light is a condition in which the snow looks perfectly smooth, regardless of its true contours. Skiing in flat light is scary. It's like driving at night with no headlights.

How is it that light can be flat? And is there anything you can do about it? The solution to the second question lies in the answer to the first.

We infer texture and shape in the snow (or anything for that matter) from the presence of shadows. When the sun is out, every little ridge and ripple in the snow casts a bit of a shadow. When the sky is heavily overcast or, worse, the air is foggy, the snow is illuminated uniformly from all directions. Hence, there are no little shadows and the snow looks smooth, regardless of its actual shape and texture. Fog is the worst, and coastal climates like those in the Pacific Northwest and coastal British Columbia can produce absolutely terrifying whiteouts. To combat flat light, you need to find a place to ski where the snow is not illuminated so uniformly. Skiing close to the side of a tree-line trail is your best bet. Here, the trees block light from hitting the snow from one side, and so the snow can cast some feeble shadows. The narrower the trail, the better. Stay away from open slopes, especially ones above tree line.

Orange, yellow, or vermilion colored goggles or sunglasses help a bit, too. Much of the light that is so uniformly illuminating the snow is light that has been scattered after hitting the snow itself. This light tends to have a lot of blue in it because snow is actually somewhat

When the light gets flat, stick to the side of the trail. Notice how there is much more detail in the snow near the trees than out in the middle of the run.

bluish. Since orange, yellow, and vermilion lenses block out more blue light
than other colors, such lenses help reduce
some of the scattered, uniform light,
enabling you to see a little bit better.

COLD

The skiing can be really good when the
weather is really cold. The snow is dry and
the hill is empty. So put that hood up and
strap on your boot muffs. You're going to
be wearing more clothes, so accept that
you may not ski with quite the pizzazz you
would on a warm spring day. You may
look like the Michelin Man, but who cares?

I've lived and skied in Minnesota,
so I've been through some cold weather.

Savvy Yankee friends from the upper
reaches of New England, Peter Howard of
Maine and Bill McCollum of Vermont,
have shared their wisdom, too. Here are a
few tricks to staying warmer:

Ride Lifts that are Protected

If they are available, ride gondolas and
trams rather than chairlifts. Surface lifts
should be your next choice, since they will
keep you out of the wind and working
your legs a bit. If you must ride chairs, stick
to ones that are protected by trees and
are lower on the mountain. If there are
many people skiing, avoid lifts that cater
to novices and intermediates, as they are
more likely to stop.

Enjoying Yourself in Challenging Weather

Wide-open alpine slopes like these are great when the sun's shining, but should be avoided on cloudy days when the light is flat.

Keep Your Core Warm

No one ever complains that his or her chest is cold. And yet, putting more insulation around your chest has a decided effect on the warmth of your hands and feet. Keeping the core of your body warm enables more heat to be distributed to the outer reaches of your anatomy. So adding a fleece or down vest is always a wise move.

Peter Howard, the Staff Training Coordinator at Sugarloaf, Maine, recommends cutting the legs off an old pair of looser long johns just above the knees to create a core-warming pair of long john shorts for those extra-layer days. It will also help keep your behind warm and dry on snowy chairlifts. Peter also notes that these make your thighs look bigger, too, which you might consider a bonus.

Keep Your Head Warm

Wearing a warmer hat will keep everything else on your body warmer, too. Because your brain is there, your body keeps a full supply of blood pumping to your head all the time, regardless of the temperature. Also, there is very little muscle or fat on your head to insulate it. As a result, you can lose a great deal of heat from your head without it feeling cold. The trouble is, that heat is being taken from some other part of your body. Take off your hat and your toes get cold.

By greatly reducing heat loss from your face, neck, and through the gaps in your knit hat, pulling up your hood will extend your comfort zone downward by at least 10 or 15 degrees. If your hood doesn't like to stay put while you ski, put your goggles on after your pull the hood up. The strap will keep everything in place. It should go without saying that you always wear goggles on cold days to reduce heat loss from your face and the likelihood of frostbite.

A hat with a fabric or leather shell and earflaps, à la Elmer Fudd, will make the rest of your body remarkably warmer.

Eating and Drinking

Sports physiologists say it is unclear whether hot liquids such as hot cider or soup make you warmer or colder. They make you feel good initially, but don't put all that much heat in your body. On the other hand, they can make you perspire, which takes heat away and reduces your clothing's insulation ability.

If it's time to refuel, eat light. A cookie and an apple will stave off your hunger during a day of skiing, give your body ready fuel to burn, and help keep your blood in your limbs instead of your guts. Digesting a hamburger and fries requires your body to work harder than it should while it's trying to ski and diverts much of your blood to your digestive tract, setting you up to get cold.

Shivering

Your body shivers in an attempt to warm itself, signaling that your core is cold. Get some more clothing on right away. Put on a hat. Pull up your hood. Put on your goggles. Cover any part of you possible with more insulation. Then get inside.

Frostbite

Frostbite can nip you even if you're wearing warm clothing and your fingers and toes feel fine. Your exposed skin is at greatest risk—particularly your cheeks, nose, and earlobes. Frostbite is insidious, because that skin is numb well before the frostbite strikes. You may feel "pins and needles" in your fingers or toes before they become frostbitten, but I have never felt them on my nose or earlobes.

You can help prevent frostbite by putting Vaseline or a greasy sunscreen on your exposed skin. You can also cover your face with your gloved hand while riding the lift.

Your best defense against frostbite is the person you are skiing with. Frequently ask him or her to check the color of your nose, cheeks, and earlobes. Keep an eye on his face, too. Pink is good. White is bad. If you or your companion see any waxy white areas, sound the alarm. White skin indicates the beginning stages of frostbite. Cover it immediately with your gloved hands. If it's your nose or cheeks that are affected, your breath behind your gloves will help warm the skin.

If you are feeling pins and needles or are battling white spots, get inside. Do not rub the affected areas in an attempt to warm them. If frostbite has set in, this will damage the skin. Instead, soak the affected areas in warm water if they don't warm up quickly on their own. Get some warm liquids in you.

If you get frostbite while riding the chair, go in to the lift operator's shack at the top if there is no other place to go.

Keeping Your Hands Warm

The first things to get cold on most skiers are their hands. My sister suffers from a condition called Raynaud's disease, and

Heat-releasing packs like the one in the picture are effective for warming up your hands on a cold day. The black elastic band is provided to hold the pack against your wrist, where it is most effective.

Enjoying Yourself in Challenging Weather

her hands get cold very easily. Yet she skis all the time, comfortably, because she takes appropriate measures.

WEAR MITTENS INSTEAD OF GLOVES

It is no secret that mittens are warmer than gloves. While some *poseurs* might fret that mittens are a fashion *faux pas,* the true skiing elite know better. Many pros wear them, and two of the very best skiers in World Cup racing at this time, Bode Miller of the United States and Janica Kostelic of Croatia, often compete in mittens.

PUT MORE ON THE CORE

A warmer jacket or layering a vest over your sweater will keep your core and your arms warmer, and this will translate to warmer fingers. It is critically important that your jacket and gloves cover your wrists well. The blood that warms your hands flows very near the surface here, and any heat that is lost is heat that can't be used in your fingers.

PACKETS OF MAGIC CHEMICALS

Every ski shop and lunchroom sells little packets of chemical stuff that heat up

A charcoal-burning hand warmer, often used by ice fishermen and hunters. These small, inexpensive gizmos pump out a lot of heat.

when exposed to air. They are particularly good for warming your hands. Put them in your palms for the lift ride. For the run down, move them to the backs of your gloves or mittens where they won't affect your grip on your poles. Some people put them in their boots on top of their forefeet, too. They also come in handy for heating up exposed parts of your face that show signs of frostbite.

But please, please don't throw the wrappers or expended packets on the ground!

ICE FISHERMAN'S HAND WARMER

I lived for a few years in Minnesota, where temperatures that folks in other parts of the country call cold are considered barbecue weather. While there, I picked up a charcoal-fueled gadget that Minnesota ice fishermen use to stay warm. I'm told people use them at football games, too.

It's a little flat steel box covered with velvet where you put a specially formed stick of charcoal, about three inches long and one-half inch wide. You light the stick, blow on it until the end glows, and put it in the box. You then close up the box. The stick burns slowly for several hours, putting out a remarkable amount of heat. If you want even more heat, light both ends.

You can carry the box in an inside pocket. The heat put out by the charcoal warms your core and quickly finds its way to your extremities. If you get too hot, just move the box to an outside pocket. These things are inexpensive, around $5 with a supply of charcoal sticks, and effective, putting out more heat than the little magic chemical packets. And there is no trash to send to the landfill. Extra charcoal sticks are around $.20 apiece. You can find them in sporting goods

Enjoying Yourself in Challenging Weather

Swinging your arm in a big circle for a half-minute will force blood intro your fingers, warming them up considerably.

stores that carry hunting and fishing gear and from various online vendors.

IF ALL ELSE FALLS . . .

If you don't have any fancy hand-warming gizmos, you can always warm up your hands by swinging them in a circle.

Centrifugal force will push blood out to your fingertips, warming them up. Fifteen seconds of this on each arm will do wonders. You won't feel the effect immediately, but within thirty seconds or so of stopping, your hands should feel much warmer. And they'll stay that way for a while, too.

If your hands are toasty but those of your companion are cold, swap gloves on the lift. Your friend's hands will warm up considerably by the time you start skiing again.

Keeping Your Feet Warm

Your entire body perspires when you ski, even on a cold day. Your feet have the hardest time getting rid of the perspiration because they are enclosed in waterproof material. Your socks' ability to keep your feet warm is based largely, then, on their ability to absorb perspiration and pull it away from your skin. Unlike a sweater or jacket, through which moisture can transpire to the open air, a sock cannot get rid of the moisture it takes from your feet. So keeping your feet warm requires using your socks' moisture-storing capacity wisely.

There are many things you can do to keep your feet from getting cold short of buying heated ski boots or giving up skiing in favor of watching TV:

- Don't put on your ski socks until you put on your ski boots.
- Never drive to the ski area in your ski socks if it is more than ten minutes away.
- Never wear a pair of socks twice without laundering them.

Boot muffs provide more warmth than you'd think. They are inexpensive and durable, and never need recharging.

Enjoying Yourself in Challenging Weather

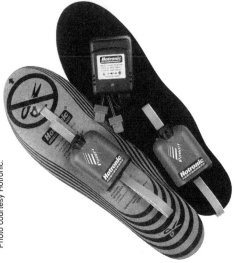

The ultimate solution to cold feet: Electrically heated insoles for your boots with rechargeable batteries.

- Never wear cotton socks. Wear a single pair (never layer your socks) of "thermal" ski socks with a high fiber content—70 percent or more—of wool, polyester, or other wicking fiber.
- Spray your feet with antiperspirant. Even when your feet are cold, they perspire, and moisture is anathema to warmth. To convince yourself that this works, try spraying one foot and not the other the next time you go skiing. You will feel the difference within minutes.
- Wear warmer pants, long underwear, and a warmer hat. Keeping everything else on your body warmer lets it allocate more heat to your feet. If you ski in a headband and stretch pants, I have no sympathy for your cold feet.
- Go inside and take your boots off. I have found that when my feet are really frigid, they just will not warm up inside my boots. Just be careful to keep your stocking feet off the floor so your socks don't get wet.
- Dry your socks under a restroom hand dryer.
- Talk to a good boot fitter. There are certain crucial spots on your feet that must not be pressed on hard by your boots,

lest the flow of blood to your tootsies be restricted.
- Get a pair of boot gloves or something similar. These are neoprene covers that strap onto the front half of your boots. They work remarkably well, require no batteries, and are pretty economical.
- If all else fails, battery-operated heated insoles, such as those from Hotronic, work quite well. They are widely available and adaptable to most boots. You must be careful, though, not to overwork the heaters, or your feet will perspire too much, leaving you in a worse fix.

SKIING IN THE RAIN

This is a common condition on the West and East Coasts, and it drives many skiers indoors, leaving the lift corrals empty. The snow is usually fine, however. The trick is to dress in a way that allows you to enjoy it.

Gore-Tex and its sibling fabric laminate membranes rule. It's worth the investment if you live in a coastal area. Make sure the garments have taped seams. Wool remains warm but is still less than wonderful when it's wet. Fleece is the way to go.

Visibility can be a problem. Carry a goggle squeegee (see "Goggle Squeegee" on page 93) and wear a baseball cap under your hood to keep rain off your goggles.

Insulated fisherman's rubber gloves are an inexpensive alternative to ruining your good ski gloves, and they will keep your hands warmer, too. If you don't have clothing made of Gore-Tex or another high-end waterproof-breathable fabric, get yourself a garbage-can liner, punch holes in it for your head and arms, and go for it!

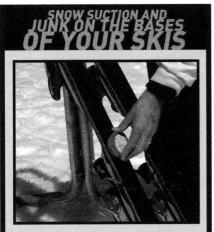

SNOW SUCTION AND JUNK ON THE BASES OF YOUR SKIS

Spring snow is wet snow, and wet snow is slow, so it pays to wax. For this sort of snow, there are a number of good products that you can carry with you and apply on the hill. Some come in tubes, some are impregnated in cloths packaged in foil pouches. Katie Fry, director of the Aspen Highlands Ski School, says that, in a pinch, sunscreen lotion will do.

Sometimes the bases of your skis will pick up dirty, oily gunk from the snow. No one I've talked with really knows where it comes from, if it's the dust that each snowflake forms around, exhaust from snowcats, lubricant from snow-making equipment, all of the above, or none of the above. But there it is, dragging on your skis.

As the snow in contact with the air melts and seeps downward, the snow beneath it strains out this noxious goop, so that by late season, it's concentrated, waiting to attach itself to the bottoms of your skis like barnacles to the hull of a ship.

Not only does this stuff ruin your skis' gliding qualities, it is hard to get off. Waxing only works for a while, until the wax has picked up even more crud. The best solution to this is to scrape your skis, clean them with base cleaner if you have some, and wax again. In severe cases, a dry, unwaxed base may work best. In any case, clean the junk from your boards and wax them before putting them away for the summer.

Skiing in a Group

Skiing is a social sport. People from a wide range of ages and abilities can ski together. Because you don't keep score, it's not particularly competitive. You get to talk with each other on the lift and switch around on each ride so nobody gets excluded, and everyone talks with everyone else.

When I lived in Aspen back in the late 1960s and 1970s, there were loose confederations of people who always skied together. Some were so identifiable and cohesive that they had names, like the Bell Mountain Buckaroos and Flynn's Flyers. Some of these people are still skiing together. Stu Campbell, longtime instructions editor for *SKI* magazine, who lives in Stowe, skis with a group called the "10-by-10 Club." They get on the lift when it opens, and make 10 runs by 10 o'clock. Like many such groups, they don't stop to talk on the hill. They save the chatter for the chair.

Whether you ride regularly with such a posse or just want to go out and have a good time with your family and friends, you should observe a few guidelines.

GETTING GOING

If members of your group differ in the intensities of their desire to get going first thing in the morning, let them start at their own pace. I like to get going early and become frustrated and antsy waiting for dawdlers. So oftentimes the best plan for me is to make a few runs by myself or with the other early risers in the group, then meet everyone else midmorning.

MEETING UP ON THE HILL

Before you and your cadre take your first run, pick a time and place to meet later in the day. Do this even if you intend to ski in a group all day. Nothing frustrates people more than standing at the bottom of the lift waiting for friends who took a wrong turn coming down and ended up at another part of the mountain.

Be very clear and methodical in your meeting plans. Specify the corner of the base lodge to meet in so you won't have to wander around and possibly miss each other. Specify how long people should wait before assuming that the others have missed the rendezvous. If you are meeting around lunchtime, decide whether you should have all eaten before you meet, or will eat together. Devise a Plan B in case someone gets lost, gets stuck in a mammoth lift line, or runs into someone else they'd like to ski with for awhile. And finally, make a Plan C that says where you will meet at the end of the day.

Everyone in the group who is not intimately familiar with the mountain should have a trail map and know where the designated meeting spots are, so if they get separated they can rejoin the group.

When you pick a meeting spot, choose one that is centrally located. That will prevent people from showing up late because they found themselves on the other side of the ski area fifteen minutes prior to the agreed-to rendezvous time. A place where the tops of several lifts converge is good, if the weather allows it. Another good option is meeting at the top of a lift that has a good run beneath it. That way, if your friends are late you can ski down under the lift and look for them riding up.

Be aware that most skiers, especially less experienced ones, underestimate how long it will take them to get from one place on the mountain to another.

GROUP SIZE

I find groups of two to four perfect. Once groups get larger than that, you must be prepared to do more waiting and less skiing. If you have a large group (greater than four) that wants to ski together, consider adopting one or more of the following tactics.

Take a run or two with everyone at the start of the day, then break up into smaller, special-interest groups, then meet for lunch.

When you meet for lunch, do it earlier than 11:45 or later than 12:45. Otherwise, you might not get to sit together.

Take a run or two together after lunch, then break up again into smaller groups.

Meet at the end of the day, perhaps for a last run down as one big group. Be sensitive of the ski patrol, however. Their job includes the end-of-the-day *sweep*. The patrollers spread out and make the last run down every trail on the mountain, sweeping everyone else off the hill ahead of them. A big group that dawdles its way down the mountain after the lifts have closed places an unfair burden on patrollers who are trying to get their work done.

SKIING IN A GROUP OF VARYING ABILITIES

The single most important rule of skiing in a group is that no one should be asked to ski on terrain that is outside his or her comfort zone. Pushing anyone to ski terrain above his or her head is guaranteed to put a damper on the whole group's day. Those who have to wait get frustrated, but it's worse for the odd man out, who suffers the double whammy of fear and embarrassment.

A good tactic is for the group to occasionally split at the top of the lift, with a plan to meet at the bottom of the lift. The

THE SEASONS
OF SKIING

EARLY SEASON: OPENING DAY TO THANKSGIVING

On the first day of the season, two things always surprise me. The first is that I haven't forgotten how to ski. If I don't think about it too much and just let my body do what it knows, I can still ski pretty well. The second is that it's more fun than I remember.

Partway through that first day, I'm also reminded of some of the distinctive characteristics of early-season skiing. The snow is hard. Your skis chatter and your teeth rattle, so get your skis tuned ahead of time and keep them that way.

Every day you should run a pocket stone over the edges to knock the burrs off. (See pages 50 and 103.) Waxing your skis every day or two is a good idea, too. At least every second or third day, your skis should see a file.

Those first couple of days can be hard on your feet, too. Your boots feel tighter, so wear your thinner socks. Because you've been wearing more forgiving footwear for the last four or five months, don't clamp your boots down really tight. The top buckle in particular should be loose, giving your ankles extra leeway.

November and December are dark months, and you spend much of the day in shade and flat light. It's time for amber, rose, or orange lenses in your goggles and glasses.

The best tactic for finding the softest snow is to get out on the hill early. The night before, grooming machines have done their best to make your day a good one,

but once the throngs of early-season eager beavers have hit the hill and scraped it down, the snow turns to Formica.

Unless the slopes have been getting a lot of natural snow, I recommend sticking to groomed runs, in particular those that have machine-made snow. Moguls of any significant depth will be rocky until more snow has fallen.

Stop in for a visit at the ski patrol and ask where the skiing is good. They'll know. It's also a good idea to keep an eye on the base depth at the ski areas you frequent and learn how much is needed to make different parts of the mountain skiable. You'll soon learn that certain runs are fine when the base depth is 30 inches, but others are to be avoided until the base is past 45.

EARLY WINTER: THANKSGIVING TO NEW YEAR'S DAY

I can take it or leave it during Thanksgiving and Christmas. If the snow is great, I can get enthused, but years of working on the hill have, unfortunately, led me to view these as periods of work rather than play because of the huge holiday crowds. If you've got an itch to ski that must be scratched, Christmas and New Year's mornings are good times to get in a lot of miles, but otherwise you are just going to have to be philosophical about sharing the hill.

From the Monday after Thanksgiving until

The Seasons of Skiing

THE SEASONS
OF SKIING

the Saturday before Christmas, however, I have had some of the best skiing of my life. It's cold and it's dark, but many years the snow is very good, and you've generally got it to yourself. One career heli-skiing guide told me that this is the best time to book a week of Canadian backcountry powder skiing.

MIDWINTER: NEW YEAR'S TO EARLY FEBRUARY

Midwinter is one of my two favorite times to ski. I've got my ski legs under me by now, and enough snow has fallen that all the runs on the mountain are open and well covered. Because it is the coldest time of year, the snow falls dry and soft, and stays that way for a long time. The cold weather, Christmas's financial hangover, the NFL playoffs, and the Super Bowl keep the less committed skiers at home.

Me, I'm out skiing.

Because it is traditionally a slow time for ski areas and resorts, many have better rates than in December and February. Some also have promotional events and carnivals, like Aspen's Winterskol.

This is the time of year to wear warm clothes. Don't trade comfort for style. You might think you look cute in that headband and stretch pants but nobody looks good when they're shivering. If your hands get cold easily, break out the mittens. Put on fresh, clean socks every day.

Even on sunny days, you'll often be skiing in the shade because the sun is low in the sky, so always carry goggles or glasses with amber, orange, or rose lenses.

If you ski in New England, do your skiing before the last week of January, when nine seasons out of ten the weather cycles through the classic *January Thaw*. It brings rain and fog and steals the snow from the mountain.

LATE WINTER, EARLY SPRING: FEBRUARY THROUGH EARLY MARCH

This is the meat of the season, when the snow is sure to have hit its stride and the weather perks up. On the days the sun is out, it is high in the sky, so you don't need goggles with lenses that turn everything an unnatural color. When it's cloudy, it's snowing. As we move in to March, the layers of clothing get lighter and fewer. We're skiing better, so it's that much more fun.

The crowds during the week of Presidents' Day rival those of Christmas week. Ski schools run out of instructors and lodges run out of beds. If you want to take a ski vacation in February and don't have children, pick a different week. If that's the week you're going, plan ahead. Things get busy again in March as schools cycle through their spring breaks, but since they are staggered across two or three weeks, their impacts on lift lines are moderate.

SPRING: MID-MARCH TO END OF SEASON

Swap your knit hat for a baseball cap. Break out the nylon shell and the light gloves. Put away the goggles and slip on those stylin' shades. Spring is here, and you've been liberated from all that insulation. Spring skiing is one of life's great joys.

Weather in the spring is more variable than at any other time of the year. A warm, sunny morning can quickly devolve into a cloudy, windy, and chilly afternoon. So, when you head out for a day of spring skiing, it pays to plan.

I usually start out with a sweater and light shell. As the day gets warmer I roll the shell up and tie it by the sleeves around my waist. I wear a light ski cap and stick a baseball cap in the waistband of my pants. If the weather looks potentially cool, I'll throw on a fleece vest, too. When I don't need it, I stash it in the trees. Oftentimes I'll take a small day pack with me with goggles, fleece vest, warmer gloves, some food, and maybe a camera. I pick a centrally located spot on the mountain and hide the pack in the trees. It beats skiing down to the bottom of the mountain and walking to the car if you need to add or shed clothing and gear.

This time or year, it's okay to sleep in. Yesterday's slush froze overnight, and is now this morning's coral reef. Few skiers will really enjoy this snow until it has softened up a bit. When you do get onto the hill, pick your runs by the direction they face. If the slope you are on hasn't yet softened to your liking, find one that faces toward the east. If you're mired in slop, migrate to a more westerly exposure. Sometimes moving just thirty feet to the left or right will deliver you from purgatory to nirvana.

You *must* be conscientious about sunscreen in the spring. Waterproof sunscreen will last longer, but in any case, you should apply it at least once an hour. And remember those parts of your head that may not be covered by a hat in the spring: your ears and the back of your neck. These spots burn easily. You also *must* wear eye protection. A baseball hat will give extra shelter to both your face and your eyes.

Spring moguls, like tomatoes and peaches, reach the peak of ripeness just before they fall apart completely. As long as the snow isn't too sloppy, this is a special time to ski moguls. Instead of knocking you back when you confront them, they yield and reward you with a spray of refreshing slush. It's like having a water fight with the mountain.

The best thing about spring moguls is the variety of lines you can ski in them. Wet spring snow is slow when compared to midwinter packed powder and hardpack. This means you can ski lines that would be too fast in the winter. The so-called zipper line (a path straight down the hill) doesn't punish you like it does in January, and certainly not like it did in December. A round line in spring snow is smooth, relaxed, and low intensity. (See "Moguls" on page 197.)

stronger skiers can beat themselves silly on a tough run, while the weaker ones enjoy themselves on something mellower. Make sure that each subgroup has at least one person in it who knows the mountain well, and who is clear on just where the rendezvous point is. This helps ensure that the group won't get permanently separated. Make sure you have a plan B and everyone knows what it is.

GROUP ETIQUETTE AND SAFETY

When skiing down the hill, try not to pass the people with whom you are skiing. It is disconcerting for them and dangerous for both of you. If you ski faster than others in the group, either start off ahead of them or give them a big head start. If you find yourself catching up, either slow down or stop for a moment. Don't ski close behind another skier, either. If that person should stop suddenly or fall, you'll hit him.

Always stop below the group or off to the side. Never stop above them. If you should happen to slip and fall trying to stop above them, you stand a chance of causing a bad accident. I know a ski instructor whose skiing career was ended when he was struck in this manner by a student in his class.

Similarly, never play the prank of spraying someone with snow when you ski up to them. If you blow it—and it happens all the time—you'll hit them like Ty Cobb sliding in to second base with his cleats up.

Keep an eye on your skiing partners' zippers. If one is open, let the owner know. That could be the pocket with his car keys in it.

STOPPING AND STANDING

Do not stand in a knot in the middle of the trail, where you obstruct other skiers.

This is particularly dangerous on groomed runs, where you are more likely to be in the path of an out-of-control skier. Adding to the danger is the fact that people in groups often converse on the hill and are less aware of other skiers.

Skiing with Kids

As soon as your children can walk, they can ski. However, most ski schools will not take children until the age of 3. If and when you do send a toddler to ski school, it may be best to start them out with a few private lessons if you can afford it. Otherwise, there may be too much standing around for a child who has little or no attention span.

Annie Black, a friend of mine who is a master ski and snowboard instructor and the mother of three, believes it is best to start children on skis rather than snowboards. Her experience is that skiing is easier for them to learn, and they will be on their own sooner. Children learn to use the edge of a ski more effectively and with more subtlety than they do the edge of a snowboard. Once they have reached a level of competence on skis, the skills they have learned are easily transferred to a snowboard.

When children are just learning to ski, poles are more of an encumbrance than an aid. A good rule to apply is this: Until children can carry their own equipment with ease, they should not bother with poles. And if you use this as a carrot, you may get out of the business of schlepping your kid's gear sooner, too.

Up until the age of five or thereabouts, children don't see skiing at all like their parents see it. Adults want to be *good skiers*. Kids want to *play in the snow*.

Adults fancy themselves in TV commercials, swooping and darting with elegance or ripping and hucking with extremity. Kids fancy themselves in *Mister Roger's Neighborhood*, playing with King Friday. My own daughter was five years old and had been on skis for a couple of years before it occurred to her that turning was something she might want to do. Up to that point, it was more like sledding to her: Go fast in a straight line. This was fine with me.

Let them play. Don't fashion them in your image. Resist the urge to live vicariously through them.

PARENT-CHILD TECHNIQUE

When your child is just learning to control his or her skis, try one of these techniques to help him along. Note that you must be a strong skier yourself to do these.

Ski in a snowplow with your child in front of you and between your skis. Hold your ski poles horizontally in front of her where she can hang on to them and you can hold her up.

Use a leash and harness made specifically for skiing with children. This will not prevent your child from falling down (like the ski pole technique described above does), but it will prevent him from flying off down the mountain out of control.

RIDING LIFTS

Well before you get to the loading area for a chairlift, arrange yourself and your child so he or she is on the outside of the chair, on the side where the lift attendant is standing. The attendant will help your child onto the chair. He will be able to do this best because of where he is standing, the fact that he is not wearing skis, and

because he does it for a living. If your child is very young or inexperienced, tell the attendant well in advance so he can slow the lift down.

When my daughter was young, I used to pick her up under my arm when we got to the top of the lift and ski with her over to a safe area before I set her down. If you are capable of this, it may be an easier way to get a three-year-old off the lift than asking her to ski.

HOW CHILDREN SKI

Children are intuitive about skiing and don't need much technical direction. Let them ski with their skis in a "pie" (a wedge or snowplow shape) at first, then you can gently encourage them to make "French fries" with them (skis parallel to each other). But if they gravitate to the "pizza," don't worry. The mountain itself is the best teacher; and just starting them young and imbuing them with a love of the sport is the best guarantee you can have that they will grow up good skiers or snowboarders.

If your children are using the proper equipment, don't be concerned if they adopt decidedly nonadult techniques. Kids naturally appear to sit back when they ski, due to several factors. Their body-mass distribution is much different from that of adults, with their heads accounting for a much larger percentage. Their legs are also relatively short when compared to adults. Add a helmet, and a child's center of gravity may be farther forward than you might think from looking at the position of his or her hips. Complicating this are stiff skis and plastic ski boots. As I've mentioned in chapter 1 (see "Children's Boots" on

Ski school teaches kids not just to ski, but to love skiing. Preparation and planning are key, and that's the parent's job.

page 14), put your children in boots that let them bend their ankles, but make sure you put them on real skis and real boots. Mushy toy boots and plastic skis just don't work the same and will teach your kids the wrong skills.

WHERE KIDS LIKE TO SKI

Children like to ski in very different places than adults do, so let them show you around the mountain. You will find yourself in narrow slots through trees that you would not have considered skiable. You'll be dragged halfway across the mountain just to hit a little jump that they know

about. If you're lucky, you might feel like a kid yourself.

While part of your job as a parent is humoring their tastes in terrain, another is to educate them on the risks of their choices. Children seldom have an adequate appreciation of the dangers of jumping into a blind landing or whistling along a rollercoaster track through trees. You should imbue them with the proper sense of caution without dampening their enthusiasm.

Because they are more cavalier than adults, it is a good idea for children to wear helmets. If they ask you why they have to wear helmets but you don't, tell

Skiing with Kids

them it's because you've seen enough carnage over the years to keep you from doing things that could crack your noggin. Better yet, buy a helmet for yourself and use it.

LETTING THEM GO OFF ON THEIR OWN

When I was young, my parents let my sister and me go off and ski by ourselves long before they would let us go into town by ourselves. A ski mountain is a good place to give your children some measured independence.

Ski at smaller areas where you can give your kids more freedom. They will be less likely to get lost and will feel more comfortable. It is also more probable that you will occasionally meet up with them on the hill, which gives them a real kick. Give them trail maps on which you have highlighted your designated meeting place. Show them what the ski patrol and instructor uniforms look like, and tell them how to ask for help. If they get lost, they can show their maps to a patroller. Another great way to let your kids be kids on the mountain is by enrolling them in a multiweek program. (See "Extended Children's Programs" on page 218.)

Keeping in Touch on the Mountain

I remember when cell phones and personal walkie-talkies first started appearing at ski areas. They met with a lot of resistance and downright antagonism from the locals, who saw them as a cultural invasion from vacationing urbanites. Most people seem to have gotten over that by

now. And although some still gripe about it, no one complains when their car has broken down and someone comes along with a cell phone.

Far from being nuisances, these devices keep you connected with your friends and family on the mountain. And that means you can enjoy skiing more. I'll often call friends who I know are already out skiing, for example, and arrange to meet them on the hill. This sort of thing is impossible to do without cell phones or radios.

CELL PHONES

Cell phone coverage is getting more and more common at ski areas. And that's a good thing. If you need to hook up with your wife or friends for lunch or after skiing, they are great. If you have children in ski school or in day care, they are virtually required.

Add a short list of important local phone numbers to your phone book. The number of the ski patrol is a must. If you have children or a spouse in ski school, put that number in, too. Other suggestions are your hotel or condo and restaurants you like.

Cell Phone Etiquette

Using a cell phone on a chairlift or anywhere else for important communications is perfectly acceptable. Tracking down people in your skiing party from whom you've become separated, calling the ski patrol to report an accident, or getting a call from the ski school that your child is sick all qualify. On the other hand, many skiers consider it a breach of outdoor etiquette to make social or business calls from the chairlift when you're riding with strangers.

Here's my take on the issue. By all means, carry your cell phone with you if

For me, it doesn't get any better than this. Helicopter-serviced skiing, or *heli-skiing*, for short, is so wonderful that it's hard to believe you're actually doing it. Here you are in the midst of mountains that stun you with their beauty every time you turn around. The snow and the slopes are like nothing you've skied anywhere else. The lift (i.e., the helicopter) gets you to the top of the mountain in less than five minutes in the most astounding and spectacular fashion you can imagine.

Could life possibly get any better? Stunning mountains, acres of unskied snow, and an ultrahigh speed ski lift to take you to a new peak for every run.

And when you get there, you've got the whole place to yourself.

A week of heli-skiing changes you as a skier. You come back feeling comfortable in all sorts of natural, unmanaged snow conditions. What used to feel funky and uncomfortable now feels like a play-ground. Most of all, you come to under-stand that skiing is something you do on a *mountain*, not some snow-covered, man-ufactured, and manicured theme park attraction. You will never forget it.

If you get a chance to go on a heli-skiing trip, you should know that it will be quite different from one to a conventional resort. Plan accordingly.

Be prepared to be outside all day. There are no restaurants out there, no base lodges, no places to stop in for a cappuccino. You go out early, ski your butt off, eat a fabulous lunch out in the middle of nowhere, then ski some more. If you're feeling tired, you can usually go back to the lodge after lunch, but you probably won't want to.

This means a few things. Get in shape before your trip. Take clothes that you know cover a wide range of conditions and temperatures. You will be working hard when you're skiing and may get a little damp. When you climb into the chopper, you will be in close quarters with six to ten other sweaty people. By the end of the day, your clothes may be ripe and may not dry out by the next day. The moral of the story is to bring at least two of everything other than your jacket and pants—extra hat, gloves, sweater, etcetera—so you can rotate them, giving them a full day to dry out if needed.

You will be spending time standing in the snow throughout the day. Pack a clean, fresh pair of socks for every day you will be skiing. If your feet are prone to getting cold, bring boot gloves, boot heaters, or whatever works for you.

You will fall. And when you fall, loose snow will find its way into every nook and cranny you offer it. Most people like one-piece ski suits because they provide the best defense, but there are heli-aficionados who prefer to two-piece it. If you do, it is advisable to wear a jacket that has an inner powder skirt. In either case, your pant legs must have a robust elastic cuff that will grip your boot tightly and must be long enough for the cuffs to stay put when you ski. Long gauntlet-style gloves or mittens that overlap your sleeves by at least several inches are a good idea.

Heli-skiing operators typically provide skis and poles appropriate for the conditions, so you don't have to worry about bringing your own. Some operators provide them as part of the package; the others will rent them to you. If you take your own poles, be sure to put powder baskets on them before you go. The little racing disks you get on some poles these days work on packed snow, but are useless when you need to manage your affairs in the backcountry.

When the helicopter takes off, it blows snow into every nook and cranny of your clothing. Dress accordingly.

The food is often spectacular, but the ambience is never fancy. Take casual clothes, including a swimsuit for the hot tub and sweats for stretching. Most operations hold voluntary stretching sessions in the morning, prior to liftoff, and it's a good idea to go to them.

You might take a small pack for carrying stuff during the day, but understand that the helicopter is not spacious, so when I say small, I mean it.

Finally, take a camera with lots of film or memory cards. But don't be surprised when you find yourself incapable of making your friends back home understand what a wonderful time you had. It simply defies description.

Heli-skiing

Regardless of where, when, or how you ski, a little youthful exuberance always seems to be part of the package. So go ahead: jump for joy!

you like. If you have an important call to make, go right ahead and use the phone. But be polite and keep it short. If you need to make a call on the chairlift or gondola, first ask those with you if they mind. They won't, of course, but they'll appreciate you asking. By the same token, I think it's rude to gab on and on into the phone while in the company of strangers. And keep your voice down. Talking into a cell phone as if no one were next to you shows disregard for your lift companions.

Walkie-Talkies

Walkie-talkies have become very popular at ski areas and are a good alternative to cell phones if you have children or ski at an area that does not have cell phone coverage. Sometime in 1990s, the Federal Communications Commission (FCC) set up what is called the Family Radio Service

(FRS), a standard for short-range (up to two miles) two-way radios that you can own and operate without a license. Sometime later, the FCC established another standard called the General Mobile Radio Service (GMRS), intended for purposes similar to FRS, but with a longer range of up to five miles. Before you operate a GPRS radio you are supposed to get an FCC license to operate the thing. The license costs $80 and is good for five years. I'm told instructions for obtaining it come with the radio.

The two radio services have some overlapping channels and so can interoperate. Also, you can buy a single radio that operates in both domains.

Most of these are *line of sight* radios, meaning their signal does not bend very well around large obstructions, such as mountains. Still, they are light, small, easy

Keeping in Touch on the Mountain

to operate, and relatively inexpensive (you can get a good pair for around $60 online), and if you have friends who own FRS or GMRS radios, you'll be able to communicate with them, too.

A few tips on selecting a walkie-talkie. Make sure you get a model that has *sub-codes*. This will greatly increase your ability to find a channel that no one else on the hill is using. Get a model that can ring, like a telephone. This will help you hail the others in your group much more easily than yelling, "Hey Bob! Can you hear me?" into the thing over and over. Check that the buttons and knobs are set up in such a way that if the thing is bouncing around in your pocket, the channel won't be inadvertently changed, the volume turned down, or the radio turned off.

As with cell phones, you should observe certain standards of deportment when using walkie-talkies. Keep your conversations short. Don't use them to conduct conversations on the hill. They are just as obnoxious to those around you as cell phones. More important, you may be sharing your radio's frequency with others on the mountain. At a large ski area, this is likely. If you decide to have a conversation with someone using your walkie-talkies, anyone else whose radios are set to the same frequency will hear your every word, which they almost certainly do not want to do. They can't turn their radios off, because they have to be able to get important calls from others in their party.

ALTIMETER WATCHES

These gizmos are useful not just because they can tell you how high above sea level you are, but because they can also help you predict the weather. All such devices determine altitude based on barometric pressure. If the altimeter says that the top of the mountain is a few hundred feet lower than it was two hours ago, it means the barometer is rising. That indicates a high-pressure system is moving in, so the weather should be stable. If, on the other hand, the altimeter indicates you are gaining significant altitude steadily, the barometer is falling, and you can expect the weather to worsen. ♦♦♦

Why are Phil and Steve Mahre smiling? Probably because they ski so well. And the better you ski, the more fun it is. If you skied as well as these guys (they've won Olympic medals, world championships, World Cup titles, and things like that), you'd smile a lot, too.

SKIING BETTER

I am a terrible snowboarder. Still, I like to snowboard, mostly because every time I do it, I do it better than the last time. And getting better is fun. That's why beginning skiers enjoy themselves so much. Every hour they're doing things they've never done before. That they don't necessarily do them very well is beside the point.

Skiing is such a rich and varied sport that you can ski for decades and still discover new things. Take, for example, one of my best friends, Curt Chase, who grew up skiing in New Hampshire in the 1930s. He served in the 10th Mountain Division in World War II and afterward was director of the Aspen Ski School for 20 years. Now in his 80s, he continues to live in the mountains and ski almost every day of the season. As the saying goes, he has probably forgotten more about skiing than I've ever known. Still he's always getting excited about some new technical nuance he has uncovered and incorporated into his skiing. After more than 70 years of skiing, he is still getting better.

The Essentials

This section is about the most essential techniques that every skier must master. No, it's not about bending your knees, turning your feet, or planting your pole. It's about putting on your skis, putting on your poles, and getting up after you've fallen. Because if you can't do those things, you can't do anything else.

GETTING SNOW OFF THE BOTTOM OF YOUR BOOTS

Before you step into your bindings, you've got to make sure there is no snow stuck to the soles of your boots. Otherwise you stand a good chance of your ski falling off when you least expect or want it to, like when you're going hell-bent-for-leather fast. Listen for the solid snap your binding should make when it closes properly on your boot. If it doesn't make that sound, either there is snow or dirt stuck to the boot sole, there is snow on the ski between the toe and heelpiece, or you didn't get your boot in straight. Step out of the binding, scrape your boot sole, and try again until you hear that nice, satisfying clunk that says you're good to go. If you're sure the boot is clean but there's still no clunk, look at your heel to see if it's centered in the binding. If it is, it's time to visit a ski shop.

The most popular way to remove snow from ski boot soles is also the worst. It involves balancing on one leg like a flamingo and whacking away at the bottom of the other boot with the shaft of your pole.

There is a much better way: Scrape the sole of your boot across the top of your binding toepiece, front to back, as

The Flamingo Technique: Whacking the sole of your boot with your pole to knock off the snow is ineffective and frustrating.

Scraping your boot across the binding toepiece is the best way to remove snow stuck to the sole.

shown in the picture. The binding's ski brake will hold the ski in place, and the snow will fall off in front of the binding, keeping the area where your boot goes clear of snow.

A tip for parents: You can't count on small children to know when their bindings close properly. Watch and listen as your kids step into their skis and carry something you can use to scrape snow and ice off the bottoms of their boots. A small windshield scraper, a plastic ski-wax scraper, or an old credit card will do the trick.

PUTTING ON SKIS IN TOUGH SITUATIONS

If you find yourself needing to put a ski on in the middle of a bumpy or icy run, you'll find the job a lot easier if you move to the side of the trail first. The snow will be smoother and softer here, and there will be less traffic.

Putting on a downhill ski is hard because it is angled away from you. Instead of struggling like this, turn around so the ski you need to put on is uphill of you.

STEPPING INTO A SKI ON A SLOPE

First, place the ski uphill from you and pointing across the hill. Fifty percent of the time, this means you will have to turn around first. Why bother, you ask? If the ski is on your downhill side, the binding will be angled away from you, and it will be hard to get your boot lined up properly. When the ski is uphill of you, the binding is naturally angled toward you, and the task is much easier.

MAKING A SKI STAY PUT WHILE YOU STEP INTO THE BINDING

If your ski just won't stay put while you try to step into it, stick the tail in the snow. This has the added benefit of keeping loose snow out of the binding area.

PUTTING ON A SKI IN POWDER SNOW

This sticking-the-tail-in-the-snow trick works in powder snow, too, as long as it's not too deep and light. If you're in powder that won't support the ski firmly enough, try the following approach: Stamp out a hole in the snow about two feet across, then lay the ski down so the binding is suspended over the hole. Now the binding will stay clear of snow while you step into it.

PUTTING ON BOTH SKIS ON A SLOPE

When you lose both skis on the hill, you can do one of two things: You can put on your uphill ski, then turn around so the other ski becomes your new uphill ski; or you can stand downhill of both skis and swing your downhill foot uphill, across your uphill foot, and put it into the downhill ski.

The Essentials

If your ski won't stay put or snow keeps getting in the binding, stick its tail in the snow, then step into it.

With the ski's tail in the snow, stepping into the binding is easy.

Step one for putting on both skis: Stand downhill of both skis. Swing your downhill foot across and step into the lower ski.

Step two for putting on both skis: Step into the upper ski.

The Essentials

This will be easy because of the angle at which the ski sits on the snow. Once that ski is on, you can put your other foot into the uphill ski.

PUTTING ON YOUR POLES

The correct way to put on a ski pole is not obvious. The secret is to understand the strap's purpose. Not only does the strap keep you from dropping the thing; it provides support when you push on your poles. The force you apply to the pole when you push across a flat or make a turn with a solid pole plant should be transmitted by the strap, so you don't have to grip the pole like a vise.

The strap must go around your hand as shown in the photos at right. Start by reaching up through the strap, then bring your hand down on the strap and around the pole handle.

A tip for parents: This whole procedure is too complicated for small children. They can just stick their hands through the straps and grab the handles.

GETTING UP FROM A FALL

Every instructor knows that getting up is surprisingly difficult to both teach and learn. When I took ski lessons from the Aspen Ski School in 1958, I was taught a technique that didn't work. When I started teaching skiing in the Aspen Ski School in 1970, I was told to teach beginners that same technique. If you spent your seminal hours on skis in a ski school class, you may well have been taught the same questionable maneuver.

Here's how it goes: Get your skis together, downhill of you. This much is good advice. Now, you take both your

Step one for putting on a ski pole: Reach up through the strap so your hand is above the pole.

Step two for putting on a ski pole: Bring your hand down so it grips the pole and strap together.

This is the method that is traditionally taught for getting up. No experienced skier does it this way.

pole straps off, plant your poles uphill next to your hip, and hoist yourself up, as shown in the pictures on the left.

In all my days of skiing, I have never seen an experienced skier get up off the snow in this manner, unless he was an instructor demonstrating this method to his hapless students. To figure out how people really get up after a fall, we need to understand a little bit of physics.

The central issue in getting up is getting your center of gravity, which is some-where in the vicinity of your derriere, over your feet. Once your butt is over your feet, it is easy to get the rest of your body there.

So here is how to get up. Get your skis together, downhill of you. It is very impor-tant that they are not pointing uphill or downhill, by even the smallest amount. They must be perfectly level across the hill or they will slide away from you as you rise. Put your hands down on the snow next to and slightly in front of your hip. Now, turn your head and shoulders toward the snow, and swing your rear end up over your feet. Walk your hands toward your feet until you feel balanced enough to stand up.

There is one more good method for getting up. It's hard to describe, but easy to understand from the pictures on page 194. One of the best things about this technique is that, as you start to get up, your skis don't slide to one side or the other, because they are braced in a "V."

The steeper the slope, the easier it is to get up, because you are starting with your center of gravity closer to your feet.

If all else fails, the most reliable strategy is to take off one ski. Once that's done, rearrange yourself so both feet are downhill

The Essentials

There are two keys to getting up. First, make sure your skis are directly across the hill, so they won't slide away. Second, keep your chest down while getting your hips over your feet. Once they are, you can stand up easily.

It may look inelegant and strange, but this method of getting up works very well, especially for novice skiers.

of you, with the foot still in the ski farther down the hill. From this position, it's a simple matter to stand up and just slightly more challenging to put the ski back on.

If you happen to be skiing with an adult who has fallen and is having trouble getting up, don't try to help by lifting the person. It's easy to hurt yourself. As an instructor, I used to do this occasionally, and thought I had a foolproof technique for it. Then one day I got a hernia helping a woman get up who couldn't have weighed more than 120 pounds.

The Essentials

The Basics

Skiing is a richly technical sport, requiring all manner of unintuitive movements that are alien to other human activities. There are, however, some simple, fundamental technical points that are not exotic, complicated, or hard to understand. And they apply to skiing at all levels.

MAINTAIN AN EFFECTIVE, BALANCED STANCE

My first year as an apprentice ski instructor was spent in the Aspen Ski School during the 1970–71 season. Curt Chase, the director at that time, told us, "You can always improve a student's skiing by improving their basic stance."

Quality of stance is hard to pin down, but there are some key characteristics. Do you have an athletic and proactive posture on your skis, or are you passive and reactive? Are you typically forward on your skis, in the middle or on your heels? How much does your stance shift and vary as you ski?

The best skiers have athletic stances. The two adjectives I think best describe such a stance are *forthright* and *ready*. Picture a top tennis player getting ready to receive a serve, a soccer goalie anticipating a shot, or a linebacker just before a play. What you see is a person whose joints are flexed to a moderate degree, and who is balanced on the balls of the feet with arms up and in front.

Adopting a neutral or "home-base" posture in which every joint in your body is flexed and ready for movement is one of the two best things you can do to improve your stance.

The other is to get your hands and arms, which are key to a skier's stance, in a good place and keep them there. The best skiers keep their hands well in front of them at all times, about halfway between their waist and shoulders, and a bit wider than shoulder width. The left hand is at the same level as the right hand, and when the hands do move, they move in unison.

Quiet arms are another hallmark of a fine skier. When your hand or arm moves, the rest of your body is sure to follow, disturbing your stance and balance.

Have you ever been told to reach forward to plant your pole? This bromide treats the symptom rather than the illness. If you have to reach forward to get your arm to the right place from which to plant your pole, it was in the wrong place to begin with. If your arm had been in the right place to begin with, reaching forward would put it in the wrong place.

Hold your arms in the right place all the time and you won't have to move them at all to plant your poles properly, other than to roll your wrist a bit to bring the tip of the pole forward.

To sum up, nothing shouts "hacker" more loudly that standing up straight, hands straight out to your sides or, worse, below your waist.

Another telling characteristic of a skier's stance is its width—how far apart his or her feet are. Many recreational skiers think that a very narrow stance is a sign of a good skier. Few great skiers, in fact, ski with less than six inches of space between their feet; most ski with wider stances than that. With your finger, find the bony points on the front of your hips. If you ski with you big toes about that far apart, you're in the ballpark.

The legendary Norwegian racer Lasse Kjus does it right: A simple, solid, athletic stance without flourishes or affect.

Skiing is a sport of style. We all like to feel elegant and graceful, and maybe that is why so many skiers yearn for nothing more than to ski with their feet pinned together, and rate themselves by their ability to do just that.

This is an artificial aesthetic. There are few situations in which having your feet close together is functionally superior to having them at least six inches apart. The paradox is this: If you focus single-mindedly on skiing with your feet together, you'll never ski well on challenging terrain. If you keep your feet apart and use them independently, you may become a very good skier indeed and will then also be

able to ski with your feet together if and when you so choose.

SKI WITH YOUR FEET

Like soccer, skiing is a sport you play with your feet. The finesse and technical sophistication of a great skier happens mostly from the hips down.

Most of a skier's weight, on the other hand, is from the hips up. Gross movements above the waist cause big changes in balance and should be avoided.

The look of a great skier is one of a quiet upper body and active legs. And as I mentioned earlier, quiet arms engender a quiet upper body. More subtle, but just as important, great skiers use their feet and legs independently. The foot and leg that is to the outside of the turn do the lion's share of the work on packed snow, bearing most if not all of the skier's weight. The inside foot has a role to play, too, guiding and edging the inside ski through the turn and carrying more or less weight depending on the specific turn.

For some reason, many skiers think that the trick to making a turn on skis is "shifting your weight." When I see these people ski, I see them gyrating with their upper bodies, twisting and turning their shoulders and hips in order to turn their skis.

Good skiers don't ski this way. They turn their skis with their legs and maintain their balance with conservative movements of their upper bodies.

This approach requires what ski instructors and coaches refer to as *upper and lower body separation*. This is strikingly evident in a good skier when he or she makes short turns on a steep hill. The skier's upper body moves little, facing more or less down the hill at all times, while the skier's legs turn back and forth underneath. If you were to see that same skier making big, round turns, his or her torso might not be facing down the hill. It won't be facing down the hill, but more in the direction of the ski tips. But even then, the upper and lower bodies will be working independently.

MOVEMENT

Who do you look like when you ski? Barbie or Ginger Rogers? Ken or Fred Astaire?

Phil and Steve Mahre, the two most successful male alpine ski racers this country has ever produced, once told me that, in their opinion, hardly any skiers flex and extend their bodies enough when

they ski. Most restrict their movements to tiny ranges that don't come close to meeting the needs of good skiing.

Sometimes you must fold and crouch very low, and sometimes you must stand tall. Just as important as the range of movement is the smoothness of the movement through that range. Good skiing is not done as a sequence of positions (think of a walking robot) but as a continuous movement (think of Tiger Woods swinging a club).

Moving your body on skis requires coordinated actions at all your major joints. To move up and down through bumps, for example, you must flex and extend at the ankles, knees, waist, and lower back, all at the same time. To learn these coordinated motions, you should practice by exaggerating them on easy terrain. Start each day with an easy run or two on which you loosen up with long, fluid movements. By extending your range of motion, you'll extend your skiing.

Advanced Topics
MOGULS

During the years I taught skiing, it seemed that 90 percent of the advanced students who came to me for private lessons wanted to ski better in moguls. I enjoy moguls. Every set of turns is a little puzzle. When I'm really tuned in, it seems I'm not thinking about where I'm turning or the line I'm taking. I'm a spectator watching some inner subconscious intelligence pilot me through the terrain. It takes awhile to get to that point, but there are things you can do to get there quicker.

To ski moguls well, your body and the line you travel must conform to the terrain. Think about driving a car on an old dirt road full of potholes and big rocks. The car's suspension works in concert with the road so you don't get bounced and jarred while you direct the car on a line that skirts the big bumps and dips. When you ski, your body provides its own suspension system. To conform to the terrain, your body must flex and extend through a long range of motion without your balance being disturbed in any way. This means going from a very short stance to a very tall one and back again in a very short period of time, over and over, without your balance moving fore and aft or side to side. You can get a start on developing this skill by making turns on smooth slopes with grossly exaggerated up-and-down movements.

Finding your line requires understanding that there is only one really good place in a mogul turn to check your speed, and that trying to keep a lid on your velocity the rest of the time will cause you trouble. Weak mogul skiers are afraid of picking up any speed in the bumps, and so they try to keep it in check throughout the turn. The seasoned bumpster understands that the right place to exercise speed control is at the end of the turn, when you ski up against the uphill shoulder of the next mogul, and the best thing to do up

Good skiing isn't a series of positions, it's a continuum of fluid movement.

Advanced Topics

Donna Weinbrecht shows how to flex and extend in harmony with the bumps. Her center of gravity (roughly at hip level) barely moves up and down. If you can't flex this deeply without losing your balance backward, check the forward lean in your boots (see p. 25-26). Donna is the most successful mogul skier in World Cup history, with 5 overall titles, 46 World Cup wins, and an Olympic gold medal, to boot.

to that point in the turn is to fit your skis into the smoothest line possible that will take you to that control point. You may pick up speed along the way, but you won't be jarred and jostled by the terrain, your edges won't catch in the trough, and you'll be in a good, stable position to clamp down on the speed at the end of the turn. This line also presents you with fewer rocks and less hard snow and ice.

In practical terms, this means you need to look ahead. Riveting your eyes to the mogul right in front of you is like looking at the hood of your car while driving in highway traffic. You're always in reaction mode. Pick the place you are going to finish your turn well before you start it. Once you know where the turn will end, plan a line that will take you there. Since you know from the get-go where you will check your speed, you will be more com-

fortable going with the flow in the first three-quarters of the turn.

When people are first taught to ski moguls, they are often told to turn right on the crest of the bump. This works because the tips and tails are free of the snow, making the skis easy to turn. Also, it provides a clear timing cue and easily applied heuristic technique by which to pick a line through the bumps.

However, this rule of thumb applies only in the simplest, easiest mogul fields, skied at low speed. When the bumps get bigger, this tactic leads you to turn too soon and on the wrong part of the bump. Swiveling your skis on the top of the bump leaves you with your skis sideways on the steep, often icy flank of the mogul. From here, you slide sideways down the side of the mogul and bang into the bottom of the trough. That sideways ride down the flank

Advanced Topics

Kurt Fehrenbach, a PSIA Demo Team member, threads his way through a steep field of deep moguls on Aspen Mountain by going around, not over, them.

Advanced Topics

of the bump is usually rough, and there are often rocks between where you start and end your slide. When you hit the trough, your edges may catch and throw you for a loop. By aiming for the crest, you confront the most dramatic part of the mogul. This is ok when the moguls are small, but when they get big, that's just the place you want to avoid.

POWDER

If you don't like skiing in powder snow, it's only because you haven't yet had the *transformative experience*. This comes on the day you make twenty consecutive linked turns through untracked fresh snow and feel the bliss of that virgin soft stuff under your skis and around your legs.

Once you've had this experience, the hook is set. It's barbed and you can't shake it. You now seek powder rather than avoid it. You plan on getting up early if you think there's going to be fresh snow. You eschew the groomed runs. You start to think about getting powder skis. (Which you should do, because they make it easier and more fun.)

Skis

Back in the day, I used to think that a good skier could handle powder just fine on any ski. Then my brother-in-law loaned me a pair of 185-cm Volant Chubbs to use for a day of powder skiing in the trees. I became an instant believer in short, fat skis.

There is no question that powder skiing is easier, and therefore more fun, on skis that are made for it. But pure powder skis are not good for much else, and most of the days you ski powder, you also spend time on some packed snow. The best

Think that powder skiing looks great? It feels even better. It's easier than you might think, too, especially with modern skis.

approach for most skiers is a pair of skis around 115 to 120 mm wide at the tip, and around 80 to 90 mm at the waist. Some of these models are known as "fat skis." They are not to be confused with the ultrawide skis designed strictly for powder skiing by Atomic in the 1980s, which were instantly dubbed "fat boys."

If you want a pair of skis that are suited to spending half their time on packed snow and the other half in powder and crud, take a look at "midfat" skis. These have waist widths in the 70- to 80-mm range and have become very popular all-around skis in the western United States.

You don't need to run out and buy a brand-new pair. Powder skis seldom get skied enough to wear out. The condition of the edges is not critical, either. An inexpensive alternative is a used pair of intermediate-level shaped skis. Because the tips

It's important to maintain a rhythm in powder. Use the pressure that builds up at the end of one turn as your springboard into the next.

and tails are wide and the skis are soft, they bend easily in soft snow, and the sidecut makes them turn well on the groomed snow.

A good idea for skis 80 mm or wider at the waist is to put a lifter of 10 mm or so under the bindings. This gives you much better leverage on the edge for packed snow and has no noticeable effect in the powder and crud. It makes a good off-piste ski a much better ski for navigating the packed runs between your sojourns into the unpacked.

I also recommend going short with powder skis. Those wide skis have a lot of surface area, so they needn't be long. The great thing about a short powder ski is that you can ski trees that are inaccessible to other people. You can turn through tight tree lines without fear of hitting anything hard enough to hurt yourself. And this is where the powder lasts.

Boots

Powder conditions favor a looser, softer boot. I've known heli-guides who ski powder in boots a full size larger than the ones they use on packed slopes. The extra size translates to extra warmth, too. If you plan on doing a lot of powder

Advanced Topics

skiing, consider getting a pair of the new "soft boots." They are perfect for this.

When your boots are down in the snow, instead of on top of it, they seem to get cold more easily. If you have a tendency toward cold feet, consider getting muffs or battery-powered heaters.

Poles

You don't need special poles for powder, but baskets bigger than the ones that usually come with high-performance poles are very helpful. I have a set of small-diameter baskets I use for most of my skiing, and I carry a larger pair in my boot bag for powder days. They are easy to swap and make a real difference, not only for turning, but also for walking, hiking, and pushing yourself around in deep snow.

Lots of pro skiers recommend taking your pole straps off when skiing in the trees to avoid hurting an arm or shoulder if a pole should get hung up. Since poles baskets have evolved from open rings to disks, I don't worry much about this. Rather, I worry about losing a pole in a place I can't get back to, so I seldom take my straps off. Follow your own intuition on this one.

Goggles

Tighten your goggle strap for powder skiing. If you fall, or rather *when* you fall, your goggles are less likely to come off and fill with snow. If they should happen to get snow in them, shake out as much as you can before you wipe them. If it is snowing, hold them with the inside of the lens down while you wipe them, so more snow doesn't fall in them. If they get steamed and just won't clear, take them off and wave them around to circulate air through them. As a last resort, put

them inside your jacket for a while to warm the lens up. Carry a chamois and a bunch of paper napkins.

Powder Technique

If the snow has no firm base, split your weight evenly between your feet so your skis stay at the same level in the snow. Skiing with your feet a bit closer together will reduce the chances of crossing your tips. If you are skiing powder on top of a packed base, you can use a hip-width stance and put more weight on the downhill ski—the same stance and weight distribution you would use on packed snow.

A lot of people will tell you to sit back. This is probably the most common piece of misinformation in ski technique, and it's spouted mostly by people who don't

Heli-skiing guide Bob Rankin prepares to launch into the powder by kicking his tails into the snow. When he starts, he won't have to make his first turn from a traverse, which is difficult.

really know how to ski in powder. It is very difficult and tiring to turn a pair of skis from the *backseat* position.

Stand in the middle of your skis and crank 'em. You have to get used to the fact that you need some momentum to make a turn in powder, and that you can't turn on a dime. So let yourself go and be patient.

Point your skis straight down the hill when you take off. This will make your first turn only a half turn, and much easier to execute. A good trick is to kick your tails into the snow with your tips suspended in the air as you prepare to take off. When you're ready to go, simply push forward and you're on your way. Avoid starting from a traverse if you can. But if you must, your first turn will be easier if you start by stepping the tail of your uphill ski out to the side.

Let yourself pick up some speed before making your first turn. Bouncing up and down in rhythm with your turns will often help, especially if the terrain is not steep. Feel free to swing your shoulders and hips into the turn to help get it started. This is considered poor technique on packed snow, but in powder, whatever works is okay, and this often gets the job done.

Don't turn too far out of the fall line. And keep turning—make the end of one turn be the start of the next. Pick a rhythm and stick with it. Whatever you do, don't go into a traverse at the end of a turn. Making a turn from a traverse is much harder than making one that is linked with the one before.

Finding Your Skis and Getting Them Back On

Falling in powder rarely hurts, but finding your skis can be a nightmare. You can get

When you fall and lose a ski or pole in powder, it usually submerges uphill of you and can be hard to find.

long leashes for your skis that attach to your bindings, making them much easier to find. You tuck the leashes inside the powder cuffs of your pants. Simply follow the leashes to find your skis. An inexpensive and practical alternative is plastic surveyor's tape, attached in a similar fashion. A couple of bucks will buy you a lifetime supply.

If you don't have powder leashes, the best way to find a sunken ski is by raking through the snow with a pole. This also works for finding an errant pole.

Just getting yourself collected after a fall in powder can be exhausting. You can't stand, and you can't walk. You need to have your skis on to have any mobility at all, but getting them on is challenging, too. Snow keeps falling on top of the ski, and when you try to step down on the binding, the ski sinks deeper into the soft snow.

Advanced Topics

The easiest way to locate an invisible ski or pole is by raking through the snow with a pole. If both poles are lost, use the tail of a ski.

If you need to get up the hill to retrieve a ski, make an "X" with your poles to help you climb.

In the words of The *Hitchhiker's Guide to the Galaxy* by Douglas Adams, "Don't Panic!" It may take you awhile to get just ten feet back up the hill to where you think your skis are, but you'll get there. Make an "X" with your poles to help you get more purchase in the snow if you have to climb up to retrieve a ski.

If the snow is very soft, fluffy, and deep, stomp out a hole in the snow a couple of feet in diameter and place your ski across the hole so the binding area is suspended in the air. Push the ski down until it's got some support under the tip and tail and you can get your foot into the binding. Once you've clicked in, put the other ski over the hole and repeat.

Skiing the Trees

Because it is protected from wind and sun, the best powder is usually in the trees. It also lasts longer there, because a lot of skiers who will pursue powder on an open slope will not go into the woods to find it.

Before you make that first turn in the trees, study the hill below you and plan a line. If you can't see beyond a tree four turns down the hill, plan your line so the second or third turn puts you where you'll get a better view. As you head down the hill, focus your attention on the spaces between the trees, not the trees themselves. Half the time you will be scrambling for a Plan B by the third turn, but after a while, you'll get good at forecasting your path and finding long, continuous lines.

If your line closes out on you and you're not sure you can stop quickly enough, just sit down. The last thing you want to do is ricochet off an aspen or fall into the tree well under an evergreen.

Advanced Topics

I have six important cautions regarding skiing in the trees.

- First, don't ski under any ropes. Closed areas are closed for your safety.
- Second, don't do it alone, and keep in constant voice contact with your companions. Many heli-guides yodel occasionally as they ski through the trees so that their group knows where they are. It's a good idea. If you're not a yodeler, carry a referee's whistle, walkie-talkie, or cell phone (if there is service on the mountain).
- Third, don't go into the woods early in the season. Submerged rocks and logs are very dangerous. Early in the season, there is usually enough snow to hide them from sight but not from your skis. When in doubt, ask the patrol.
- Fourth, be sure you know how to get back to the regular slopes and lifts. Know where your lowest possible traverse line is, and don't ski past it. I have made the mistake of skiing too far on more than one occasion, tempted by the lure of just a few more marvelous turns. It's very difficult and tiring to climb uphill in powder snow. Going just 50 feet too far could put you in a spot you might not be able to get out of.
- Fifth, be very cautious around tree wells. These are the bowls that form in the snow around large evergreen trees. If you fall into one, you will have a very hard time getting out. You may, in fact, never get out. Your buddies won't see you, and might not hear you either, because of the muffling qualities of the snow and trees. If you fall in headfirst, you could suffocate. This has been known to happen. Be careful!
- Sixth, wear a helmet. Those trees are hard.

SKIING ON ICE

I grew up in Colorado skiing on soft, packed powder snow. As an adult, I spent some years in New York State and came to the realization that sometimes you have to ski on ice. Real ice. Ice you can see into. I also learned that skiing on ice is not only possible, it is potentially enjoyable.

First and foremost, keep your skis sharp. Skiing on New England ice with dull edges is like running the Grand Canyon in a deflated raft. Your edges need to be sharpened at least every other day. Serious skiers will file them every night and touch them up at lunch with a pocket stone.

Second, your boots have to fit well and be canted properly (see "Tuning the Fit" on page 27 and "Tuning the Shell Setup" on page 21) properly. If they are loose, the liners are flabby, the shells are undercanted, or your footbeds don't support you, it's like trying to carve wood with a rubber-handled knife. Boots don't have to be particularly stiff in the front, but they must be stout on the sides.

Finally, assuming that the hardware is right, you have to ski right. Nothing punishes poor technique like ice. A little too far forward and the tail washes out. Too far back and your outside ski shoots away. Precise pressure control is paramount.

You must tilt your skis up on their edges. Many people think this means cranking their downhill knee inward as much as possible. Getting your knee in is important, but so is getting your hip in, and getting your weight out over your outside, or downhill, ski. Generally speaking, most people get maximum grip when they have all their weight on that ski. The more you put on your inside, or uphill, ski, the more difficult it will be to make your skis hold on very hard snow.

The best tactics for ice depend on whether the ice appears in patches or is wall-to-wall. If it's patchy, plan your turns so the ice comes in the first third of the turn. Look for softer spots on which to finish them. If you find yourself in the middle of a turn staring at a glossy patch of blue, let up and ski straight over it, and revisit the rest of the turn once you crossed over to something more tractable.

If the ice is wall-to-wall, be attentive, stand on your downhill ski, and get used to sliding some if you have to. Stay flexed,

supple, athletic, and poised, and make the skid look good.

HANGIN' AND HUCKIN' IN THE TERRAIN PARK

If you have some adventure in your soul, you should try your hand in a beginners' terrain park. They are generally harmless and a lot of fun. The jumps are usually well designed and quite safe, but can still make your toes curl.

The most common mistake made by people new to terrain parks, particularly those who have an adult's healthy sense of mortality, is not taking enough speed

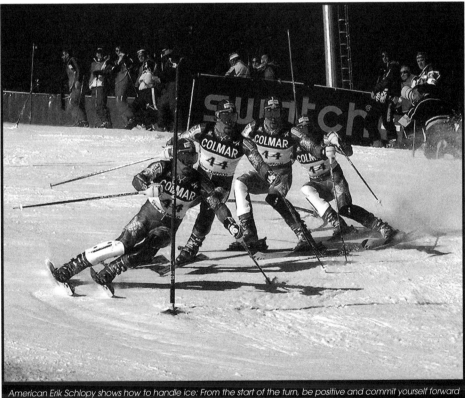

American Erik Schlopy shows how to handle ice: From the start of the turn, be positive and commit yourself forward and down the hill, getting your skis up on edge early. At the end of the turn, focus your balance on the downhill ski.

Advanced Topics

You don't have to be this extreme to have a good time in a terrain park. Basic jumping is easy and fun (not to mention thrilling), and a terrain park is the safest place to do it.

photo: Martin Olson

into a jump. When it comes to jumps, the safest landing is a steep one. But between the lip of the jump and the knuckle of the landing hill is a flat area that will give you a good smack if you land on it. Watch several people take the jump first. See where they start and where they land. What you are looking for is someone who skis straight to the jump without doing anything to speed up or slow down, who doesn't spring hard off the lip, and who clears the knuckle to land safely on the steep part of the landing hill. When you've seen a couple of people do this, you'll know where to start, yourself. All that waiting and watching may let you work up a healthy level of anxiety prior to your leap, but don't slow down as you approach the jump.

The first time you ski up to the jump, do it at full speed, then stop just before the lip. This will let you know what it will be like when you do it for real, the next time.

The second most common mistake is going off the jump on your heels. This will put you into the air in poor balance. Focus on driving your hands forward and down as you hit the lip.

You don't need to spring off the jump. Just ride it. You'll be scared the first time. Heck. I was scared my first five times. But once you get the hang of it, the beginners' terrain park is a real hoot.

Now, intermediate and expert terrain parks, that's another story . . .

Advanced Topics

Your Body: Fit to be Skied

Investing some time and sweat getting your body ready for skiing will pay off as well or better than investing money in new gear. The better your physical condition, the better you ski. The better you ski, the more fun you have. Therefore, the better your physical condition, the more fun you have. Simple, isn't it?

STRENGTH AND POWER

Skiing is a sport that favors power more than raw strength. Technically speaking, power is the exertion of force through a distance over a period of time. If you stand up from a chair slowly, you don't put out much power. If you leap up from that chair, you put out a lot. Based on that simple explanation, you can deduce that weight lifting workouts involving many fast repetitions of moderate weight will prepare you better for skiing than will workouts using near-maximum weights.

Dr. Sue Robson of the U.S. Ski Team points out that skiing has another, more curious characteristic that should have bearing on your training. Skiing requires your muscles to work *eccentrically* much more than other sports. Eccentric (pronounced "ee – sen – trick") muscle effort is that done while a muscle is getting longer. When you lower yourself into a chair, your thighs are working eccentrically; when you stand up, they are working concentrically (meaning they are getting shorter). Since skiing places such high eccentric demands on your legs and lower back, the StairMaster or exercise bicycle won't help you all that much to get ready for skiing. Instead, take an elevator to the top of a large office building and walk down. This will do more for your ski legs than walking up.

If hiking is part of your dryland training, plan your hikes so you come down by the steepest routes.

In the gym, try doing squats with light weights. Push up in the normal manner, but when you lower your body, do it on one leg, alternating legs each time.

DEALING WITH HIGH ALTITUDE

Unfortunately, you can't prepare for high altitude by training at low altitude, says Robson. Physiologists today agree that your body's ability to deal with changes in altitude is determined genetically. You can embark on an extensive aerobic training program in Florida three months in advance of your ski vacation in Jackson Hole, and you will suffer the same altitude-related effects when you get there as you would if you had spent the time bowling.

The only thing that helps is acclimatization, and that takes most people three to six days. Once you've spent enough time at altitude, your body will function just like it did at sea level. There is little you can do to accelerate the process. You can keep the effects to a minimum, however, by keeping yourself well hydrated. When your body is stressed by typical ski-mountain altitudes, its respiratory processes shift in a way that demands more water intake.

Ski School

Regardless of your skiing ability, you will get better with advice from a good instructor or coach. The best racers in the world get constant coaching. My instructor friends and I constantly give each other constructive criticism. The main things holding most skiers back from taking a lesson now and then are, I believe, expense, being afraid they won't get that much out of a lesson, and pride and vanity. When you consider how much a season of skiing costs, the cost of a good lesson or two looks pretty reasonable. The guidelines in this section should help you get a lot out of your lessons. Pride and vanity? Learning to deal with them might be the most valuable thing some people get from a lesson.

Be a savy student and become a better skier.

HOW TO GET A GOOD LESSON
Your Point of View

Most people put themselves at the mercy of the ski school and the instructor. They figure the instructor knows best and should set the agenda. This is the wrong attitude. Remember, you hired the instructor. Treat him or her as a consultant. If you hired an architect to help you plan a house, you would expect a lot of back and forth, right? You would expect the architect to be very solicitous. It would be his or her job to figure out what you really like and design your house accordingly.

On the other hand, don't pester the poor instructor, especially if you are in a group lesson. Most people learn a lot more by watching and emulating than by listening and thinking. Remember that. If you get an instructor who spends a lot of time explaining things, you should suggest, in a polite way of course, that he shut up and ski. If the instructor won't heed you, ask for a different instructor.

Take a positive mind set to the lesson. You and the instructor should focus not on what you are doing wrong, but what you can do to ski better. I have had countless students who began their lessons with a statement like, "I've taken lessons before and I know what I'm doing wrong." Their idea of their deficiencies was often accurate, but it didn't help them improve.

YOUR EXPECTATIONS

Expect to come away from a lesson with a clear idea of what you should be doing, and the ability to tell when you are or are not doing it. After the lesson, you won't have the instructor to watch you and tell you when it's right and when it's wrong. You have to be able to judge for yourself. So it's more important that you know what it feels like than what it looks like. If you are not getting this from your instructor, let him or her know.

YOUR EQUIPMENT

If you are a novice, make sure before you show up for your lesson that your equipment is set up properly and that you know how to deal with it. Nothing ruins a lesson, especially a group lesson, like a binding that keeps coming off or won't close.

If you do have a binding problem, do not ask your instructor to adjust it. If he knows what he is doing, he will refuse. If he adjusts them he could be liable for an injury you might suffer.

A good ski lesson will increase your enjoyment of the sport for the rest of your life.

Ski School

TIME OF YEAR

If you can swing it, take lessons in the first half of December or in mid-January. Why? These are the leanest times of the year for the ski school, and the best, most senior teachers are the ones who get assigned the work. During busy times, like Christmas and the President's Day week in February, ski schools are scrambling to find enough instructors. The best are booked a year in advance with repeat customers, and walk-in pupils end up in a crapshoot for teaching talent. This is especially unfortunate for beginners and intermediate skiers, who often end up with the least experienced instructors.

During slack times, ski schools often run multiday clinics targeted at locals. These are great for any experienced skier. You will get more of an insider's view of the mountain and the town, and probably get a top-flight instructor.

DAY OF THE WEEK

If you have never skied before, get into a class your first day on the hill. Carol Levine, the staff training manager for the Vail/Beaver Creek Ski and Snowboard School, recommends you stay in ski school for at least three days before you venture off on your own. Carol points out that you will learn much more than how to make a good turn to the left and one just as good to the right. You will learn how to enjoy being in the mountains, which is at least as important as learning

to make those turns. The best instructors do what they do because they love the whole skiing package, and they will share that passion and devotion with you.

If you are an experienced skier on a vacation of four or more days, you might wait until the second day of your trip to take a lesson. Spend the first day acclimating and getting your ski legs. Go on a skiing tour of the mountain if one is offered. Take a lesson the second day, practice on your own the day after that, then go back for another lesson on the fourth day.

PRIVATE OR CLASS LESSONS?

Generally speaking, class lessons are a better value for beginning and intermediate skiers. The scale begins to tip in the other direction as a skier gets to the advanced and expert levels. At any level, private lessons are better for skiers who are very timid or very aggressive for their experience level or have very specific goals.

There are, of course, differences in cost. Group lessons at major ski areas run in the range of $70 a day, while private lessons are more in the neighborhood of $120 an hour, or $400 a day. Private bookings allow you to add more people to the lesson (usually up to a total of four), for a small surcharge. "Never-evers" often get special group lessons, with insanely discounted lift-lesson-equipment packages. I've even seen them given out for free. In between are the semiprivate lessons that some ski schools offer, primarily for advanced skiers. They are generally priced more like group lessons, and have a limit of six or so students. A lot of times you will end up with only a few people in the class, so you essentially get a private lesson.

If you are vacationing alone or with just one or two friends, taking a class lesson can help you enjoy your vacation more. You'll meet some other skiers of your ability level with whom you can ski and *après-ski*. If you sign up for a group lesson on a slow day, you may end up with a private lesson.

Many ski schools offer workshop-style classes for advanced skiers. These are smaller classes aimed at developing specific skills, like moguls, steeps, or powder skiing and are a good value.

The minimum length for which you should book a private lesson is two hours. Anything shorter will only just get you started. You may get a diagnosis but are unlikely to get much in the way of a remedy.

Don't plan on coming away from a two-hour private lesson having improved dramatically. Expect to have one or two things to focus on that you understand well and some exercises to practice. Think of such lessons like you would think of private instruction for a musical instrument. You meet with your teacher. He or she makes recommendations and assigns you etudes and short pieces of music that will help develop the skills you need. Then you are expected to practice.

STRATEGIES FOR SKI SCHOOL

Go to ski school with a well-formed purpose. That could be as seemingly vague as, "I want to feel more confident," or as specific as "I want to ski Outer Limits at Killington without falling or feeling foolish."

If you don't have something in mind, you are counting on your instructor to decide for you, which is not being fair to yourself or your instructor.

Here are some possible objectives to consider:

"I want to . . .

- Get from the top of the mountain to the bottom.
- Ski better on ice and hard snow.
- Beat my friend (or kids, or girlfriend, or husband) in the NASTAR race.
- Ski moguls better.
- Ski without being afraid.
- Control my speed on steep slopes.
- Learn my way around the ski area.
- (add your own here . . .)"

If you are an experienced skier with a brand-new pair of skis or boots, spend a day on them before taking a lesson.

INSTRUCTORS
PSIA and CSIA

The Professional Ski Instructors of America (PSIA) and the Canadian Ski Instructors Alliance (CSIA) are the organizations primarily responsible for codifying ski instruction in North America. They publish educational materials for instructors and conduct training clinics and certification exams.

Certifications for ski instructors are a lot like those for other professions. Not all the worthy practitioners out there have formal credentials, but all the ones who do have the credentials are good practitioners.

Most instructors who are serious about their work pursue certification, and each organization has several levels of certification. Most instructors reach their first level after a year or two, which classifies him or her as an apprentice. The second level of certification indicates an instructor is like a licensed journeyman. An instructor with this level of qualification has been around the block more than a few times and can be counted on to be very experienced with beginning and intermediate skiers. Level three is the highest level of certification offered by PSIA and designates a master instructor. Many instructors never reach this level. CSIA has an additional level, four, which requires extensive training and demanding skiing exams that include benchmarked performance in racecourses.

If you are a skier of intermediate-level or better, I recommend you ask for an instructor certificated at level two or higher. If you are a seasoned veteran who can make it down most of the black-diamond runs on the mountain without trauma, a level-three certified instructor will be able to expand your skiing horizons.

Finding the Right Instructor

Not all good instructors are created equal. Some work well with aggressive skiers, others with timid ones. Some are great at teaching people to ski moguls, others are masters of carving the groomed runs. Some are great demonstrators, some great explainers. Some work best with men, others with women. And there are the rare few who can do it all.

If you are taking a group lesson, get to the ski school meeting place early and talk with one of the ski school supervisors. They are responsible for grouping the students into classes and assigning them to instructors. They usually wear uniforms similar in style to those of the instructors but different in color. Tell the supervisor what sort of skier you are, what you are hoping to get from your lesson, and what you know about yourself that might be important in selecting an instructor.

If you are going to take a private lesson, tell the person doing the booking what you want to get out of your lesson, what sort of person you are, and the sort of instructor you'd like. If you have a particular instructor in mind, be sure to say so.

How do you find a good instructor? Ask people coming away from ski class at the end of the day. When instructors and students are milling around, getting ready for classes to be divvied up, look for the instructors who are talking cheerfully with students, not the ones who are off to the side, being clubby with the other instructors. Get recommendations from friends if

Good instructors are drawn to the profession not only by a love of the sport, but by a love of seeing others enjoying it. They keep the talking simple and short and focus on skiing.

you can. Ask instructors who *they* would take a lesson from.

Once you've got an instructor, get to know him, and treat him like a colleague, not a king or a servant. Great athletes collaborate with their coaches. They do not throw themselves at their coach's feet, nor do they treat their coaches like the hired help.

Video

World Cup coaches videotape their athletes and review the footage with them daily. If your lesson comes with the option to be videotaped for review with your instructor, do it. If you aren't sure, ask.

Watch out for an instructor who goes off the deep end and overloads you with information when you're reviewing

the videotape. Make him back up and simplify. A good review should identify no more than one or two salient features of your skiing, and they should be clearly visible to you. You're not looking for a treatise on biomechanics, you're looking for practical advice.

Instructor Overload

Beware the instructor who tries to teach you too much or is confusing you with words. A good instructor will keep it simple and only work on one or two things at a time. If you feel like you've gotten the wrong instructor, tell the ski school and get a different one. If you end the day dissatisfied, don't be afraid to go to the ski school and tell them so. If your beef is reasonable, they'll give you either a free lesson at another time or your money back.

Ski School

Kids and Ski School

If you love skiing and have kids, you want them to love skiing, too. Children's ski school is a good way to increase the likelihood they will. You need to be part of the equation, though. Prepare your children for ski school and pay attention to a few details.

PARENTAL BLUNDERS

Anne Hirn, a supervisor in the Vail Children's Ski School, warns parents to avoid the two great parental blunders: pushing and dumping. Many parents overestimate their child's ability and interest in skiing. Let your kid ski for fun, not for fame and fortune. If your child wants to sit inside and drink hot chocolate rather than ski all afternoon, let him. Another adult motivation that sometimes deposits children in ski school is the parents' desire to go skiing in places and at paces that children can't handle. My advice is to split your kids' time between ski school and skiing with you. They'll love you for it, and they'll love the sport.

DON'T BE LATE

Show up early to give yourself plenty of time to fill out the requisite paperwork and for your child to get her bearings. Andrea Quirt of the Breckenridge Children's Ski School says the single biggest problem they have is parents leaving without completing the administrative stuff. John Gillies, the Eastern

Ski school is fun for kids, especially if their parents do their part to make the experience stress free. Get them there in plenty of time, with the right clothing and equipment, and the skiing school will see to it that they learn to ski and learn to love skiing.

Program Director of the Canadian Ski Instructors' Alliance, recommends enrolling your child the afternoon before the lesson, if possible. You will have time to fill out your paperwork without the pressure of wanting to go skiing yourself, and your child will get a look around the place so he or she will feel more comfortable in the morning. Some ski schools provide the option of enrolling over the Internet.

Show up on time to pick up your children at the end of the lesson. This may take you off the hill earlier than you would like, but picking your kids up late makes them feel abandoned and is unfair to the instructors. A child sitting all alone in the ski school after all the other kids have been picked up is sad sight to see.

YOUR KID'S GEAR

Label all your children's personal items and gear and give them a basic equipment orientation before ski school. The less of this the instructor has to do, the more successful the lesson will be for everyone. The design of some children's ski boots makes it hard for kids to tell which is right and which is left, even when they are on their feet. It is not uncommon for them to put them on the wrong one. Make sure your children know the difference, so if they take them off during the day in ski school, they get them back on correctly. Put stickers on the boots or draw on them with permanent marker, then tell them "the star goes on this foot, and the flower goes on that one."

Essential Items

Find a safe, zippered pocket in your child's clothing where you can put the following items, and make sure he or she knows where it is. A good solution is a small zippered pouch that hangs on a neck strap under your child's jacket.

- Sufficient money for lunch, snacks, and the occasional video game
- Their lesson ticket for the day. If you have bought tickets for several days, only give him or her one at a time.
- The ski school release form
- The name and phone number of the place you are staying
- Information on how to contact you; this could be your cell phone number or the name of your instructor if you are in ski school, too.

Some ski schools now require children to wear helmets. They will rent them to you, but your child is better off with something fitted specifically to him or her. Children's helmets are not very expensive, either, so after a couple of days, you've paid for it.

Don't expect the ski school to provide any equipment or clothing, especially eyewear. This is your responsibility, not theirs. Send your child with ski gloves, not fleece or knitted wool gloves. And only put one pair of socks on your kid, but make sure they are real ski socks and not made of cotton. Two pair won't keep his feet warmer and will cause problems.

Err on the side of too much stuff. The ski school will have a cubbyhole for your kid to store the excess.

LUNCH

Kids' ski schools have limited menus. It may just be a hot dog, fries, and a soda. If your kid is a picky eater, pack a lunch. The instructor is not going to be able to buy a separate meal for your child.

Most ski schools require children to wear helmets. Although you can usually rent one, it's best to buy your own.

CONTACTING YOU

The ski school will need a way to contact you during the day. Cell phones are good if there is coverage on the mountain, but you've got to remember to leave your phone on and check it regularly, because you won't hear it while you're going down the hill. Some ski schools have pagers for rent.

KIDS AND HIGH ALTITUDE

Andrea Quirt warns that children often suffer from the effects of altitude, even when their parents don't. If your kid feels tired, nauseated, or cranky the first day in

the mountains, let him or her stay at home for at least a half day to get acclimated. Don't put him into ski school. Andrea notes that drinking lots of water that first day helps a lot. This is especially important for families coming from sea level.

EXTENDED CHILDREN'S PROGRAMS

Since the 1950s, the Ski Train has run from Denver to Winter Park, Colorado. On Saturdays through the 1950s, '60s, and '70s, it teemed with young members of the Eskimo Ski Club: Denver schoolchildren whose parents wanted them to ski in a supervised setting. Programs throughout the country like the Eskimos were, and still are, responsible for teaching tens if not hundreds of thousands of kids to ski and to love skiing.

These programs typically run as short as three to as long as eight weeks in length. Some are run by local clubs, and some are run by the ski areas themselves. If there is a particular place you and your family like to ski, ask the ski school there about such programs.

Being in this type of program will make transporting your child to the hill much easier. Some are served by public transportation. An example is the Trek program at Eldora Mountain Resort, 20 miles from where I live, which has public bus service from our city. If public transportation isn't available, you can be sure that there will be plenty of carpooling among the parents.

The kids learn a lot more about skiing than how to turn left and right. They learn the ins and outs of a particular mountain and they develop friendships with other kids in their group.

Specialty Clinics and Camps

For every possible subgroup of skiers and types of skiing you can think of, there are specialty clinics and camps. There are women's clinics, extreme-skiing camps, race clinics, and terrain park camps. There is even a season-long series I know of called the Over-the-Hill-Gang, of which you must be 55 or older to get into.

The best way to find out about them is through the magazines whose target markets are the people who would go to such things. If, for example, you are interested in attending a masters' racing camp, pick up an issue of *Ski Racing* magazine. Want to send your teenage son to a half-pipe and terrain park summer camp? Check out *Freeskier* or *Freeze* magazines. Would you like to make your toes curl in an extreme-skiing clinic? Look in *Powder* or *SKIING* magazines. And of course, there is always the Internet.

Adults can humor their interests during the winter, but kids in school are generally more amenable to summer camps. Most of these are held in the Pacific Northwest and the Sierras. Mammoth Mountain, California, plays host yearly to camps in May. After that, the action picks up in Bend, Oregon, and Whistler/Blackcomb, British Columbia. These venues have exceptionally dependable snow through July and are the homes of many camps, from introductory programs to training sessions for national ski teams.

Other Info

MAGAZINE ARTICLES

Every month, ski magazines run instructional articles. They tend to be short, punchy, and focused on one particular skiing situation, movement, or principle. The magazines each have their cadres of writers. Some they use frequently, others they use now and then. If you find an article that pitches something that really works for you, take note of who wrote it and watch for more pieces by him or her in the future. You can help get more of your favorite guru's wisdom into print by sending your kudos for that writer to the editor.

BOOKS

There are many, many books on the market on skiing. My collection numbers well over 100 titles. Some of them are very helpful. Some of them are not. Some of the best are no longer in print but, with a little literary archaeology, can be found in used bookstores.

Here are my favorites:

Teach Your Child to Ski by Barbara Ann Cochran (Stephen Greene Press, 1989). Down-to-earth advice from a woman who grew up with three brothers and a sister who all competed at the top level of international skiing. Barbara herself won the 1972 Olympic gold medal in slalom. The book is not about grooming champions, however. It's about learning and loving to ski.

Learn Downhill Skiing in a Weekend by Konrad Bartelski with Robin Neillands (Knopf, 1992). Hands down, the best book I've ever read for the never-ever skier. Read this one before your trip.

The All-Mountain Skier by R. Mark Elling (Ragged Mountain Press, 1997). A book of practical wisdom for serious skiers who want to master powder, crud, moguls, and steeps. Includes a good section on boot fitting.

Teach Yourself to Ski by Georges Joubert (Aspen Ski Masters, 1970). In my opinion, this is the best self-teaching book ever written on skiing, from perhaps the best technical analyst and teaching methodologist the sport has ever known. It proves that the fundamentals haven't changed in over thirty years. If you can't find this book, Joubert's *Skiing—An Art, A Technique* is a close runner-up. Every serious student of the sport must read one of these.

World Cup Ski Technique by James Major and Olle Larsson (Poudre Publishing, 1979). This book contains the largest and most inspirational collection of photomontages, or sequence photos, ever published, including many of Ingemar Stenmark, the best technical skier the world has known. The book's text is a spot-on technical analysis of the highest levels of ski technique.

The Skier's Edge by Ron LeMaster (Human Kinetics, 1999). This book, which I wrote, focuses on the *why* as well as the *how* of making a good turn on skis and it provides analyses of ski technique not found elsewhere. A popular volume among coaches, instructors, and skiers.

Breakthrough on Skis: How to Get Out of the Intermediate Rut by Lito Tejada-Flores (Vintage Books, 1986). An unsurpassed classic by the most literate of ski writers. Lito connects with every intermediate and advanced skier seeking the next level of skill and ecstasy. He has published a newer version, but this one is my personal favorite.

Learn to ski, and the mountain becomes your playground.

ADVICE FROM FRIENDS, SPOUSES, AND SIGNIFICANT OTHERS

Out on the mountain, I hear people giving their friends bad advice all the time. Just because some people ski better than you doesn't mean they are really all that good, know what they are talking about, or can teach it to you. Many people are more than willing to give you advice who are less than qualified to do so.

There are problems with taking advice from people you know well or with whom you have a relationship other than instructor-student. It's hard to be an effective instructor, or an effective student when the other person means more to you than that. It is hard to both give and take critical advice dispassionately in such situations, and doing so often has a negative impact on the other relationship.

I have taught skiing and coached racers at many levels for over twenty-five years. When it comes time for my wife to get some coaching, I send her to friends who I know are great instructors. Other than giving simple tips and comments, I don't coach her myself. ◆◆◆

American Bode Miller displays a combination of exemplary technique, aggression, and finesse on his way to winning a World Cup giant slalom race. Miller has won multiple Olympic medals, World Championship, and World Cup titles.

RACING

Competition, whether with others or just with yourself, is fun. Watching the best skiers in the world, which is what the best racers are, is exciting and inspiring. And yet, while tens of millions of people in the United States ski, ski racing goes largely ignored in this country. It's a shame, because ski racing is an exciting and beautiful form of competition. It's fun to do, fun to watch—and both doing and watching it will improve your skiing. I think American skiers are indifferent to ski racing because they don't understand it. Big jumps and crashes aside, a typical skier hasn't a clue as to why one skier is faster than another or why one part of a course is critical to the outcome of the race.

Do It Yourself

First and foremost, racing is fun. Flying down the course with the poles whizzing by gives you a rush that you won't get anywhere else. Friendly competition with your family and friends is great fun, too. Plus, other than buying the right boots and getting them set up properly, nothing improves your skiing like racing. If you can execute a dependable parallel turn, an hour spent making four or five runs through a racecourse will tune up your skiing in ways you never would have thought. Your technique, judgment, and confidence will all improve considerably.

Once you've had the experience of "running gates," you'll enjoy watching ski races, too, because you'll understand what these guys are doing, and maybe learn a thing or two. Watching great skiers, you

The start gate for this World Cup racecourse is similar to what you will find on just about any racecourse (minus the advertisements). The thin horizontal rod is the wand (see text), and the dark patches below it are where the racers pushes off with their poles.

The turns in a slalom course are marked by single poles with no flags.

Turns in most types of racecourses are prescribed by panels: pairs of poles joined with flags.

pick up subtleties of stance and movement, which can find their way into your own skiing without you having to think much about it.

THE BASICS
The Course

Ski racing, or more properly *alpine* ski racing, involves timing a bunch of people skiing, one at a time, through a course defined by poles, or *gates*, set into the snow.

The *start gate* has two short posts set vertically about two feet apart on a flat spot in the snow, with a small stick between them, called the *wand*. The wand pivots at one end, where it is attached to a switch. You begin with your legs behind the wand, then as you push off onto the course, your legs bump the wand open, and the clock starts. The finish gate is much like the finish line for a footrace. A small bright light shines across the track along the finish line and a photodetector on the other side of the track senses it. When you ski through the light beam, the photodetector stops the clock.

There are a number of different ways that courses are laid out between the start and finish gates, but for now we'll

Do It Yourself

focus on the types you are most likely to find yourself in as a recreational skier.

SINGLE-POLE COURSES

Recreational racecourses are almost always single-pole courses. Each gate is defined by a *panel*: a pair of poles set in the snow about two to three feet apart with a flag tied between them. The gates alternate red and blue in color. You turn to the left around one gate, then right around the next, and so on. It is usually obvious on which side of each panel you are supposed to ski.

DUAL COURSES

A dual course consists of two single-pole courses set in parallel, so as to be as identical as possible. Pairs of skiers race head-to-head, usually taking one run on each course. In recreational races, the sum of each skier's two runs determines his or her result when compared with the rest of the field. In professional-level dual races, a more involved, double elimination system is used. Parallel racing is exciting and gives you the opportunity to try showing your kid sister a thing or two.

HOW TO GO FAST

It's fun to just ski through a course, but it's more fun to ski fast. And it's more fun yet to ski faster than the last time. The most fun is to ski faster than everyone else. So how do you go faster on your next run and win back that beer you lost to your sister on the last one?

The Start

The easiest way to lower your time is by improving the way you start, which is not obvious to many people. Almost everyone

This racer has bumped the wand open with her shin before she's really gotten started, costing her significant time.

Save time at the start by keeping your shins behind the wand while you get your upper body going down the hill.

blows significant time at the start until they learn the proper techniques.

Recall that when you push on the wand with your leg, the wand springs open and the clock starts. It just takes a light tap to do, and you probably won't feel it. A lot of inexperienced racers push one leg forward and bump the wand open before they need to. The best approach is to lean out over the wand with your upper body, keeping both your feet well behind the wand, then give a good hard push with your poles, pulling your legs through at the last possible instant.

Once you're on your way, don't just coast to the first gate, *charge* to it! Make two or three strong skating steps to pick up as much speed as you can. Just make sure you've stopped skating and are ready for the first gate well before you get there. To get ready for the race, practice poling and skating on the flats at the bottom of the mountain and on gentle roads.

The Finish

This is another place people lose a lot of time. For some inexplicable reason, a lot of skiers start to turn and slow down before they cross the line.

Don't be one of them. Imagine that the finish line is 10 yards farther down the hill than it really is, and don't turn to a stop until you've passed that imaginary line. This will help you beat a lot of people who otherwise ski every bit as well as you.

Line

So far, we've talked about the simple stuff that experienced racers take for granted. Now we get down to the nitty-gritty that the very best racers in the world constantly tinker with: line. Other than your basic ski technique (which we won't go into here), this is the most critical factor in how fast a time you post.

Anyone who enjoys driving fast on a curvy road understands what line is about. What is the shortest path through the corners that allows the highest speed without skidding? The puzzle is the same when you ski through a racecourse. To be fast, you must minimize skidding. A good

line will enable you to make your best, cleanest turns. A bad line forces you to make turns that scrub away your speed.

Given any specific combination of pitch, speed, and hardness of snow, there is a minimum radius of turn you can make without skidding. The keys to picking a good line are knowing the shape of that turn for each gate and knowing where to make it. Making your turn in the wrong place either forces you to try to make a tighter turn than you can hold without skidding, or forces you to travel a longer path down the course.

Looking ahead is the single best thing you can do to help find the optimum line. Before you start a turn around a gate, you must look ahead to see where the next gate is. Its position determines, as much as anything else, where you should

The ideal line is the one in the middle. The one to the right is too round, but still leaves you in a good spot at the end of the turn, without skidding. The left-most (as you look at the page) turn starts too soon. As a result, the skier must tighten up the radius when he reaches the panel, and as a result ends up skidding sideways, losing speed and getting too low for the next gate.

Do It Yourself

Blind spots—places where the hill gets steeper—deserve special attention during course inspection, as these coaches and racers are doing.

turn. Experienced racers look two gates ahead or more.

Two of the most common line errors, at all levels of competition, are going too straight at the gates and turning too soon. Both of these errors force you to make a tighter turn than you can hold cleanly when you get to the gate. As you try to tighten the arc, you skid and lose speed. The better approach is to err on the conservative side, making the turn well above the gate, "setting up" as it is called, and making the arc of the turn in such a way that you "come back" at the

pole, passing it two-thirds of the way through the turn or more, and without having to tighten the radius.

When a racer blows out of a course or slides low in a gate, the problem can very often be traced to an earlier gate where the competitor was too aggressive, going either too straight or turning too soon.

You must be most attentive to your line at those places where the course changes *rhythm* (the turns either tighten up or lengthen), and where the hill changes pitch.

You need to see rhythm changes at least one gate ahead of time and adjust

Do It Yourself

your line in preparation for them. If the course tightens, set up more and make a more conservative turn in the preceding gate, or you'll get caught going too straight at the gate where things tighten up. If the rhythm loosens, you can make time by going a bit straighter at the gate before the rhythm changes.

Places where the hill gets steeper usually present you with a *blind spot*: a place where you can't see the next gate until it's too late. When you inspect the course prior to running it, assess the blind spots by stopping at them, getting a good look at the next couple of gates, then walking back up the hill a little way to see what the blind spots look like from above. Now you should be ready to race over them.

Places where the hill flattens are crucial to fast times. You want to carry as much speed as possible off the steeper pitch onto the flat. This means setting up a couple of gates above the transition so you can make as clean a turn as possible with as direct a line as you can in the last gate or two of the steep. This will launch you onto the flat with the maximum speed. Once you're off the pitch and onto the flatter section of the course, it is most critical to make clean turns and maintain your speed because it is so hard to get it back.

Technique

There are no style points awarded in a ski race. Racers win or lose based on the effectiveness of their technique, as judged by the clock. Good racing technique is the same as good recreational technique for packed snow. This is why ski instructors and experts have always studied the skiing of the world's best racers. For an in-depth treatment of technique in general and

racing in particular, I recommend my book *The Skier's Edge.* (see page 220)

Fundamentals

- Economy of motion. Every movement has a functional purpose. Nothing is done for style.
- Weight on the outside ski. To achieve the best grip on hard snow, most, if not all, of the racer's weight is balanced on the outside ski.
- Quiet upper body, active legs, and feet. Because small movements of the upper body translate to big changes in balance, racers keep movements of the arms, head, and torso to a minimum. In contrast, the racer is constantly moving from the hip joints down, adjusting, twisting, and tilting the skis.
- Forward pressure early in the turn, finish in the middle. To get the skis arcing early in most turns, racers put pressure on the forebody of the ski. As the turn progresses, they move progressively back toward the middle of the ski.
- Aggressive movements linking one turn to the next. Racers don't finish one turn and just wait for the next one to come to them. They dive across their skis into the coming turn.

Tucking

The one racing technique with which everyone seems to have some familiarity is the *tuck*. This is that characteristic crouch with the poles up under the armpits, the chest down just above the knees, and the hands together out in front of the face. While it looks really cool, it is ineffective at speeds under 20 miles per hour or so. If you're going much slower than that, it's better to skate than to tuck.

Do It Yourself

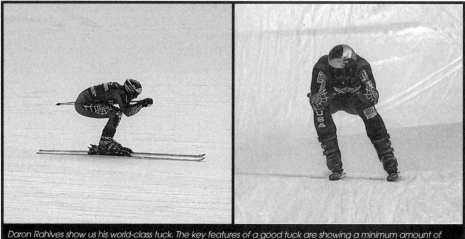

Daron Rahives show us his world-class tuck. The key features of a good tuck are showing a minimum amount of surface area to the wind as you move forward, while letting your skis and legs work freely and fluidly with the snow.

To be fast in a tuck, your back must be flat so that your chest does not catch any wind. The most common error people make is to drop their butts and raise their shoulders, exposing their torsos to the oncoming air. Get your butt up, your head down, and reach forward with your hands so your elbows are in front of your knees.

Turning well in a tuck requires a lot of practice. Unless you are an experienced racer and really know what you are doing, you will always be faster if you simply spread your arms, stand up a bit, and just make a good turn. That tuck may look cool when you're coming down the course, but a faster time definitely looks cooler when you're in the finish area.

Gliding

Gliding is the art of allowing your skis to run as freely on the snow as possible, especially when you're going straight on a flat ski. This may sound elementary, but it's not. In the highest levels of World Cup

downhill and super G racing, the events where good gliding is most important, some racers are known to be good gliders, while others are not. There are competitors who rank among the fastest gliders, but who have never placed in the top twenty in a race.

To get a sense of what good gliding is about, ski straight down a moderately pitched road and tune into your feet and shins. Are you riding a bit on your inside edges? This is quite common, because it keeps your outside edges from catching unexpectedly. It is also quite slow, because the steel of the edges is much slower than the plastic of the bases. Are you pressing against the fronts of your boots? This is slow, too. It's like standing on your tiptoes in sand—the increased pressure causes them to sink in farther than they would if you were standing flat-footed. This makes the skis run slower, too.

Seek a neutral stance that puts your skis perfectly flat and lets them swim a bit side to side. Your legs should not press on either the front or back of the boot, and your ankles should feel loose and floppy. Whenever you are running straight in a racecourse, you should focus on gliding.

Now try to glide in a tuck. This is much harder, but equally important. Next, try doing it on ice at 70 miles per hour. Now you're racing.

HOW TO GET STARTED WITH RECREATIONAL RACING

There are opportunities everywhere to race an easy course, get a time, and compare yourself to your friends (or enemies, as the case may be).

Ski schools everywhere have racing clinics. This is the best way to become acquainted with racing. Many of the most important elements of success are not at all obvious, and you will spend inordinate time floundering down courses if you try to figure them out on your own. You should come away from a race clinic with the skills to go ski in NASTAR, a series of local low-key league races, or the fun race at your company's spring skiing party.

Some ski areas have a setup that is commonly called *pay-to-race*. This is the simplest and most informal setup you are likely to find for running gates, consisting of a single-pole course, a timer, and a box into which you stick a dollar bill. When you feed the box a bill, the timer is enabled. You make your run, and your time is displayed at the finish area.

NASTAR

The NASTAR system (short for National Standard Race) is a good way to entertain your urge for competition, whether it's a casual interest in seeing if you can ski better than you did a month ago,

fulfilling a secret desire to kick your brother-in-law's butt, or satisfying an urge to see where you stand in relation to the best racers on the U.S. Ski Team.

The genius of NASTAR is that through its handicapping system, described below, it compares you with every other skier in the country who races in NASTAR. Depending on how you compare on any given run, you might win a gold, silver, or bronze medal—or simply bragging rights.

The courses are straightforward single-pole affairs designed to be navigable by any advanced skier. Some ski areas set dual courses. The hills used vary, and if there were one complaint I have, it would be that sometimes the slopes chosen are too flat, so that good wax and physical bulk will have an inordinate advantage over skiing skill. Many areas, on the other hand, hold their NASTAR races on interesting terrain that rewards sound technique and savvy tactics.

Pace-setting and Handicapping

Every ski area that conducts NASTAR races has ranked pacesetters on its staff. Every year they participate, along with racers from the U.S Ski Team, in a pace-setting camp. Here, they establish handicaps relative to the fastest skiers at the camp. They then return to their home areas and, for the rest of the season, set the pace times for the NASTAR races held there. Because their handicaps have been well established, it can be fairly well estimated what time the fastest racer in the country would have gotten on each NASTAR course. By inference, you too can rank yourself in relation to the fastest feet in the nation, as well as anyone else participating in NASTAR.

(and enjoy it)

Although it doesn't get much airplay from the major TV networks in the United States, World Cup ski racing does get a lot of play on the Outdoor Life Network (a Canadian channel carried by most cable companies in the United States).

But ski racing is not like drag racing: It's not always obvious who's winning. It's even less obvious to most spectators why. And while ski racing gets a modicum of coverage on TV in the United States, the sportscasters' commentary doesn't always help much.

The margins separating the top finishers in most World Cup races these days are remarkably small. The difference between winning and finishing out of the top ten can often be attributed to a single error in line in a single turn. Even so, there are noticeable differences in the techniques and tactics applied by skiers who consistently wind up on the podium.

Watch carefully for the lines taken through the course by different racers. Line tactics employed by various racers are some of their most interesting differentiators. Some, like American star Bode Miller, ski consistently aggressive lines, taking the risk that they will occasionally go a little too straight at a gate and lose some time to skidding. On balance, they hope the time they save on the turns they do pull off cleanly will more than make up for the sporadic losses. At the other end

of the spectrum are skiers like the legendary Swiss Michael VonGuenigen, now retired, who for years won World Cup giant slalom races with a more conservative line than anyone else in his class.

Most courses have at least a couple of critical spots, and paying close attention to how the different competitors negotiate them will tell you a lot about how they finish. Here are some places to watch for:

- Places where the course comes off a pitch onto a flatter slope. The ones who are fast across the flat are the ones who find the best line through the last few gates on the steep. And because it is very hard to pick up speed on a flat, the ones who come onto it fast will likely finish ahead of those who don't.
- Blind spots where the hill gets suddenly steeper and the racers can't see more than one gate ahead of them. Some will be too aggressive going over the break and have to jam on their edges to stay in the course. Others will set up more than they need to, taking an overly conservative and long line.
- Places where the rhythm or shape of the turns changes suddenly. If three or four consecutive turns of the same shape and size are followed by one or two that are much tighter or quicker, you'll see some racers that account for the change effectively, and some that don't.
- Places where the course goes from sun to shade. Some skiers have trouble seeing

Turning too soon here, results in skidding

Even World Cup champions and Olympic medalists like Martina Ertl of Germany make mistakes. See how she turns her skis a bit sideways and skids a little in the first turn? It's because she started the turn a little too soon. (See the diagram on page 227). The second and third turns are spot-on. Ertl had the 3rd fastest time in this section of the course.

irregularities in the snow in such places and get rough on their skis. This is a particular problem in super-G and downhill.

■ Quick combinations of slalom gates, especially those that are followed by a sharp turn. Some racers are masters at slithering through the quick gates with barely a change in direction, yet make the next turn without jamming. Others who try the straight line don't fare so well. Still others ski a slightly rounder line through the quick gates to reduce the risk.

The first time you ski in a NASTAR race you supply some registration information. You are given a handicap based on your age and gender. From then on, you're in the system, and your results in NASTAR races anywhere in the country will be tracked for you.

Each time you race, your time and handicap are run though the handicapping system, along with that of the pacesetter, to see where you rank in the NASTAR universe. If you rank high enough, you earn a gold, silver, or bronze medal.

Frosting on the Cake

It's pretty simple. But the NASTAR folks have figured out some surprising ways to extend and embellish the basic concept. There is a national NASTAR championship every year that draws thousands of skiers from all over the country and U.S. National Team celebrities as well.

What is really interesting is the way NASTAR has leveraged the Internet. You can track your race record there, and that of anyone else you know, regardless of where in the NASTAR galaxy they may have raced. But wait, there's more! You and your friends can establish a NASTAR team and compete with other such teams without any two people competing on the same day or at the same ski area. By using the nationwide handicapping system, the Internet, and some over-caffeinated computer programmers, NASTAR maintains something like a fantasy football league for you and your friends. The only thing NASTAR won't do for you is make book on your wagers.

TYPES OF RACING
Downhill

Downhill is the fastest event. The course is determined largely by the shape of the mountain itself. Speeds are high, upward of 80 miles per hour on some World Cup courses. At downhill speeds, the effects of terrain are amplified immensely, so the racer must deal deliberately with every variation in the shape of the hill. Rolls in the mountain that might go unnoticed by a recreational skier become jumps that project the racer a hundred feet or more through the air.

It is a spectacular event, and generates the most interest in Europe. There is no other sport I know of where competitors go as fast in as dangerous an environment with as little protection.

Competitors participate in mandatory training runs on the course prior to the race. The practice runs, skied at near-race speeds, give the racers and their coaches an opportunity to tweak their lines through the course and the moves they must make through the terrain.

Super G

This discipline was created around 1980 to fit somewhere between downhill and giant slalom. It took a few years for it to mature, but now is a unique event that places unique demands on the racer. John McBride, the U.S. Ski Team's head men's World Cup coach for downhill and super G, considers it the most difficult event in which to excel. Speeds are high, over 50 miles per hour much of the time, making the effects of terrain considerable. But in contrast to downhill, the racers do not get to train on the course prior to the race. This places great emphasis on the skier's ability

Downhill racing involves big speeds, big turns, and big air. Daron Rahlves, the most successful American down-hiller in history, and a World Champion in super-G, negotiates the Hundschopf jump on the classic Lauberhorn course in Wengen, Switzerland.

Stephan Eberharter finds the line through the big turns of a super-G course. Eberharter is former World Cup champion and World Championship gold medalist in the event.

Types of Racing

to anticipate how fast he or she will be going at every point in the course, and what effects the terrain will have on them as a result, based entirely on inspecting the course prior to the race. The entry and exit points of every turn must be estimated so that when the racer is coming down at full speed during the race, he or she will be on the fastest tenable line.

Giant Slalom

Of the alpine racing disciplines, giant slalom (or GS as it is usually called) most closely resembles the skiing we mere mortals do. It is also the size of turn most commonly set for NASTAR and other recreational racecourses. Speeds in World Cup GS races reach up to around 45 miles per hour.

Many coaches think that of all racing disciplines, giant slalom requires the best in fundamental ski technique. World Cup champion and Olympic medalist Janica Kostelic of Croatia shows how it's done.

Types of Racing

Slalom demands the shortest, quickest turns of all events. Ivica Kostelic (Janica's brother), a world champion and World Cup champion in the event, is one of the best.

Types of Racing

In contrast to downhill and super-G, and in kind with slalom, a giant slalom race comprises two runs on different courses. A racer's time for the race is the sum of his or her times for the two runs.

Many coaches consider giant slalom to be the most demanding event. Making a good GS turn requires exemplary technique, finding the optimum line requires considerable judgment, and making continuous turns at giant slalom speeds for well over a minute requires more strength, power, and stamina than any of the other disciplines.

Giant slalom skis and their detuned relatives make good skis for cruising, especially at speed and on harder snows.

Slalom

Slalom requires the racer to make the smallest, quickest turns of any discipline. The racers systematically knock down the poles as they pass, hitting them with their shins, knees, hands, chest, or whatever happens to cross the path of the gate at the time. The poles are hinged at the snow line, and have internal springs that set them upright after the racer has passed. Racers wear special padding and hard plastic shields to take the impact of the pole.

Interestingly, I believe more coaches and instructors ski on slalom skis and their derivatives than any other single type. They are particularly good for short- to medium-radius turns on hard snow.

Combined

The combined event is a horse of a different color: It is a *paper race*. The results are determined by adding the racers' times in a downhill and slalom. In most cases, these are complete downhill and slalom races in their own rights that take place on the same weekend at the same ski area. Results are determined and awards given out for the individual races, as well as the combined. In the Olympics and World Championships, the combined events have their own separate downhill and slalom races on which they are based.

ORGANIZED AND SANCTIONED RACING

Organized ski racing is, for the most part, a club sport rather than a school sport. There are high school leagues in some parts of the country, and the NCAA has Division I and II interscholastic competitions, but they take a backseat to club racing for most serious competitors.

If you are looking for a way for you or your child to get involved in ski racing beyond the recreational level, you need to find a Buddy Werner or USSA club.

Buddy Werner League

The Buddy Werner league is a good way to introduce your child to ski racing. Buddy Werner clubs comprise kids from second to eighth grade and organize races that are low-key and local in scope. The nationwide league's namesake grew up in "Ski Town USA," Steamboat Springs, Colorado, in the 1940s and 1950s, and developed into one of the best racers in the world. In addition to being athletically talented, Werner was a leader and mentor to younger racers, and it is for that as much as anything that the league is named for him.

Buddy Werner League is a great way to get a kid started in ski racing. The emphasis is on fun, sportsmanship, and developing good skiing skills.

USSA

The United States Ski Association (USSA) is the governing body for serious ski racing in the United States. It is also the Olympic Governing Body (OGB) for this country, which means it is responsible for fielding our Olympic team. Everything from organized club racing for 12-year-olds to masters events for octogenarians are governed by USSA. If you're serious about racing, contact USSA on the Internet (www.ussa.org) or by phone at their headquarters in Park City, Utah (435-649-9090), and get the names of the club programs in your area that participate in their sanctioned events.

Hermann Maier almost single-handedly raised the level of competition on the World Cup in the late 1990s with the overpowering ability to match technical precision and tactical risk. With 4 overall World Cup titles, 10 World Cup discipline titles, and numerous Olympic and World Championship medals, he continues to be a dominant force on the World Cup today.

Organized and Sanctioned Racing

FIS and the World Cup

USSA is also our country's connection to the Federation International de Ski (FIS), which is the governing body for international ski racing. Among other things, FIS runs the World Cup of skiing, which is the connecting thread of the most important ski races in the world each year. Every year FIS awards a World Cup trophy to the men and women with the most cumulative World Cup points in each of the alpine racing disciplines: slalom, giant slalom, super-G, downhill, and combined as well as men's and women's overall World Cup titles. If you have an opportunity to see a World Cup race, either on television or live, you are watching, without argument, the best skiers in the world.

For the inveterate race watcher, FIS has a Web site (www.fis-ski.com) where you can find detailed, up-to-the-minute results and analyses of all FIS-sanctioned races worldwide. ◆◆◆

Snow, sun, and skiing are the ingredients for great pictures, and you don't need fancy gear to take them. I shot this with the simplest camera I own: a little 30-year-old Rollei 35. No autofocus, no autoexposure, no nuthin'.

PHOTOS AND VIDEOS

S kiing makes great subject matter for pictures. Subject matter alone, however, does not make great pictures. Here are some tips and tricks for bringing those great days on the hill back home.

Still Photos

You don't need a Nikon F5 with an eight frames-per-second motor drive and 300-mm lens to take compelling pictures. A good point-and-shoot camera will render good pictures if used with some thought.

EXPOSURE

The term *exposure* refers to how much light is allowed to hit the film (or the CCD sensor if you have a digital camera), and getting it right is important to getting a good picture.

You cannot rely on a completely automatic exposure setting for pictures taken on snow. The brightness of the snow will dominate the scene to the extent that everything else—people, trees, and so on—will be too dark. You must figure out a way to tell the camera to compensate. If your camera has a snow, sand, or *backlight* setting, that will probably do the trick. If you have more manual control over the camera, you can get the same effect by telling it to shoot one to two full *exposure values* (EVs) more than the average light meter reading would dictate. If you have full manual control over the camera, open the aperture one to two full f-stops larger than the average reading indicates.

Another good trick is to use your flash to throw some additional light on your subjects, so they are closer to the snow in brightness. Professional photographers use this technique, called *fill-flash*, all the time, particularly for portraits or head shots. Many cameras have a built-in fill-flash setting. If yours doesn't, it probably has a setting that will force the flash to fire regardless of how bright the scene is, and this will work also.

When you rely entirely on your camera's automatic exposure system, this is what you usually get: a picture that is too dark.

This picture was taken by "overexposing" two full exposure values (EV) above the camera's automatically determined exposure.

To get a sharp picture of someone skiing, use a shutter speed of 1/500th of a second or faster. If you want to use the automatic-exposure system in your camera, set it to *shutter priority* or *sports action* if it has such a setting, and make one of the exposure adjustments mentioned earlier, so the image isn't too dark.

When in doubt about exposure, follow these rules of thumb:

- It is better to overexpose print film than underexpose it.
- It is better to underexpose a digital photograph than overexpose it.
- It is better to underexpose slide film than overexpose it.

And finally, don't despair if you wind up with a picture that is wonderful in every respect other than the exposure. Ask a good photo lab to reprint the picture and correct for the exposure problems. You'll be surprised what they can do.

FILM AND FILTERS

If your ultimate goal is to make prints, shoot print film rather than slides. Print film is more forgiving than slide film in terms of exposure and will make better prints for less money. Professionals who have not moved to digital media (most have) usually shoot slides, but they are willing to throw away more bad pictures than you are, and they're usually shooting for magazine publication, which is a much different animal than a normal photographic print.

There is usually plenty of light on the ski slopes, so you should use film with an ISO speed rating between 100 and 400. ISO 200 print film is a good all-round choice.

At high altitude, ultraviolet light (UV) can affect photos, so put a UV filter on your camera. It will have no negative effect on any pictures, so you can leave it on all the time.

DIGITAL CAMERAS

All the professional ski photographers I know have switched to digital cameras. So have I. And while digital cameras are wonderful in many respects, they have their quirks. Consumer-oriented digital cameras, in particular, require some operator savvy of their own.

WHITE BALANCE

Digital cameras are very sensitive to what is called *white balance*. This specifies the color in the scene that the camera thinks is white—an even mixture of all colors. On a bright, sunny day, the automatic white point setting for most digital cameras will provide good results. Shooting on snow in the shade is a different matter. The automatic white balance setting on most digital cameras will result in a picture that is too blue and cold looking. Changing the setting to that for shade will usually warm up the picture and make it look more natural.

FOCUSING AND PREFOCUSING

The biggest shortcoming of consumer-level digital cameras is the time lag between when you push the shutter release and when the camera actually takes the picture. This lag is due in part to slow auto-focusing.

The best approach to reducing the lag is to *prefocus* the camera. Point it at a stationary object that is the same distance from you as the skier will be when you want to snap the picture and press the shutter release partway. The camera will have some sort of indicator, usually a light, that tells you when it is focused and ready to shoot. As long as you keep the shutter release depressed partway, the focus will be locked. Now aim the camera in the direction of the picture you want to take and let your subject know that you're ready to shoot. When you want to snap the picture, push the shutter release the rest of the way down. The camera should fire immediately.

Optical Viewfinders Versus LCD Displays

Digital cameras all have LCD displays. Point-and-shoot varieties allow you to use the display as a viewfinder, and many people seem to like this. LCD panels are, however, impossible to see on a bright, sunny day. Get used to using the optical viewfinder. Be aware, however, that all point-and-shoot cameras take a larger picture than you see in the optical viewfinder, so compose your pictures accordingly.

Digital Zoom

Many digital cameras have both *optical zoom* and *digital zoom*. Optical zoom is a wonderful thing to have, but digital zoom is not. It makes the picture "soft" and indistinct, like tabloid pictures of famous people shot from too far away and blown up too much. If your camera has this so-called feature, I recommend turning it off, so you won't inadvertently use it.

PHOTOGRAPHING PEOPLE

Everyone seems to think that taking group pictures is easy, but there are a few subtle tricks that will make everyone look better.

The "firing squad" pose: Line 'em up and shoot 'em. People seldom look their best this way. The background is busy and distracting, too.

Still Photos

- Get everyone to stand close together. Closer than they normally would.
- When taking a picture of just a few people, turn the camera 90 degrees and shoot a vertical frame.
- Avoid the "firing squad" pose. Have people turn slightly sideways or shoot the group slightly from the side. People generally look better this way than when their bodies face the camera directly.
- Pose your group with the sun coming from the side, not straight into their faces. Direct sun makes people squint and makes their faces look flat.
- Have everyone take their goggles and sunglasses off, if you can.
- People generally look much better without helmets. Have your subjects take theirs off.
- Unless some mountain or other feature is important to your picture, fill the frame with the people. Amateur photographers commonly stand too far back and surround their subjects with too much irrelevant background. If you're really interested in the people, try getting in close and shooting them from the waist or bustline up.
- Take the picture before 10 in the morning or after 2 in the afternoon. When the sun is high in the sky, people's noses and eyebrows cast unflattering shadows. The snow also usually looks best early in the day, and you will have fewer people cluttering your background.
- Take at least one shot for every two people in the group. It's your best hope of getting one picture that flatters everyone.

People look better when they stand a bit sideways, get close to each other, and take off their sunglasses. I got a better background simply by walking to the other side of the group and shooting in the other direction.

Still Photos

- Be careful with your background. Buildings, chairlifts, and other people pull attention away from your subject and make for weaker pictures. Distant mountains and trees are great.
- If you want to get in the picture yourself, ask a stranger to shoot for you. But make sure to set up the shot ahead of time and tell the stranger-photographer exactly where to stand.

SHOOTING LANDSCAPES

Skiing is done in some of the most beautiful places in the world. But that beauty is not easy to capture in a photograph. One of the main reasons is that a photo is two-dimensional and lacks the depth you see with your eyes. Here are a couple of

The mountain in the background is certainly beautiful, but the photo would look flat and dull without the tree in the foreground.

Landscapes are most appealing when the main subject is not smack-dab in the middle of the frame and another element is placed in the foreground to add depth and scale.

Still Photos

Shoot landscapes early or late in the day, when the shadows add depth and drama. Note that the key elements of this picture are placed about a third of the way across the frame and a third of the way down.

things to keep in mind that will improve your chances of getting good pictures.

- Shoot early and late in the day. This will provide more dramatic and depth-invoking shadows than midday sun.
- Compose your picture with something in the foreground. A tree, rock outcropping, or other object close to the camera will give the picture a sense of depth.
- To get a better idea of what the scene will look like in a photo, close one eye. This will flatten the image you see, much as a photograph will. Make a rectangular frame with your hands and look through it to give yourself a better idea of how the picture will look.

TAKING ACTION SHOTS

The first thing to remember is to be safe. When you are concentrating on setting up and taking a picture, it's easy to ignore other things, like the fact you might be standing in a spot that can't be seen from above. If you do want to shoot a skier from such a spot, have a third person stand in a place where they can see both you and the skiers from above and manage the traffic. The third person can also coordinate you and the skier you are shooting so that your subject goes when you are ready, and you will know when he or she is just about to come into view. Have the spotter hold up

Still Photos

Shooting from the side will help you catch some snow flying in the air, conveying action.

his arm, then drop it just before the subject comes into view.

Camera Angle

The worst camera angle for an action shot is the one most people naturally use: shooting straight up the hill at the skier. This seldom results in a good picture.

Be creative. Get up on a bank on the side of the trail and shoot from the side and above. Shoot from the side with a ridgeline in the background. Get on the other side of a gully and shoot the skier directly across from you. Shoot from behind as your subject skis over a drop-off, with the mountains across the valley for a backdrop.

Pay attention to your background. People and trees seldom make good background material. Blue sky, distant mountains, and rock outcroppings work well.

Jumps

To make a jump look bigger, shoot up from a low angle. Use a wide-angle lens setting. Because you will usually be shooting from

Still Photos

a blind spot, you should always have a spotter. If you are using an auto-focus camera, prefocus on the lip of the jump.

Making the Hill Look Steep
It's hard to make the slope look as steep in a photograph as it does when you're really there. Shooting up the hill, in particular, flattens the picture considerably.

Shooting across the hill from the side lets the viewer see the slope's pitch, especially if there are a few trees or other vertical objects in the background to provide reference. If you shoot across the hill, make sure you hold the camera straight, so that your vertical reference objects are vertical in the picture. Shooting down the hill is often effective, too.

If the steep pitch ends in a flat, try skiing out onto the flat a ways and shooting back at the pitch. This will give you a more accurate representation of the slope's true steepness. A telephoto lens helps convey steepness in such a shot, too. If you can shoot from the other side of a gully, you can make the slope look really steep.

HANDLING A CAMERA ON THE HILL
Snow, Humidity, and Cameras
Cameras don't do well when they get wet. In fact, getting one wet can easily ruin it, so be prepared to deal with the possibility of your camera being dropped in the snow or getting sprayed by the subject of your picture. The best thing for drying off a camera is a big piece of chamois. This will double as a cloth for cleaning your lens. If you don't have one, carry a bunch of paper napkins to towel-off your camera if needed. Do not,

Although this was shot on a rather steep slope, it looks flat because I shot straight up the hill.

The angle from which this shot was taken, from above and behind, makes the hill look steep and adds a sense of action.

Still Photos

Shooting from across a gulley and putting a vertical reference, such as a tree, in the frame, tells people how steep the hill really is.

Still Photos

however, use paper napkins to clean the lens unless you have absolutely no alternative. They often contain hard fibers and microscopic grit that can scratch the lens.

Snow or water drops on the lens will ruin your shot. If you take pictures on a snowy day, always hold the camera with the lens pointing down or hold it inside your jacket, Napoleon-style, until just before you want to take the picture. Use a lens shade to shield the lens from the falling snow. If you don't have a lens shade, hold your free hand above the lens to protect it.

High humidity will also harm your camera. For this reason, carry it in an outside pocket. Avoid carrying a camera inside your jacket if possible, especially if you are skiing hard and working up a sweat. Things can get steamy enough inside your jacket to temporarily disable and possibly even damage a camera. Video cameras are especially vulnerable.

Cold itself does not hurt a camera or film, but when you go inside on a cold day, don't take your camera out of your pocket or pack until it has warmed up to room temperature. This can take twenty minutes or more. The warm air hitting the cold camera will cause moisture to condense on and inside it, including its delicate mechanical and electronic parts. This can wreck havoc on the camera. An alternative tactic is to carry a plastic freezer bag with you. Before you go inside, put the camera in the freezer bag and seal it. When you get inside, you can bring the bag and camera out into the room-temperature air without a worry, and the camera will warm up much more quickly than if it were still in your pocket.

BATTERIES

Always carry extra batteries. Cold reduces the juice in most batteries, so you won't get the same life from them that you do at home. The special rechargeable batteries that most digital cameras use can be expensive, but some have equivalent alkaline batteries that can be purchased in supermarkets and discount stores. These are inexpensive alternative backups.

Because of cold's effect on batteries, carry your extras inside your jacket if possible. The best type of nonrechargeable batteries for use in the cold are lithium, not alkaline. Energizer is the only brand I know of who makes them. Lithium batteries are more expensive, but they last much longer and are not affected by cold. Two other benefits are that they are much lighter than alkaline batteries and do not get progressively weaker as they are used. They hold the same level of strength until they die, and then they die quickly.

Still Photos

Video

Many of the special considerations for taking skiing photos apply to shooting skiing videos. You need to exercise the same control over exposure that I described earlier for photographs. Basically, you need to increase the exposure one to two exposure values (EVs) from what the camera wants to do on its own. As with digital photographic cameras, use the eyepiece viewfinder: LCD screens don't work well for ski videos.

Moisture and humidity are especially dangerous for small video cameras. Most have sensors built into them that will cause the camera to shut down if they sense excessive humidity inside the camera. If you turn your camera on and it refuses to do anything, the problem is likely to be this or a dead battery. Don't put the camera inside your jacket. The humidity in there can easily get to an unsafe level.

SIZE MATTERS

I recommend buying a small video camera that you can carry in an outside pocket because you will be much more likely to take it with you. Larger cameras get left at home.

VIDEO FORMAT

There is a confusing array of video formats out there right now, but the best by far is Mini DV. This is a completely digital video format that has many advantages over the other consumer video formats such as VHS, Hi-8, or Digital-8.

IMAGE STABILIZATION

Image stabilization systems make your videos look sure and steady, even if you have the shakes and are shooting at the telephoto end of your camera's zoom range. There are two varieties: so-called *optical image stabilization* and *electronic image stabilization*. While they are both good, the optical stabilization type is markedly better.

SHOOTING TIPS
Length of Takes

Each segment of video you shoot, from the time you start the tape rolling until you stop, is called a *take* or a *clip*. As a rule of thumb, never shoot less than ten seconds of video at a time. Clips shorter than that will make your viewers nervous or seasick. Many shooters say that twenty seconds is the minimum.

Not all the good skiing pictures are taken out on the hill.

Zooming

Keep your zooming to a minimum. People overdo it because they think it will keep the viewer interested. What keeps the viewer interested is, first and foremost, the subject matter of the video, not the camera work. One or two smooth, continuous zooms to get from one subject to another or to follow a subject are acceptable. More than that weakens your video.

As with digital still cameras, digital video cameras usually have a digital zoom feature. As with digital still cameras, you should avoid using it.

Fading In and Out

Most consumer video cameras have a feature that will cause the image to fade in when you start shooting and fade out when you stop. This single feature will make your videos more watchable than any other little trick. Learn to use it.

Videos of Snow and Your Feet

I have shot hours and hours of skiing video, and I still make the same mistake occasionally: I start the camera shooting when I think I'm stopping it. It's because you press the same button in the same way to both start it and stop it. I think this is bad design, but video cameras force you to live with it.

Most cameras can be set to beep when they start and stop, and the beeps are usually different. Train yourself to listen for them. I've been trying to train myself for years, and I still come home with a lot of pictures of the snow around my feet. Or, as Martin Andersen, a coach with the Norwegian Ski Team likes to call them when he's ribbing me, "snow crystal studies." ◆◆◆

SOME THINGS NEVER CHANGE

O ver the years a lot of things have changed. The equipment we use. The techniques we employ. Even the technology of the clothes we wear. But much of the practical lore of the sport, which has been the subject of this book, hasn't.

I recently heard a piece on National Public Radio about today's young extreme skiers and terrain park jibbers and a guy named Warren Miller. Miller, now in his 70s, is a patriarch of the ski bum subculture. The young turks are still impassioned about their sport with a depth of commitment that precludes financial security. So they practice a ritual similar to one I picked up in the late 1960s. When these guys get hungry, they economize by going to the base lodge, grabbing a handful of saltines, some pickle relish and honey, and making sandwiches.

The only difference is that I used ketchup instead of honey. And I still would.

ABOUT THE AUTHOR

Ron LeMaster

Ron LeMaster has been an avid skier for almost fifty years. He has been an instructor, race coach, writer and photographer, and regular contributor to the major North American ski magazines. Ron lectures internationally on ski technique and is a technical advisor to the United States Ski Team and the Vail/Beaver Creek Ski School. Ron has written technical manuals and articles for the Professional Ski Instructors of America and is the author of *The Skier's Edge,* an in-depth book on ski technique and biomechanics.